THE 14 CODES

Published by Spines
ISBN 979-8-89950-018-3

THE 14 CODES

THE BLACK AMERICAN MAN CONSTITUTIONAL CODE OF CONDUCT

TREY (SON OF RA) STEVENS

CONTENTS

DEDICATION

To the Black Woman—
The ones who carried our families on their backs, whose
strength never needed applause because it was built into their
bones. Your wisdom, your grace, your fire, and your fight—
may it echo in every generation that rises.

To the Black Man—
Those who stood tall through storms meant to break them.
Who held the line when the world told them to fold. This is
for you—for your endurance, your honor, and the weight you
carry with pride.

To My Ancestors—
You walked through fire so I could speak freely. You bore
chains so I could lift mine. Your blood is the ink in these
codes. Every lesson, every sacrifice, every unspoken truth is

carved into this foundation. I see you, I feel you, and I move with you.

To My Panda—
May these codes be a shield around you and a compass for the men who seek your presence. Let them be the measure. May no man enter your world without these principles etched into his soul.

When I'm gone, let these codes live on—
Not just as words, but as law for the right kind of Black man: one who is unbreakable in spirit, unshakable in purpose, and unapologetic in his standard. Let them serve as the line in the sand. Only those who live by it, deserve to stand on it.

THE PURPOSE OF THE BOOK AND THE CODES

Black men must return to their true selves. The time for softness is over; it's time to become the strong, resilient figures that the world tried to take away. This rebirth isn't just for Black men; it's for the future of the Black community. It's for the generations that will come after, who will know exactly what a solid Black man looks like because the blueprint will have been passed down. It's time to repair the broken pipeline and restore that which was once lost. The era of clay molding clay is over. It's time for steel to shape steel.

The transformation of Black men to malleable, soft individuals is a direct result of modern social influences. From the moment we step into society, we are bombarded with images of weakness disguised as strength, misdirection wrapped in self-help, and a culture that rewards passivity over action. The media pushes narratives that strip away the toughness Black men once prided themselves on, instead promoting emotional vulnerability as a replacement for mental fortitude. The societal shift towards emotional indulgence has undermined the backbone of Black masculinity, turning men who once stood tall into figures who bend to every whim of public opinion. This softening of Black men isn't accidental; it's a direct product of a system that benefits from weak, fractured communities. A society that encourages emotional overflow and fragility ensures that Black men no longer have the conviction to stand firm in their identity.

As Black men, we've been conditioned to believe that softness is a form of strength, but it's nothing more than an illusion. We are taught to be accommodating, to be open with our feelings, and to embrace a state of perpetual vulnerability. However, this has led to a generation that cannot defend its own masculinity, let alone build its own future. The traditional values of resilience, fortitude, and independence are buried under layers of societal expectation, leaving us more confused and broken than ever before. This softening has manifested in an inability to take action or uphold the responsibilities that have historically defined Black manhood. Instead of rising to the challenges, we have conformed to a passive existence that pleases the outside world but leaves our core hollow.

There was a time when Black men were strong leaders, devoted protectors, and the foundation of their families and communities. Strength wasn't measured by how much we could bend or adjust but by our ability to shape our own fate, our own future, and those of our families. Yet, as time passed, society's influence turned Black men from rock-solid pillars to liquid clay, easily molded by external forces and social whims. Instead of standing in the face of adversity, we now find ourselves shrinking, unsure of what it means to truly be men. Our roles as leaders have been undermined by the very structures meant to uphold us, and we have internalized the narrative that our strength is dangerous rather than necessary. The result is a generation of men who, despite their potential, lack the will to resist the pressure to conform to this new, soft identity.

It's time for Black men to break free from this mold, to reject the narrative that has been forced upon us. We must return to the *"steel shaping steel"* mentality, where Black men hold each other accountable, challenge each other, and push each other to be greater. This isn't about competing with each other or tearing one another down; it's about forging an environment where every Black man is expected to stand firm in his truth and rise above the weakness that has been instilled. We are brothers, and we must make each other stronger, not more fragile. This is about reclaiming what was lost and building upon it, creating men who are not afraid to take responsibility, not afraid to lead, and not afraid to stand firm when others try to break them down.

We have the power to reshape our identity, but it requires us to look inward and confront the lies we've been told. Black men can no longer afford to live under the weight of societal expectations that seek to break us down. We have to understand that real strength comes from within and that it's forged through hardship, accountability, and discipline. It's time to remove the shackles of emotional indulgence and self-pity and replace them with the steel of determination, ambition, and unity. The responsibility for rebuilding Black masculinity lies not in external forces but within us, as a collective group, to take the reins of our own destiny. We must once again become the warriors, leaders, and protectors we were meant to be. The system has chipped away at us, piece by piece, until we no longer recognize the power that flows through our veins. It's time to take back that power, to strip away the layers of weakness, and to forge ourselves into the steel that can't be bent or broken. The *"steel shaping steel"* mentality is a call to arms for every Black man to look to the man next to him and say, *"I'm going to help you become the best version of yourself, and in doing so, I will become the best version of myself."* This is a brotherhood built on mutual respect, discipline, and unwavering support. No longer will we let the softening of Black men define us. We will define ourselves, and through that, we will uplift the entire Black community.

Our journey back to strength is not going to be easy. It will require us to confront uncomfortable truths, to discard the comfort of vulnerability that has been imposed upon us, and to rise above the temptation to fall back into old habits. But we are capable of it. We are built for this. We've survived far worse, and this is nothing compared to the struggles our ancestors faced. The question now is whether we will take up the mantle of responsibility or continue to be molded by the pressures of a society that does not have our best interests at heart. The choice is ours, but if we want to reclaim our power, we must take a stand. We've been molded by forces that have no respect for our legacy or potential. It's time to stop being shaped by these external pressures and start shaping ourselves. We need to look inward, embrace our full strength, and begin building a future where Black men rise above mediocrity, complacency, and softness. There is no reason we cannot return to the strong, resilient figures we once were. All it takes is the will to stand firm, the strength to resist, and the courage to lead with unapologetic authority. The world has underestimated us, and now it's time to show them what Black men are truly capable of when we are at our best.

Let us not wait for society to dictate our worth. Let us not wait for the system to tell us what it means to be men. We know what it means. We've always known. Now is the time for Black men to rise as leaders, to hold ourselves accountable, and to create a legacy that will last for generations. The pipeline may have been broken, but it's up to us to repair it, to reshape it, and to pass it down to our sons and grandsons. We are the architects of our own future, and the time to rebuild

Black masculinity is now. The softening ends here. The steel is ready to be forged.

This is the moment of transformation. Just like the phoenix that rises from the ashes, Black men will rise from the destruction of their identity. We will rise stronger, unbreakable, and unashamed of who we are. The time to reshape Black manhood is now, and the "*14 Codes*" provide the blueprint. It's time to build, to shape, and to reclaim what is rightfully ours. We are not clay anymore. We are steel. The purpose of this book is rooted in my deep concern for the current state of Black men in America. As a collective, we've been systematically placed in a position of weakness—physically, mentally, emotionally, and spiritually. Every corner of this society, from education to the justice system, has been designed to suppress and dismantle the Black male identity. What we see today is the product of centuries of oppression, and it's clear that the forces at play have no intention of letting us rise to our true potential. We were never meant to succeed under this system, but still, many of us have tried to defy it. This book isn't just a reflection of that struggle; it's a blueprint for how we reclaim our power.

Black men in this society have been molded into something they are not. We've been shaped by a system that profits off our weakness, one that rewards submission, confusion, and apathy while punishing strength, unity, and self-sufficiency. From the day we encountered white supremacy, we were stripped of our essence, taught to distrust our power, and forced to live in a state of constant survival. What makes this system dangerous is that it's not just about oppression; it's about creation. They've cultivated an environment where Black men don't see themselves as leaders but as commodities to be exploited. We've been conditioned to accept our fate instead of challenging it, and that's where the danger lies: we've forgotten that we are steel, meant to shape and build, not clay meant to be molded by others. The system is strategic in how it weakens Black men. It uses subtle tactics that target our self-worth, our purpose, and our sense of brotherhood. Every day, we face distractions that pull us away from our mission: to build strong, resilient, accountable lives. Whether it's through the media, the lack of representation, or the absence of positive role models, the message is clear: Black men don't need to stand strong. The system works tirelessly to keep us on the back foot, in a constant state of reaction rather than being proactive. It forces us into a cycle of dependency, seeking validation and approval from those who profit off our subjugation. This book is about breaking that cycle, shifting the paradigm back to one where we take control of our destinies.

This isn't just about personal empowerment; it's about community resurrection. I wrote this book because I understand that no Black man is an island. We're all connected, and our collective weakness stems from a broken sense of unity. The system has worked overtime to sow division among us, turning us against each other in a never-ending cycle of competition, jealousy, and distrust. But the truth is, we can only rise when we rise together. The foundation of this book is built on the understanding that, as Black men, we need each other to build, to grow, and to move forward. This is not a solitary mission; it's a collective one, and every Black man who reads this book has the responsibility to share its message and its power with others.

The strength of Black men has been demonized and distorted for so long that we no longer see the full extent of our capabilities. The system wants us to forget that we come from a rich, powerful lineage of warriors, leaders, and visionaries. It wants us to believe that weakness is a virtue, that vulnerability equals strength. But in truth, our strength comes from knowing our worth and standing firm in it. We have been silenced, yes, but we have not been broken. This book serves as a reminder of who we are, who we've always been, and what we are capable of when we are no longer afraid to fully embrace our power. This is a wake-up call for every Black man who feels lost or disillusioned with the world around him. It's a call to awaken the spirit that has been dormant for far too long. The system has done its best to drown our voices, but our voices will no longer be silenced. This book is for the men who have been told they don't matter, for the men who have been rejected by a system that never valued them. It's for the ones who have internalized these lies and now believe that they are unworthy of greatness. I wrote this book for them to understand that their worth is inherent and undeniable. This book isn't about fighting the system in the traditional sense; it's about taking the power back by recognizing that the power has always been inside us. In the past, Black men were leaders because they had no choice. They understood their responsibilities, their power, and their place in the world.

They did not seek permission or validation; they knew who they were. But over time, the system has convinced Black men that they are less than what they are, that they don't deserve to lead. This book is about reclaiming that leadership, unapologetically. It's about restoring the belief that we are born to lead our families, our communities, and our people. It's time we take our rightful place as leaders and show the world the true strength of Black manhood.

This book is not just for me, nor is it for the present generation alone. I wrote this for my daughter, to ensure she has a model for what a strong Black man looks like, even after I'm gone. It's a legacy I'm passing down, not just through my words, but through every action I take as a man. I want her to know that when she looks for a man to stand beside her, she won't have to settle for anything less than a man who embodies the principles of integrity, character, and strength. I want her to know that Black men are not weak, that we are not soft, and that she has every right to expect the best from us. This book is my gift to her, my promise to her, that the blueprint for Black manhood will be passed down from father to daughter, from generation to generation, as a roadmap for what it means to be a strong, self-respecting Black man.

As a society, we've forgotten the power of legacy. For too long, Black men have been left to wander without direction or guidance. The pipeline of wisdom, leadership, and strength has been broken, and too many men have been left to flounder without a model to follow. This book is my attempt to reconnect the dots, to rebuild the bridge between the past, present, and future of Black manhood. The wisdom of our ancestors is not lost; it's only been hidden. We must reclaim it. It's time to stop looking to others for our validation and start looking inward for the strength we've always had. This book is the first step in that process, an offering to anyone willing to take it and walk the path toward self-empowerment.

This isn't about giving Black men a new identity; it's about reminding them of the one they've always had. The codes within these pages are not a prescription for what men should be; they are a declaration of what Black men are when they live to their full potential. We have been shaped by a system that seeks to diminish our power, but this book is a call to action to rise above it. Black men are steel. Steel doesn't bend to the whims of its surroundings. It stands firm, it is strong, and it shapes what it touches. We are that steel, and it's time we remember that. We've spent too long running from our responsibilities, afraid of what it means to embrace true manhood. The system has turned us into clay, shaping us into whatever it needs us to be. But we are not clay; we are steel. And this book is the hammer that will forge us into the men we were always meant to be. It's time for Black men to stand unapologetically in our power, to build, to lead, and to restore our communities. It's time for us to return to the role we were born to play: that of leaders, fathers, and warriors. And it all starts here.

PROLOGUE

A code, what is it? The Oxford Dictionary defines a code as *"a system of words, letters, figures, or other symbols substituted for other words, etc., especially for the purpose of secrecy."* In the context of computers, code refers to a set of instructions that make up the program: a systematic collection of laws or regulations. It is essential to recognize that the design and function of computers were inspired by the human brain. (I am going to let that sink in.) Other definitions are: a set of conventions governing behavior or activity in a particular sphere; a set of rules and standards adhered to by a society, class, or individuals. Codes can be converted into a specific format to convey a hidden meaning, or they can be assigned for purposes such as classification, analysis, or identification. I define a code as a pattern of conduct. When you hear the word code the first thing that will come to a lot of people's minds is the mafia, the password to your computer, or your ATM pin or if you go back like me unlimited lives on Sonic on Sega Genisis.

In the context of this book, it is defined as a pattern or consistency of behavior. Growing up in Compton, California , *"Where you from?"* was a question that was understood; if you gave the wrong code, things turned bad fast. Growing up in and around the gangbang culture, giving the wrong code could mean having to defend yourself from getting robbed or ending up in a situation where you're fighting for your life and may not make it home that day. An incorrect code can be recognized immediately, and there is a consequence for an inaccurate code. Inputting the wrong PIN at the ATM can get you locked out of your account. A code determines who gets into the building and who does not. Who gets to sit in V.I.P and who is still waiting outside?

I did not grow up with my real pops' , but I've had many real-life examples of how respectable BLACK MEN conducted themselves, and how certain behaviors that BLACK MEN engaged in reflected poorly on us as a whole. My great Grandfather fought in WW2; uncles were gangbangers from the neighborhood I grew up in and step Pops was a blue collar guy who did not take any shit and took care of his business. I was able to get a close observation of black men coming from different environments and how they dealt with the challenges of being a Black Man in America. With the lesson I have learned from these men and my own life experiences I've would like to introduce **The 14 Codes: A Black American Man Constitution Code of Conduct**. These codes are inspired by real people and their real-life experience, illustrating how they navigated certain situations and the outcomes they faced.

Growing up in Compton in the '90s, I didn't realize the kind of warzone I was really in, at least not at first. As a kid, that chaos felt normal. Sirens at night, helicopters overhead, people moving a certain way, it was just the background noise of life. But everything changed the day I watched both my uncles get shot right in front of me. I was only six years old, but that moment burned itself into my memory. That wasn't just a traumatic experience, it was a turning point. From that day forward, I couldn't look at the world the same. I stopped seeing things like a child and started seeing reality for what it was. I learned quick that life can get taken in an instant, that love doesn't protect you from bullets, and that pain doesn't wait for you to grow up. That moment didn't just scar me, it shaped me. It taught me early that this world ain't fair, and if you don't learn how to navigate it, it'll swallow you whole. My grandmother was the cornerstone of the family; like most Black American families, she was the granddaughter of slaves from the killing fields of the South. I was 13 when she passed. I look back and realize that was when I had to learn the codes as a Black man in this country. It felt like something out of the movie

"*Soul Food*," except the family never reunited. I found myself feeling a bit paranoid, surrounded by a sea of barracudas and killer whales, and as a little piranha, if I did not learn quickly, I would have drowned. My awareness of the game had to come fast; I had to learn when I was being played, scammed, and taken advantage of. It had to be a crash course, involving ducking the police, robbers, neighborhood politics, and even family. If I wasn't able to adapt quickly, I would not be here to write these codes.

As a young Black Man in the inner city of the odds were stacked. Even though 1998 had been a record low in L.A. according to the Los Angeles Times since the 70's, there still was 414 murders that year. Based on statistics from bureau of Justice 47 % of those incarcerated were black men Nation Wide! How is that possible? If the Black American community was only 12.9% leading up to the 2000 census, if it not systematic? Is it cause black men have and inherent nature to engaged in criminal behavior? I think there has been a deep ingrained perception of the BLACK MEN in this society for centuries, and their impacts are felt today. Addressing them requires sustained efforts in advocacy, policy change, education, and a collective commitment to creating more fair systems. It is an ongoing struggle, but conversations like this one are crucial in raising awareness and inspiring action. The Black American Man is the Strongest, weakest, Admired, loathed, benign, Hostile, Revered, despise, and we cannot forget most Original being on the planet. No one on this earth has been copied more than the BLACK MEN, that is a fact!

The dynamic I just explained in the above paragraph is something that the *"Black man"* has dealt with in this country since slavery. In a nation founded on the ideals of freedom and justice, the Black American man has often been denied the full benefits of these principles. Despite this, we continue to show resilience, fortitude, and the resistance to be triumphant. These codes serve as a reminder of the rich and unique experiences that trace back to the hardships endured in the killing fields of the South. They highlight the value of integrity, respect, and community, while also acknowledging the significant challenges that Black men have faced since the inception of this nation we call the *"U.S. of A."* Our history in this country is something that we should always look back on as a people. As a history enthusiast, I have come to understand that those who came before us, from our lineage, have laid the foundation and set a key milestone from which these codes are forged. Their sacrifices, made through blood, sweat, tears, and even the ultimate price of life, have shaped the legacy. These codes now serve as a guide to foster personal integrity and community solidarity. They build self-determination while acknowledging the historical and systemic injustices we have faced.

The purpose of these codes is to foster self-determination while recognizing the historical and systemic injustices we have faced. For meaningful change in our circumstances, a shift in mindset is essential within our community. There are stages that a person goes through when learning something new.

- Ignorance - *"I don't know what I don't know."* At this stage, a person is unaware of a code.
- Aware Ignorance - *"I know there are codes, but what are they?"* The individual is aware of the existence of codes but lacks understanding.
- Aware Proficiency - *"I know that I know."* The person has knowledge of the codes but still requires cognitive effort and focus to apply them in their daily lives and interactions.
- Effortless Mastery - *"I know without thinking about it."* You relate this to learning to ride a bike; after enough practice the correct way, applying the code becomes second nature.

By making a conscious effort and progressing through the stages of competence, you will not only become more aware of when the codes are being practiced, but you will also immediately recognize violations, whether they occur by you or by others in the community. The code provides the instant feedback needed to make proper decisions based on the code. However, beyond the code itself, there must be a system of consequences for any breaches. This is something we, as Black Americans, as a community, can decide together what those consequences should be. Implementing a swift and fair punishment for violations is crucial and something we must begin to prioritize. We must acknowledge that some individuals may come among us with ill intentions, lacking any desire for the betterment of our people. Holding them accountable through clear consequences will deter them from violating even a single code.

The awareness of them being broken must be heightened because they are all one, and like a chain, one weak link or violated code compromises the structure. If the code is instituted on a regular basis, it would become part of the community culture, and with enough of us standing by the code, it would create a collective mindset that would be passed down through the generations. There was an experiment conducted off the coast Japan on the island of Koshima. These experiments were trying to find out if there is a web mind among the same species, scientist would refer to it as a *"Hive Mind."*

The Hundredth Monkey Theory suggests that once a certain number of individuals in a population adopt a new behavior or idea, it will suddenly spread rapidly through the entire population, a *"tipping point,"* even to those who have had no direct contact with those individuals. This idea is often used metaphorically to explain social and cultural shifts or collective consciousness. The story behind the theory comes from a study conducted in Japan in the 1950s by researchers studying a group of macaque monkeys on the island of Koshima. The researchers observed that one monkey, a young female, started washing sweet potatoes in a river to remove the dirt. Gradually, more monkeys observed this behavior and began washing their food in the same way. The story goes that once a certain number of monkeys (often cited as 100) started washing their sweet potatoes, monkeys on other islands who had no direct contact with the original groups suddenly began exhibiting the same behavior. This led to the notion that there was a sort of *"critical mass"* or *"collective consciousness"* that caused the behavior to spread universally, even across populations with no direct connection.

The *"Hundredth Monkey"* theory, as it is often told, has been criticized for exaggerating the findings and misinterpreting the nature of the study. The behavior spread within a group of monkeys over time, and there is no evidence to suggest that it suddenly spread to other groups of monkeys at a specific threshold or that it occurred through any form of collective consciousness. Despite the scientific inaccuracies in the original story, the *"Hundredth Monkey Theory"* has taken on a symbolic role, where enough people or individuals in a society adopt a new idea, technology, or behavior, and it suddenly spreads more widely. The idea has been popularized in self-help literature, New Age thought, and discussions of collective human consciousness. It is often used to suggest that minor changes in individual behavior can lead to larger societal shifts, particularly when a critical mass of people adopts new ways of thinking or acting. The *"Hundredth Monkey Theory"* suggests that social or behavioral change can reach a tipping point once a critical mass of individuals adopts a new behavior or idea. While it is based on a misinterpretation of the original research on macaque monkeys, the theory has become a popular metaphor for collective change and the spread of ideas in society. Think of *"social media."*

This is my purpose: to create a collective mindset that will spread. Some of these codes were instilled in me at birth, and I have always lived by them; some are codes I've violated, and some I had to learn as I navigated through life as a Black man in America. By adhering to these codes, we not only honor the legacy of those who came before us but also empower ourselves to create a future defined by progress and unity. We can cultivate a culture of accountability and respect that uplifts our communities and promotes understanding across all areas of life. I want this book to be a source of inspiration and a call to action as we navigate the complexities of our existence in a place that never had good intentions for those who look like me.

With that, I present...

The 14 Codes: The Black American Man Constitutional Code of Conduct

THERE ARE FIVE PRINCIPLES.

- Discipline
- Integrity
- Brotherhood
- Sovereignty
- Legacy

A MALE IS A NOUN, and a MAN is a Verb.

1. A Black MAN will never let anyone question his Integrity.
2. A Black MAN will never let anyone question his Work Ethic.
3. A Black MAN has Emotions, but he is not Emotional.
4. A Black MAN shows Character. Character is defined as the ability to follow through.
5. A Black MAN doesn't Gossip.
6. A Black MAN doesn't Request respect, he Commands it!
7. A Black MAN understands that a woman doesn't make him, she is only a reflection of the male that he is.
8. A Black MAN will die for his Responsibilities.

9. A Black MAN understands that if his Words mean nothing, he is Useless.
10. A Black MAN gives Reasons not Excuses.
11. A Black MAN is Proactive not Reactive.
12. A Black MAN understands that if he can't produce, he is a dead man.
13. A Black MAN holds his peers accountable.
14. A Black MAN understands that his Dick can make or Break him.

A male is what you are.
A MAN is what you do.

INTRODUCTION

In school, we were taught about slavery, and I watched movies about it. Growing up, I associated white supremacy with the word *"nigger,"* but I now realize that the issue is much deeper than that. I gained a more comprehensive understanding of the dynamic between Black American men and white supremacy through the work of Dr. Frances Cress Welsing. Dr. Frances Cress Welsing (1935–2016) was a prominent Black psychiatrist and scholar best known for her work on race, racism, and its psychological effects on Black or nonwhite people. Dr. Welsing was born Frances Luella Cress in Chicago on March 18, 1935. In 1957, she earned a B.S. degree at Antioch College in Yellow Springs, Ohio. In 1962, Dr. Welsing received her medical degree in psychology from Howard University in Washington, D.C. As a graduation gift, she took a trip to Germany in 1964 to complete a year of psychiatric training at a psychiatric hospital in Munich. She was awarded a medical fellowship at the hospital. After her training abroad, Dr. Welsing explained how she was able to observe European attitudes toward race and racial dynamics, which helped her refine her theories about white supremacy, racism, and the psychological impact of racial oppression in America. With a new profound perspective after her return to the United States, in 1970 she wrote the "**Cress Theory of Color-Confrontation and Racism**," which argued that white supremacy is rooted in a deep psychological fear of genetic annihilation due to the prevalence of Blackness and the genetic dominance of Black people. Twenty-one years later, she published her infamous book (*"to the white supremacist and coon class"*), "**The ISIS Papers: The Key to the Colors**," in 1991.

In her book, Dr. Welsing defines racism (white supremacy) as:

"The local and global power system structured and maintained but persons who classify themselves as white, whether consciously or subconsciously determined; this system consists of patterns of perception, logic, symbol formation, thought, speech action and emotional response, as conducted simultaneously in all areas of people activity (economics, education, entertainment, labor, law, politics, religion, sex, and war). The ultimate purpose of the system is to prevent white genetic annihilation on Earth- a planet in which the overwhelming majority of people are classified

as non-white (black, brown, red, yellow) by whites-skinned people. All of the non-white people are genetically dominant (in terms of skin coloration) compared to the genetically recessive, white-skinned people."

With this type of psyche how could we ever be considered equal as black people, in particularly BLACK MEN in this country. (Because we as black men carry the ultimate weapon for that genetic annihilation that the white supremacist fear so much according to Dr. Welsing). Dr Welsing also address how the BLACK MEN is perceived as a boy in the country, as our history as shown, going back to slavery all the way up to the civil rights movement BLACK MEN were referred to as *"boy."* No matter the intellect or strength. In Nelly Fullers' Book **The United Independent Compensatory Code/System/Concept (The Compensatory Counter Racism-Code)**, who was one of the first to define racism, or white supremacy, in a way that sheds light on the dynamics of this system. His work emphasizes that in a white supremacist society, Black American men are often relegated to three roles: that of an infant, a boy, or a woman. Dr. Welsing agreed with this framework and further argued that as the system of white supremacy evolves, it would push BLACK MEN to adopt more feminine roles, including wearing dresses. I must admit that these two scholars made prophetic statements that are now observable in modern society. This is no longer just a perception, but a reality that we are actively witnessing and engaging in.

Since slavery to the civil rights movement as black had not rights that a white had to respect. Statement made by Chief Justice Roger B. Taney in (Dred Scott v. Standford 60 U.S. 393) March 6, 1857. During Jim Crow, a Black man had to walk with his head down, step off the sidewalk in to gutters for white women and children. We were not allowed to raise our voice around white people and we even had to dumb down our intelligence, being an *"uppity nigga"* was a threat. History has shown us what happens to certain groups outside of the WS and within their own group. They can become very violent. The recorded record of this violent can be seen in books like **"Without Sanctury" lynching photography in America** which is a collection of photographs and postcards from lynching, primarily in the late 19th and early 20th centuries.

The images are deeply disturbing and show public lynching, often accompanied by crowds of white spectators. Also, **"100 Years of Lynching"** by Ralph Ginzburg was written in 1962. This book focuses on a detailed historical account of lynching in the United States, particularly around the same period in the late 19th century and early 20th century. It provides a chilling record of over 4,700 documented lynchings of Black American MEN and WOMEN, focusing on the years between 1882 and 1962. *"60 years of fucking recorded lynches."* LET THAT SINK IN! Having to conform to this type of environment, how could there be any progress? Dr. Welsing was also quoted in the Black community cult classic *"Baby Boy."*

Growing up in Compton, CA, the movie resonated with me on a personal level not only because I recognized the locations where some scenes were filmed, but also because many of the situations depicted were ones I had either experienced myself or witnessed others go through. In this country, Black American men are often viewed as infantile, as modern times reveal through both societal behavior and treatment. At the beginning of the movie, Dr. Welsing's idea of the Black man is that he has been made to think of himself as a baby, a not yet fully formed being who has not realized his full potential. The movie references how we as black man refer to our woman as *"Momma,"* how we call close friends our *"boys"* and how we refer to our house as the *"crib".* With a lot of this behavior being passed down through the generation and the trauma associated with it, we must recognize that our behavior contributes to this false perception and is the first step toward change. As individuals and as a community, we must be aware of both how we act and how we are perceived and be committed to altering both for our own benefit. That is what The 14 codes are about changing the behavior.

"If we continue the same behavior, we will continue to get the same results."

CODE NO. 1

A BLACK AMERICAN MAN NEVER LETS ANYONE QUESTION HIS INTEGRITY

The foundation of any structure is very important. The higher you build the deeper the foundation must be. The first 4 codes are the foundation of the fourteen, with them the other twelve are useless. The Oxford definition of Integrity; the quality of being honest and having strong moral principles; moral uprightness. #2 the state of being whole and undivided. The condition of being unified, unimpaired, or sound in construction. Integrity comes from Latin integritas, which means integer 'intact.' If you look up the work integer it means a number that is not a fraction, a whole number. The Second definition is a thing complete IN itself. When used to describe individuals it refers to a person living by their values and principles, whatever those may be. Being able to define your reality is power and the information I have gathered through books and my own life experiences, my definition of Integrity is BEING ABLE TO STAND ON YOUR SHIT. This may seem like something simple, but today in the 21st century people are afraid to be who they truly are. Integrity to me is making it known to everyone who you encounter whether in public or private, family, friends, business partner or lover where you truly stand on every issue and the receipts on why you are standing on it. As a man, once that line has been drawn it is never supposed to be crossed. Being able to display your true self in any environment is real integrity. It starts from within. BLACK MEN you should have a threshold and once that threshold has exceeded past it limits there has to be consequences. No compromising!

"Doing the right thing," some may say, is a good representation of integrity. I would ask, what is the *"right thing"*? This country thought slavery was the right thing. The *"right thing"* is subjective. An analogy I use to back this is: a man who robs a bank to feed his hungry family; in this example, what is *"right"*? Is the man wrong for robbing the bank, or is he right for trying to feed those who look to him for protection and provisions? Now society would say that the man is breaking the law (especially a Black man). As I referred to in my intro, we have to study our history, going back to slavery all the way up to modern times; all men have never been equal under the law. Under the system that

governs this country, which is White Supremacy, a Black man is never, has never been, and will never be considered an equal to the white supremacists. I like that to be understood, so we don't have to spend time on why we receive the treatment we do compare to non-black people.

I'll say it again: what is considered the *"right thing"* depends on the individual. What I perceive as the right course of action may be seen differently by someone else, who might view my approach as wrong. This also applies to groups of people. Two different groups might witness the same situation but have completely different emotional responses and ways of handling it. Consider the cases of George Floyd and Kyle Rittenhouse. Going back to my earlier point, and the understanding that the *"right thing"* is subjective and shaped by perspective, integrity is about standing firm in your personal morals and principles and being prepared for both praise and backlash for doing so. If the men in our community were open about who they are and what they stand for, nothing would be a surprise. We would be able to identify the snakes, sellouts, informants, and those with harmful behavior among us. This transparency would reduce confusion and help prevent the efforts of those seeking to infiltrate and harm our community.

"A MAN that stands for nothing, will fall for anything" like the old saying goes, no matter what the situation

you may be confronted with you have to keep the same pattern of behavior. You Have to Stand ON It!!! When faced with a decision you must make the choice based on the outline of yourself you have created from past behavior and outcomes. Whether for money, sex, status, and even for those you love there must be a consistency in the behavior patterns. Integrity is being met with the possibility of those patterns being broken and staying consistent with who you truly are. No conformity No compromise.

Christopher Dorner, Nickey Barnes, and James Baldwin are three Black American men I would like to use as examples. I chose Christopher Dorner because, when confronted with a moral dilemma, he chose to stand by his principles. His decision to expose corruption within the Los Angeles Police Department (LAPD) was based on the oath he took as a peace officer. His actions, however, took a violent turn, leading to a tragic and highly controversial outcome. The story of Christopher Dorner highlights the complexity of integrity, especially when one's principles clash with systemic corruption and institutional failure. Dorner adhered to his beliefs despite the personal and professional consequences, but his methods complicate the notion of integrity. Nicky Barnes was a Harlem kingpin, no doubt, but he's the flip side of the coin. Yeah, he had his own rules and played the game like a boss for a while. But in the end, he broke the same code he claimed to live by, just like the people around him.

When folks talk about his *"feelings being hurt,"* that tells you everything. He let emotions and the streets get to him, and that pulled him off his square. What started as a man moving with purpose turned into someone reacting outta pain and ego. He lost sight of the code, and that's when it all unraveled. This compared to Dorner's unwavering adherence to his beliefs and illustrates how external pressures, such as personal conflicts or betrayal, can erode integrity. James Baldwin went through hell, dealing with racism and having to face his own sexuality in a time where both could get you silenced or killed. But what I respect most is how he never folded. Through all that, he stood ten toes down on being seen and respected as a man, A *"Black American Man"* at that! His integrity came from that refusal to be anything less, no matter what the world threw at him. The emphasis on Baldwin's refusal to let his sexuality define him in the face of societal discrimination. His focus on demanding respect as a Black man reflects a broader principle of self-worth and dignity, and he did so in an environment that was hostile to both his race and his sexuality.

Baldwin never used his sexuality as a crutch for the unequal treatment that he faced; his commitment to integrity and his resilience in facing societal pressures without compromising his identity as a Black man. Through these figures I would like to illustrate the complex ways in which integrity is both defined and challenged. Dorner stands firm in his moral stance, but his violent methods may be questioned by some people. Barnes shows the fragility of personal codes when faced with emotional turmoil and betrayal. Baldwin, however, represents a steadfast commitment to self-respect and the dignity of Black manhood, despite the dual burdens of racism and societal expectations of sexuality. Each of these Black men's grapples with their sense of integrity in different ways, making them compelling examples of how Integrity can be tested in the face of personal, societal, and institutional forces.

Last Resort

What happens when a Black man reaches his breaking point? Christopher Dorner is a stark example of the consequences. Dorner, a former LAPD officer, led authorities on a nine-day manhunt across California that left the state's law enforcement shaken to its core. A million-dollar reward was posted for his capture. To put this in perspective, Osama Bin Laden's bounty reached $25 million, and the whole world was on the lookout for him. But the million-dollar reward for Dorner, a Black man, illustrates how deeply fearful and desperate the authorities were to apprehend him. The fear of a Black man with military training, capable of defying the system, has always been something this country has struggled to confront.

Christopher Jordan Dorner, badge #7648, was born in New York in 1979. His family later moved to

Norwalk, California, a middle-class suburb of Los Angeles. If you're familiar with Los Angeles' history, you know the region had an invisible *"Mason-Dixon line"* when it came to segregation. From the turn of the 19th century, the city systematically marginalized and mistreated its Black community. Racism within the LAPD has been a constant, dating back to Chief William H. Parker, who recruited officers from the Jim Crow South. Even with the appointment of the city's first Black police chief, Benard Parks, systemic racism persisted. This historical context is crucial for understanding the challenges Dorner faced in his career and life.

When Dorner grew up in Norwalk, a predominantly white area, he had to navigate attending mostly white schools. In his manifesto, he describes the internal conflict he experienced as a Black kid in a hostile environment, dealing with societal prejudices while trying to reconcile his own identity. He recalls how, as a child, he was often called racial slurs like *"nigger"* and how he would be punished for reacting to the insults. This internal struggle, the tension between perception and reality, is something Black men often face. As Black men, we are constantly fighting against negative stereotypes, but in doing so, we sometimes amplify those same perceptions, despite our best efforts to disprove them.

Officer Dorner graduated from high school and went on to play football at Southern Utah University.

He earned a bachelor's degree in political science with a minor in psychology. In 2002, Officer Dorner was commissioned as an officer in the United States Navy Reserve. He led a security unit at Naval Air Station Fallon in Nevada, served with a Mobile Inshore Undersea Warfare Unit from June 2004 to February 2006, and was deployed to Bahrain with Coastal Riverine Group Two from November 2006 to April 2007. He was honorably discharged with the rank of lieutenant. An unverified story from Officer Dorner's time as an undergraduate during his pilot training at Vance Air Force Base in Enid, Oklahoma, recalls an incident in which he and a classmate found a bag containing nearly $8,000.

The bag belonged to the nearby Korean Church of Grace. Dorner and his classmate turned the money over to the police. Dorner later explained their actions, stating, *"The military stresses integrity."* He added that his mother had taught him the importance of honesty and integrity. During his time in the Navy Reserve, Officer Dorner earned the Navy Rifle Marksmanship Ribbon and the Navy Pistol Shot Ribbon, achievements that would later be referenced in the unfolding of his story. From February 7, 2005, to January 2, 2009, Officer Dorner served as a patrol officer for the Harbor Division of the Los Angeles Police Department (LAPD). His tenure ended after he was terminated for allegedly making a false claim against his field training officer, Teresa Evans.

Officer Dorner accused Officer Evans of kicking a suspect multiple times, including once in the head, while the suspect was handcuffed. The internal affairs investigation found insufficient evidence to support Dorner's allegations of excessive force, leading to his dismissal. Dorner appealed his termination, but the Los Angeles Supreme Court upheld the decision. At this point in his career, Officer Dorner felt he was being punished for doing the *"right thing."* However, his actions violated the unwritten code of silence within the police force, what is often referred to as the *"blue line."* This breach would have significant consequences for him and set the stage for what followed.

On February 3, 2013, four years after Officer Dorner was let go from the Los Angeles Police Department, Monica Quan and Kenneth Lawrence were found shot to death in their car in the parking structure of their apartment complex in Irvine, CA. It was later found that Monica Quan was the daughter of Capt. Randel Quan, who was Officer Dorner's representative during his hearings in front of the Board of Rights (BOR). *"BOR,"* as it is referred to, is the disciplinary appeal board that has the ultimate say in whether a LAPD officer accused of misconduct may remain in the force or what reprimand an officer may receive. According to Officer Dorner's manifesto (I will dive into the manifesto later in the chapter), he became aware that two of the officers on the BOR were close acquaintances of Officer Teras Evans. On February 6,

Officer Dorner posted his infamous manifesto on the social media website Facebook, taking responsibility for the murders of Monica Quan and Kenneth Lawrence. A few days before the manifesto was released, the National City Police Department in California (located 88 miles from Irvine, where the murders took place) discovered a police uniform bearing Officer Dorner's name. Officer Evans, upon learning this, informed the investigators handling the murders that Dorner might be connected to the killings of Monica Quan and her fiancé. Given the close timing of these events, Officer Dorner quickly became the primary suspect in the case.

On February, 07, 2013 Two LAPD officers were in route to a protection detail, assigned to provide security for an officer possibly targeted by Dorner, when they were flagged down by R. L. McDaniel around 1:00 AM. McDaniel reported seeing a man matching Dorner's description at a gas station in Corona. The officers investigated the tip and were following a pickup truck when the driver suddenly stopped, got out, and opened fire with a rifle, grazing one officer's head. About 20 minutes after the shooting in Corona, two Riverside Police Department officers were ambushed and shot while stopped at a red light in their marked patrol vehicle. Officer Michael Crain was fatally shot, while the other officer was critically injured but survived after emergency surgery. Around an hour and 25 minutes later, at approximately 3:00

AM, a man matching Dorner's description attempted to steal a boat in San Diego, telling the boat's captain that he intended to take it to Mexico. On the same day, a federal criminal complaint was filed against Dorner for allegedly fleeing California to evade prosecution. Hours later, the charred remains of Dorner's vehicle, a dark gray 2005 Nissan Titan, were discovered by local resident Daniel McGowan on a remote fire trail near Big Bear Lake, about 80 miles from Los Angeles. Investigators immediately began searching the area, with around 125 officers canvassing homes door-to-door. All schools in the Big Bear Valley Unified School District were placed on lockdown.

On February 12, deputies from the San Bernardino County Sheriff's Department (SBSD) responded to a report of a carjacking involving a white Dodge truck at 12:22 PM and immediately began searching for the vehicle both on the ground and from the air. The truck's driver was unharmed. Fish and Wildlife officers were the first to spot the vehicle and recognized Dorner as the driver. Officers from various agencies pursued Dorner to a cabin near Big Bear Lake. Dorner opened fire on two SBSD officers, wounding both. The officers were airlifted to Loma Linda University Medical Center, where Detective Jeremiah MacKay was later pronounced dead. The SBSD confirmed to the media that Dorner was barricaded inside a cabin near the manhunt's command center, located in a mountainous rural area northeast of Angelus Oaks. The cabin was surrounded by law enforcement, and reports indicated that there might be hostages inside.

A three-mile perimeter was established around the cabin, and nearby residents were instructed to stay indoors with their doors locked. The police first attempted to force Dorner out by deploying tear gas and making loudspeaker announcements demanding his surrender. When he did not respond, law enforcement used a demolition vehicle to knock down much of the cabin's walls. They then fired pyrotechnic tear gas canisters, known as *"burners,"* into the cabin, causing a fire. Soon after, a single gunshot was heard from within the cabin. As the fire spread, ammunition inside the cabin began to explode, making it hazardous for officials to attempt to extinguish the flames. There was some debate among law enforcement experts regarding the justification for using pyrotechnic devices to end the standoff rather than waiting for Dorner to emerge. Later that evening, both the LAPD and SBSD denied reports that Dorner's body had been recovered from the burned cabin. LAPD Commander Andrew Smith confirmed that nobody had been removed from the scene, as the area was *"too hot to make entry."* On February 13, reports surfaced that human remains had been found in the remains of the cabin, along with a wallet containing a California driver's license bearing the name *"Christopher Dorner."* That same day, San Bernardino County Sheriff John McMahon denied rumors that deputies had intentionally set the cabin on fire. It was also revealed that deputies had earlier knocked on the cabin's door during their search for Dorner but left after receiving no response. On February 14, medical examiners confirmed through dental records that the charred remains found in the cabin were those of Dorner. The following day, the SBSD announced that the autopsy revealed Dorner died from a single self-inflicted gunshot wound to the head.

Now that you are familiar with his story, I'd like to explore why I chose this Black man as an example of integrity. I want us to understand the mindset of a Black man who feels he has no other option. The events leading up to his alleged suicide paint a picture of someone willing to demonstrate, even to the world, that he would die for his principles. This is clearly seen in his manifesto, which not only explains the reasoning behind his actions but also reveals how he exhausted every possible measure before sparking a nine-day manhunt across the state of California. The manifesto delves into his political views, particularly his feelings as a Black man navigating the bigotry and racism in this country. It also highlights the cognitive dissonance and confusion he grappled with as he fought against the stereotype of the *"Big Black Angry Nigger."*

In his manifesto, Officer Dorner states that one of the key motivations for his actions was the injustice and corruption within the LAPD. He claims he was wrongfully terminated after reporting police misconduct, specifically an incident in which he accused a fellow officer of using excessive force against a suspect. Dorner also describes experiencing systemic racism and discrimination within the LAPD, which he believes contributed to his unfair treatment and eventual dismissal. He names several officers whom he accuses of corruption, dishonesty, and misconduct, which he asserts the LAPD failed to address. In his manifesto, he also details how various classifications within the department were complicit in these behaviors. Here's an excerpt from the manifesto addressing this issue:

"Those Caucasian officers who join South Bureau divisions (77th,SW,SE, an Harbor) with the sole intent to victimize minorities who are uneducated, and unaware of criminal law, civil law, and civil rights. You prefer the South bureau because a use of force/deadly force is likely and the individual you use UOF on will likely not report it. You are a high value target. Those Black officers in supervisory ranks and pay grades who stay in south bureau (even though you live in the valley or OC) for the sole intent of getting retribution toward subordinate Caucasians officers for the pain and hostile work environment their elders inflicted on you as probationers (P-1's) and novice P-2's. You are a high value target. You perpetuated the cycle of racism in the department as well. You breed a new generation of bigoted Caucasian officer when you belittle them and treat them unfairly. Those Hispanic officers who victimize their own ethnicity because they are new immigrants to this country

and are unaware of their civil rights. You call them wetbacks to their face and demean them in front of fellow officers of different ethnicities so that you will receive some sort of acceptance from your colleagues. I'm not impressed. Most likely, your parents or grandparents were immigrants at one time, but you have forgotten that. You are a high value target. Those lesbian officers in supervising positions who go to work, day in day out, with the sole intent of attempting to prove your misandrist authority (not feminism) to degrade male officers. You are a high value target. Those Asian officers who stand by and observe everything I previously mentioned other officers participate in on a daily basis, but you say nothing, stand for nothing and protect nothing. Why? Because of your usual saying," I......don't like conflict". You are a high value target as well. Those of you who "go along to get along" have no backbone and destroy the foundation of courage. You are the enablers of those who are guilty of misconduct. You are just as guilty as those who break the code of ethics and oath you swore."

One thing I noticed is that the groups Dorner named all have a history of mistreating and displaying a vitriolic attitude toward Black men and the Black community. As a Black man, this is the reality we face while trying to uphold the so-called *"blue line."* Dorner frames his violent actions as a form of retaliation for the injustices he believes he suffered at the hands of the LAPD. He argues that his career and reputation were ruined by false accusations, and he felt it was his duty to expose and seek justice for what he perceived as systemic corruption. Dorner viewed his actions as self-defense against a corrupt system, and after exhausting all legal and institutional avenues, he saw taking matters into his own hands as his last resort. He demanded accountability for the LAPD officers involved in the alleged misconduct and called for broader reform within the police department and justice system. Dorner specifically named individuals whom he held responsible for his firing and what he saw as corruption within the LAPD. He warned of violence against these individuals and their families, criticizing the "blue code of silence," where police officers protect each other even when wrongdoing occurs. Dorner made a controversial argument that, at times, violence is necessary to draw attention to injustice and to hold corrupt institutions accountable.

Although his manifesto primarily justifies his violent actions, it also advocates for societal and institutional reform, particularly within law enforcement. Dorner expressed a desire to go out *"in a blaze of glory,"* believing that his death would serve as the ultimate sacrifice in his fight for justice. He concluded the manifesto with a farewell message, expressing love for his family and friends while reaffirming his commitment to the violent actions he planned to take. Some might view Dorner's manifesto as a controversial and tragic document, which, in his eyes, served as an act of revenge against an institution that wronged him. His actions and the resulting police manhunt brought attention to issues of police misconduct, systemic corruption, and how unresolved grievances within law enforcement can lead to catastrophic consequences. The fact that Officer Dorner exhausted every measure and felt unheard, drove him to take drastic actions that cost the state millions in a true definition of the understanding of integrity.

The manhunt for Christopher Dorner ended up costing close to $250 million, according to the Press-Telegram. It turned into one of the biggest mobilizations in California law enforcement history. LAPD, Riverside PD, U.S. Marshals, and other agencies jumped in heavy. SWAT teams, helicopters, drones, armored vehicles—the whole nine. Cops were working nonstop, racking up insane overtime. But in all that frenzy, the system showed its fear. In Torrance, LAPD officers shot up a truck with two innocent women inside, thinking it was Dorner. But here's the kicker: the truck didn't even match Dorner's. Different make, different model, different color. The only "*match*" was that it was a truck. That shooting wasn't about proper ID, it was straight paranoia. Cops across L.A. County were spooked, not thinking clearly, reacting outta fear and pressure. Those women were hospitalized, and the LAPD ended up in court, paying out settlements and legal fees. Internal investigations followed, plus the backlash from the public, all draining even more money and resources. The city had to eat insurance costs too. Nobody wants to talk about how fear of a Black man standing up and fighting back had the entire system in panic mode. Dorner didn't just challenge them—he exposed how far they'd go, how reckless they'd get, and how quick they'd shoot anything that moved if it even felt like a threat. That's the real cost.

The role of Black men as police officers remains a heated and often disapproved topic within the Black community. This stance is rooted in the undeniable history of U.S. law enforcement, which traces back to the South's slave-catching patrols and the legal systems that upheld slavery. Policing in America was built on racial control, with slave patrols established in the early 1700s to track down runaways, prevent revolts, and maintain the grip of white supremacy. These patrols, backed by law, laid the foundation for modern policing, reinforcing oppressive laws like the *"Fugitive Slave Act of 1850,"* which required even free states to return escaped slaves. This history continues to cast a long shadow over the relationship between law enforcement and the Black community.

Back in the day, local law enforcement was legally required to help hunt down runaway slaves. And on top of that, they had these so-called *"slave catchers"*—everyday men, often ex-slave owners or folks with money and pride wrapped up in slavery, getting paid to keep that system alive. That same mindset never really died. You still see it today in bounty hunters, vigilantes, and these self-appointed *"Karens"* who call the cops on

Black folks just for existing—knowing nothing's gonna happen to them. That slave-catching spirit still lives in the way the system polices us now. So when you talk about Black men joining the police force, it gets real complicated. There's a lot of tension there. Some feel like they gotta prove themselves by showing more loyalty to the badge than to their own people. Some even go too far, trying to earn respect from white officers by distancing themselves from where they came from. Dorner's story brings all of that to the surface. His experience puts a spotlight on what it really means to be a Black cop in a system built to work against your own. It shows how deep the injustice runs, and how the pressure to fit in can turn into a fight against your own identity.

His story also reveals the mental conflict Black officers navigate, walking the tightrope between their personal identity and their professional role. The pressure to conform, to suppress one's Blackness in order to *"succeed,"* is a battle many Black officers fight daily. The system demands allegiance while historically waging war against the very communities from which these officers come from.

From Jim Crow to the Civil Rights Movement to the present day, the mistrust between Black people and the police has been well earned. Black officers are scrutinized for their actions, their motivations questioned, and their loyalty doubted. This distrust has only intensified over the last decade, fueled by the public execution of Black men, women, and children at the hands of white or non-Black officers. The names Aiyana Jones, Rekia Boyd, Sandra Bland, Mike Brown, Eric Garner, George Floyd—and Tamir Rice—are etched into our memory like scars. Each one is a painful reminder that this system keeps coming for Black lives with no accountability. These weren't accidents—they were executions in a society that sees Black skin as a threat. And the fact that most of the killers walked free? That's the real message: our lives still don't matter to the system unless we force them to.

But Dorner was different. He refused to be a pawn in a rigged game. His manifesto revealed his inner turmoil, his disillusionment, and the depth of his conviction. A man's integrity is not just about what he says; it is about what he builds within himself. Thoughts, words, and actions must align. When a line is crossed, a real man acts. Integrity has always been a battleground for Black men. From the moment we came into contact with white and non-Black societies, our morals, values, and sense of self have been under attack. What we deem *"just"* and honorable is often condemned, challenged, or outright erased.

A Black man stands firm in his beliefs. He does not waver. He does not beg for respect; he commands it. And if necessary, he is willing to give everything, including his life, to uphold his principles. Christopher Dorner embodied this. His actions were a declaration, a refusal to bow, a refusal to betray himself. Whether one agrees with his choices or not, his story forces a reckoning with the realities of what it means to be Black in law enforcement and Black in America.

Rest in power, Officer Dorner.

Mr. Untouchable

In Black neighborhoods all across the country, young Black boys grow up watching the men around them, at home, on the block, or in the streets. With the system built to keep real Black men out of positions of power in schools, workplaces, and even the family, these boys look up to the men who seem to be winning where they can: pimps, hustlers, and gangsters. These men demand respect, control their environment, and make their presence felt. The money, cars, jewelry, and designer clothes are more than just material things; they are proof that they've figured out how to move in a world that was never built for them. In a society that denies Black men opportunities at every turn, these street legends become the blueprint for survival and success.

Since slavery, the Black man's identity has been dictated by forces outside of him. Back then, he wasn't seen as a man; he was property, a workhorse, a tool to breed. Whether he was being sold like cattle, locked into convict leasing, or lynched for something as small as looking at a white woman, his humanity was constantly under attack. Over time, that message sank in. Many Black men started measuring their worth by what they could do physically, either through hard labor, their sexual prowess, or how much money they could stack: **"Our Back, Our Dick, or Our Wallets."** That mindset didn't die with the past; it carried over. Our grandfathers came from families with a dozen kids, sometimes out of necessity for survival, and other times because having a big family was one of the few ways a Black man could feel like a man in a world determined to strip him of everything.

After Emancipation, the system kept its foot on the necks of Black men through laws and policies designed to keep us at the bottom. Jim Crow wasn't just about segregation, it was about control. It was about making sure Black men had no real economic, social, or political power. Meanwhile, our women, who had their own struggles to bear, were often forced into the role of both nurturer and provider. This wasn't by choice, it was survival. But over time, it created a dynamic where Black men found it harder to assert themselves as the head of the household, the leader, or even the protector. From the plantation to the modern-day prison system, from racist policies to expectations within our own families, Black men have never been given the space to define masculinity on our own terms. We've always had to fight for our identity, while the world told us who we were supposed to be.

"Cash Rules Everything Around Me"—C.R.E.A.M. That's what it was about: the money. As young Black boys coming up, trying to figure out what it meant to

be a man, all we had was what we saw on TV, in the music, or on the corner. And what we saw was a twisted version of manhood. In a world that kept taking power from us, we learned to chase it through money, control, and status. Manhood got tied to how much you had in your pocket, how many people feared you, and how well you could survive. Not because we were born like that, but because every other route was blocked. The system shut down access to legit success. Racism kept us out, police brutality kept us down, and the economy kept us broke. So the streets became the classroom, and crime became the curriculum. We stopped moving as one. Instead of building with each other, we competed. Instead of brotherhood, we got isolation. The world trained us to believe that if you ain't on top, you ain't a man. And the only way to the top was to dominate—by any means necessary.

This wasn't by accident. White supremacy orchestrated this system, a trap designed to keep us locked into cycles of struggle, crime, and survival. For generations, too many of us have been unable to see beyond the boundaries they set. History has given us countless influential Black figures, but let's focus on Leroy "Nickey" Barnes, a man once idolized in the Black community. In the 1970s, Barnes was one of the most notorious drug dealers in Harlem. He commanded power, money, and respect, but in the end, he violated his own code of conduct. When the pressure came down, he snitched, betraying the very values he claimed to live by. Compare that to Christopher Dorner, a man who, despite the controversy surrounding his actions, stood on his principles until the end. Coming off the high of Jim Crow, Black people in America were walking with a new sense of self-worth. We had fought, we had survived, and we expected our rightful place in this country. But just as we started gaining ground, the system struck back. White flight pulled economic resources out of Black communities, leaving us with nothing but abandoned buildings and broken dreams. That's when the drugs came in. Richard Rothstein's *Color of Law* exposes this in Chapter 6, page 96. He breaks down how the government played a direct role in robbing Black families of homeownership opportunities through discriminatory practices like the contract sale system. At first, when Black families moved into white neighborhoods, property values went up because Black buyers were forced to pay inflated prices. But once enough white homeowners were scared into selling at a loss, those falling prices were then used as *"proof"* that Black residents lowered property values. The Federal Housing Administration (FHA) backed this racist system, ensuring that Black families remained locked out of true economic stability. If not for these unconstitutional policies, Black families could have spread throughout metropolitan areas rather than being forced into overcrowded, underfunded ghettos ripe for exploitation.

With resources stripped from our neighborhoods,

an underground economy emerged. Black men, boxed out of legitimate financial opportunities, turned to the streets to survive. The Italian Mob saw this vulnerability and took full advantage, flooding Black communities with heroin. Nickey Barnes himself understood the game: *"The closer you are to the connect, the more power you hold."* That was the golden rule. After doing time in prison, he made the right connections, securing his supply from Matty Madonna, a known mobster from the Lucchese crime family operating out of Pleasant Avenue in East Harlem. The Italian Mafia had a stranglehold on the heroin trade, thanks to their infamous *"French Connection,"* a smuggling operation that funneled massive amounts of heroin from Marseille, France, into the U.S. At its peak, nearly 80% of the heroin on American streets came from this pipeline, with New York City acting as the main distribution hub. What we saw in the 1970s was not a coincidence; it was a setup. The government blocked Black men from legal wealth, and the mob handed them an illegal alternative. The destruction that followed wasn't just about drugs, it was about the system ensuring that Black men stayed in survival mode, fighting for scraps in a game that was rigged from the start.

Nickey Barnes was born in Harlem, New York, in 1933 to parents who had migrated from the South in search of better opportunities. Like most Black families back in the day, his folks got hit hard by the system racism, poverty, limited options. They ended up in

Harlem, a place full of soul but starving for opportunity. That pressure cooker created hustlers, and Nicky Barnes came up right in the middle of it. He started out using, just like a lot of people trying to numb the pain. But he was different, he peeped the business side of it. Instead of letting the drugs take him out, he flipped the script. *"Don't get high on your own supply"*—that became his code. He stuck to it, and that discipline took him from a small-time hustler to one of the most feared and respected kingpins in the game during the 1970s. He didn't just survive the streets—he mastered them, for a time.

Barnes's rise to power was not just a product of his ambition but also of strategic alliances. He built a sophisticated heroin distribution network that stretched from New York to the West Coast, demonstrating a level of organization that rivaled established crime syndicates. However, no one builds an empire alone, and Barnes knew this well. His most crucial alliances were with the Italian Mafia, particularly the Lucchese family and Joe Gallo of the Colombo family. The Italian Mob controlled much of New York's underworld, from extortion and drugs to prostitution and blackmail. Recognizing Barnes's ability to efficiently distribute heroin, they provided him with protection, smuggling routes, and large-scale shipments of drugs. Barnes, in turn, kept the heroin moving, making both himself and his Mafia counterparts extremely wealthy. By 1977, Barnes had become a national figure, even gracing the cover of **The New York Times** with the headline *"Mr. Untouchable."* This level of notoriety, however, proved to be both a blessing and a curse. Barnes began to see himself as more than just a middleman in the Mafia's operation; he believed he was on their level, if not superior. Some speculate that his increased use of *"angel dust"* contributed to this delusion, but regardless of the cause, his newfound arrogance created tension between him and his Italian connections. The Mob, historically dismissive of Black crime syndicates, was unlikely to tolerate Barnes's growing self-importance.

As Barnes' empire expanded, he sought to formalize his operation by establishing *"The Council,"* a governing body of top heroin distributors. Modeled after the Mafia's organizational structure, *"The Council"* was meant to ensure stability, discipline, and collective decision-making. Each member had a vote, but Barnes retained veto power, making it clear that he was still in charge. The Council controlled various territories: Frank James, Ishmael Mohammed (known as *"Brother"*), and Wally Rice ran Harlem's East Side; Thomas Fore (*"Gaps"*) dominated Brooklyn; Guy Fisher oversaw the South Bronx; and Jazz managed the West Side. Meanwhile, Barnes controlled the heroin market on 8th Avenue and 116th Street, considered the epicenter of Harlem's drug trade. Barnes's long-term vision for The Council was not just about dominating the heroin market but transitioning into legitimate business ventures. He saw the drug trade as a temporary means to an end, a stepping stone to real estate investments, car dealerships, laundromats, and other legal enterprises. However, his frustration grew as he realized that his partners did not share his ambition. Many of them were content with their immediate wealth, indulging in fast money, luxury cars, and women rather than planning for a sustainable future. Barnes believed that their short-term thinking made them liabilities, and this fundamental difference in mindset contributed to cracks within The Council.

A key figure in Barnes' operation was Guy Fisher, who had the intelligence and business acumen to transition into legitimate enterprises. Fisher even went on to purchase the Apollo Theater, a move that demonstrated his awareness of the power of reinvesting in Black institutions. Yet, despite his efforts, Barnes still saw him and the others as short-sighted, believing that their focus remained too deeply rooted in street-level control rather than in building a legacy. This perception of stagnation only deepened Barnes's frustration and paranoia. Over time, Barnes began to believe that his fellow Council members were not just lacking vision but were actively working against him. His paranoia convinced him that if they were not thinking about the future, they were likely plotting to overthrow him. This distrust, coupled with his growing ego, set the stage for the unraveling of everything he had built. His downfall came when he was arrested and sentenced to life in prison. From behind bars, he watched as the empire he created continued to thrive without him, further intensifying his feelings of betrayal. This sense of abandonment led him to make the ultimate violation of the street code: he became an informant. Barnes's decision to testify against *"The Council"* was driven by a mix of bitterness and self-preservation. In his mind, if his so-called brothers did not share his vision and loyalty, they did not deserve to reap the rewards of his empire. His cooperation with law enforcement resulted in the dismantling of The Council and the imprisonment of many of its members, including Guy Fisher. What Barnes failed to understand was that power without loyalty is an illusion. He had spent years commanding respect through fear and dominance, but when the tables turned, he found himself alone, abandoned by the very system he had helped create.

The rise and fall of Nickey Barnes serves as a cautionary tale about the complexities of power, loyalty, and ambition. While he was undoubtedly a mastermind in the drug trade, his ultimate failure lay in his inability to build lasting unity among his peers. His story reflects the broader challenges faced by Black men in America, navigating a system designed to suppress them while simultaneously trying to carve out their own definition of success. However, Barnes's downfall underscores a crucial lesson: without trust, vision, and integrity, even the most powerful empire will eventually collapse. His legacy remains a stark reminder that the pursuit of power without a foundation of true brotherhood is nothing more than a *"house of cards,"* doomed to fall at the first sign of betrayal.

As Nicky Barnes sat in prison, serving what was essentially a life sentence, his empire began to slip further from his grasp. What truly set him over the edge wasn't just the loss of his wealth or power; it was the betrayal he felt from those closest to him. The breaking point came when he learned that his wife and longtime mistress had moved on, finding comfort in the arms of other men, including some of his former associates. The man who once ruled Harlem with an iron fist now found himself powerless behind bars, watching his world crumble from the inside. This was when Barnes made his fateful decision; he got into his feelings and sold out for a piece of *"pussy."* One of the most significant events that pushed Barnes toward cooperation was the murder of Shamecca. She was gunned down in a hit that sent shockwaves through the Harlem drug scene. While the details surrounding her death remain murky, it was clear that power struggles within the organization had turned deadly. Barnes, already feeling abandoned, saw Shamecca's murder as confirmation that there was no loyalty left among the Council. He realized that the very people he once trusted were still profiting while he rotted in a cell. In his mind, if they had moved on, why should he continue to protect them? With nothing left to lose, Barnes made the decision that would define his legacy:

he became a government informant. His testimony led to the convictions of more than 44 people, including his former council members, his wife, and his mistress. His betrayal shook the streets, proving that even the most feared kingpin could fold under pressure. The trial marked the official end of the Council, as nearly all its members received long sentences. In exchange for his cooperation, Barnes was granted early release in 1998 and placed into the federal witness protection program. He faded into obscurity, a ghost of his former self, living under a new identity for the rest of his days.

Nicky Barnes's story is a cautionary tale about power, betrayal, and the cost of disloyalty. He built an empire, commanded respect, and structured his organization with the precision of a Fortune 500 company. Yet, when faced with the reality of losing everything—his freedom, his influence, and the women he loved—he made the ultimate violation of the code: he snitched. What makes Barnes's downfall even more significant is that it wasn't driven by the usual motives of survival or fear, but by pure emotion. His ego couldn't handle being forgotten, and rather than accept his fate like a true leader, he ensured that no one else could enjoy the fruits of their labor if he couldn't. By turning informant, Barnes committed the ultimate violation of Code #1: A Black MAN will never let anyone question his integrity. Integrity is about standing firm in one's principles, even under pressure. It's about ensuring that a man's word remains unbreakable, that his actions align with his values, and that his legacy is built on honor, not self-interest. Barnes shattered that foundation the moment he cooperated with the feds. His decision to betray those closest to him, including his own wife and mistress, proved that his sense of loyalty was conditional, dictated by his personal grievances rather than by unwavering principles. A Black man with integrity would have accepted his choices and the consequences that came with them, not sought revenge from a prison cell.

Barnes's decision to cooperate wasn't just the end of the Council; it was a shift in street culture that we still see today. His case proved that even the most respected men could fold under personal betrayal, and that set a dangerous precedent. Fast-forward to today, and the streets are filled with a new breed of criminals who embrace *"snitching"* as a strategic move rather than a last resort. Loyalty has become expendable, and self-preservation is now the ultimate law. Unlike in Barnes's era, where informants were seen as the lowest of the low, today's culture often celebrates those who *"tell first"* as long as they can still profit from it. The story of Nicky Barnes forces Black American men to reflect on the principles of integrity and accountability. His actions didn't just destroy his empire; they reinforced the idea that brotherhood is fragile when personal desires outweigh collective responsibility. If the Black community is to reclaim its strength, it must reject the normalization of betrayal and reinforce a code of conduct where honor means more than temporary gain. The lesson is clear: real men stand on principle, no matter the cost. Barnes chose to violate that principle, and in doing so, his name became synonymous with the very thing he once despised: weakness.

Notes of A Native Son

James Baldwin was a man whose voice, though soft-spoken, resonated with unshakable power. He embodied the essence of integrity, refusing to compromise his beliefs despite the challenges he faced as a Black man in America and as a gay man in a time of deep-seated societal prejudices. Baldwin never allowed his sexuality to define his manhood; rather, he remained steadfast in his identity as a Black man first, navigating a world that sought to limit him at every turn. Through his writing, activism, and interactions with the leading figures of the Civil Rights Movement, Baldwin proved that true integrity is standing firm in one's convictions, regardless of opposition. Born on August 2, 1924, in Harlem, New York, James Baldwin was raised in a home overshadowed by poverty and a strict religious environment. His stepfather, a domineering and abusive preacher, left an indelible mark on Baldwin's understanding of power, faith, and oppression. As a young boy, Baldwin found solace in literature, developing an insatiable appetite for reading and writing. His early experiences with racial injustice and the complexities of Black identity shaped his world-view, themes he would later explore in his literary works. One of the most defining moments of Baldwin's early years occurred in *"Notes of a Native Son,"* where he recalls being denied service at a whites-only restaurant in New Jersey. The humiliation and rage he felt in that moment were overwhelming, leading him to a reckless act: he threw a glass at a white waitress out of sheer frustration. However, this act also served as a lesson. Baldwin realized that unchecked anger could be destructive, and instead of allowing it to consume him, he resolved to channel his emotions into his writing. His ability to transform personal pain into intellectual power became one of his greatest strengths. Baldwin's first major exploration of his own upbringing and racial identity came in *Notes of a Native Son* (1955), where he dissected his relationship with his father, the racial climate of America, and the psychological toll of being Black in a white-dominated society. Even as a young man, Baldwin exhibited a deep understanding of the systemic issues plaguing Black Americans, refusing to turn a blind eye or soften his critique to gain favor with mainstream audiences.

In 1948, at the age of 24, Baldwin made a life-altering decision to leave America for France. His departure was not an abandonment of his people but rather a necessary step to find his voice as a writer without the immediate weight of American racism suffocating him. He realized that the system of white supremacy had always kept Black Americans in a perpetual state of survival, making it nearly impossible for individuals or their communities to establish and sustain something lasting and meaningful. France provided him with a temporary escape, yet he never lost sight of the struggles Black people faced in the United States. Baldwin used his time abroad to sharpen his critiques of American society, producing some of his most profound essays and novels that tackled race, identity, and the moral contradictions of the nation. However, Baldwin's experience in Europe was not free from racism. In *"No Name in the Street,"* he recounts an incident in Switzerland where he was arrested simply for existing in a space where Black men were rarely seen. While the racism in Europe was often more subtle than in America, it was still dehumanizing. Unlike in the United States, where racial oppression was explicit and systemic, European racism often manifested through exclusion and the fetishization of Black identity. Yet, Baldwin never succumbed to bitterness, he observed, adapted, and continued to use his voice to expose injustice on both sides of the Atlantic.

His exile also allowed him to live more openly as a gay man, but Baldwin never let his sexuality overshadow his primary identity as a Black man. Unlike many modern activists who lean on intersectionality as a shield or excuse, Baldwin never sought to diminish his Blackness by conflating it with other struggles. He understood that racism in America was a unique and deeply rooted issue, distinct from other forms of discrimination. He remained committed to addressing the plight of Black Americans first and foremost. Baldwin returned to the United States in the early 1960s, fully immersing himself in the Civil Rights Movement. Unlike some leaders of the movement who were political strategists, Baldwin was a moral compass, challenging both white America and the Black community to engage in deep introspection.

James Baldwin's relationships with prominent Black leaders such as Malcolm X, Martin Luther King Jr., and Medgar Evers were complex yet rooted in mutual respect. Malcolm X, known for his militant stance, did not agree with Baldwin's lifestyle, but he respected him as a man because Baldwin stood firm in his beliefs. Baldwin understood that their struggle was the same: the liberation of Black people. This mutual respect highlights a crucial lesson in integrity: real men do not have to agree on everything to fight for a common cause. James Baldwin and Elijah Muhammad came from vastly different ideological backgrounds, yet their meeting symbolized a mutual respect that transcended their differences. Baldwin, a brilliant writer and social critic, was deeply invested in the struggle for Black liberation through literature and intellectual discourse. Elijah Muhammad, as the leader of the Nation of Islam, preached Black self-sufficiency, discipline, and separation from white society. When Baldwin met Muhammad, it was not as adversaries but as two Black men who recognized the gravity of their shared mission: uplifting their people, even if their methods and philosophies differed. This respect was rooted in an understanding that both were fighting against the same oppressive system, just on different battlefields. During their interaction, Baldwin was struck by Muhammad's unwavering conviction and the discipline he instilled in his followers. While Baldwin did not fully agree with the Nation of Islam's strict separatist ideology, he admired the strength and purpose it gave to Black men who had been broken by racism. Muhammad, on the other hand, recognized Baldwin's intellectual courage and his ability to articulate the pain of Black America in a way that white audiences could not ignore. Their conversation was not one of agreement but of acknowledgment; Baldwin saw the Nation's appeal, and Muhammad respected Baldwin's role as a voice for the Black struggle. This was a meeting of two powerful minds who, despite their differences, understood that unity among Black men was more important than ideological purity. Ultimately, the encounter between Baldwin and Muhammad reflected a deeper truth about Black leadership in America. There is no single path to liberation, and sometimes, respect does not require agreement. Baldwin continued to champion racial justice through his essays and novels, while Muhammad remained steadfast in his vision for Black economic and social independence. However, their meeting demonstrated that Black men who stand on principle, whether through words or actions, must acknowledge each other's contributions to the movement. Even with contrasting ideologies, Baldwin and Muhammad shared a fundamental respect, one rooted in the recognition of each other's power, integrity, and commitment to the upliftment of their people.

In his famous debate with William F. Buckley at Cambridge University in 1965, Baldwin masterfully dismantled the false moral superiority of white America, arguing that the American dream had been built on the backs of Black suffering. His words were unyielding, demonstrating that integrity is not about volume but about conviction. A common narrative pushed in modern discourse is that the Black community is inherently more homophobic than others. Baldwin's life and legacy challenge this assertion. The issue within the Black community has never been about personal choices but rather the imposition of certain ideologies onto society, especially onto children. Baldwin never used his sexuality as a crutch, nor did he demand that his personal life take precedence over the greater fight for Black liberation. He was not concerned with forcing acceptance; instead, he focused on the greater mission of holding America accountable for its sins against Black people. Unlike today's LGBTQ activists, who often weaponize identity politics, Baldwin's approach was rooted in responsibility. He did not seek to use his identity for special treatment, nor did he allow it to become a distraction from his ultimate goal: justice for Black Americans.

James Baldwin stayed true to his beliefs until his death in 1987. He didn't look for sympathy, didn't use intersectionality as an excuse, and never let outside forces shake his integrity. His words still hit hard today because they were grounded in truth, not popular trends. Baldwin's legacy teaches us that being a real Black man means standing firm when things get tough, speaking the truth no matter the cost, and never compromising your integrity for anyone's approval. His life embodies the essence of code number one. A Black man protects his integrity. Baldwin was not just a writer; he was an activist, a fierce advocate for truth, and, above all, a man who understood that integrity serves as the bedrock of genuine masculinity. His enduring legacy continues to inspire us to uphold this important principle.

14 Quotes from James Baldwin

"I can't believe what you say because I see what you do."

"The world is before you, and you need not take it or leave it as it was when you came in."

"Those who say it can't be done are usually interrupted by others doing it."

"To be Black and conscious in America is to be in a constant state of rage."

"There is never time in the future in which we will work out our salvation. The challenge is in the moment; the time is always now."

"You've got to tell the world how to treat you. If the world tells you how you are going to be treated, you are in trouble."

"You have to decide who you are and force the world to deal with you, not with its idea of you."

"The victim who is able to articulate the situation of the victim has ceased to be a victim; he or she has become a threat."

"The rebirth of the soul is perpetual; only rebirth every hour could stay the hand of Satan."

"Talent is insignificant. I know a lot of talented ruins. Beyond talent lie all the usual words: discipline, love, luck, but most of all, endurance."

"Sentimentality, the ostentatious parading of excessive and spurious emotion, is the mark of dishonesty, the inability to feel."

"The place in which I'll fit will not exist until I make it."

"The responsibility of a writer is to excavate the experience of the people who produce him."

"The American idea of racial progress is measured by how fast I become white."

CODE NO. 2

A BLACK MAN WILL NEVER LET ANYONE QUESTION HIS WORK ETHIC

Work is more than just a task; it is the manifestation of discipline, persistence, and commitment to excellence. True work is about never allowing anyone to question the integrity of your duty, service, or product. It is about pushing oneself beyond limits to achieve greatness. When discussing work ethic, one must look at individuals who have embodied it at the highest level: Michael Jordan, Muhammad Ali, and Michael Jackson. These men not only mastered their crafts but also set standards so high that even their harshest critics could never deny their dedication. Jordan's relentless training regimen, Ali's unshakable discipline in and out of the ring, and Jackson's obsessive perfectionism in music and dance all showcase what it means to put in the work. They understood that talent alone was not enough; it was the unseen hours of effort that separated them from the rest. In Compton, we called it *"putting in work."* That meant getting the job done and doing it right, efficiently and with pride. It was about earning respect through effort, proving yourself through action, and ensuring that no one could question your commitment. This principle applies to everything, whether it be sports, business, or community leadership. Work is more than just labor; it reflects one's character. A man's work ethic reveals his values, his determination, and his vision for the future. Those who dedicate themselves to excellence create legacies that outlast them. The great men in history who built civilizations, pioneered industries, and led movements understood that their work was not just for them but for those who would come after them. For Black American men, work has always been more than survival; it has been an act of resistance, resilience, and self-determination.

This chapter is about challenging the *"Lazy Black Man"* narrative. For centuries, a damaging narrative has been perpetuated about Black American men: that we are lazy, unintelligent, and unmotivated. This lie has been used as a tool of oppression to justify economic and social barriers. However, history has consistently proven otherwise. The very foundation of this nation was built on the backs of Black men who were forced into labor yet still displayed unparalleled resilience and ingenuity. This stereotype was deliberately constructed to rationalize slavery, segregation, and discrimination. By labeling Black men as inherently lazy, white supremacists justified withholding resources, opportunities, and economic advancement. This false narrative also served to diminish the contributions of Black men, erasing their innovations, labor, and leadership from historical records. Despite these efforts, Black men continued to demonstrate their value through relentless work, innovation, and progress. The reality is that Black American men have consistently been some of the hardest-working individuals in this country. From building the infrastructure of the United States as enslaved laborers to leading major industries post-emancipation, Black men have shown remarkable perseverance. The myth of laziness is contradicted by the undeniable fact that, even under brutal conditions, Black men have always found ways to excel. Whether it was through agriculture, craftsmanship, or entrepreneurship, they created economic opportunities for themselves and their communities. During Reconstruction, Black men built businesses, churches, and entire towns, many of which became economic powerhouses. These achievements directly challenged the stereotype of the *"lazy Black man."* Instead of being recognized, however, these thriving Black communities became targets of racial violence and destruction. The Tulsa Race Massacre of 1921, the burning of Rosewood, and the expulsion of Black residents from sundown towns were not random acts of violence; they were deliberate efforts to suppress Black economic independence and reinforce the false notion of Black inferiority. Even in the modern era, Black men continue to defy this stereotype. From excelling in the corporate world to dominating industries like sports, entertainment, and technology, Black men have repeatedly proven their drive and ambition. The problem has never been a lack of work ethic; rather, it has been the systemic barriers designed to obstruct progress. When given access to resources and opportunities, Black men thrive. The challenge now is to reclaim and reinforce the truth: Black men are builders, innovators, and leaders whose contributions are undeniable.

Black Innovation and Work Ethic

Black American men have proven their ingenuity through thousands of inventions that have shaped the modern world. Consider the fact that Black Americans hold over 53,000 patents, a testament to their innovation and work ethic. Despite systemic barriers, Black men have invented, engineered, and revolutionized countless industries. Some notable examples include:

DR. DANIEL HALE WILLIAMS – Performed the first successful open-heart surgery.

Dr. Daniel Hale Williams was more than just a surgeon; he was a revolutionary force in medicine. Born in 1856 in Hollidaysburg, Pennsylvania, he refused to accept the barriers placed on Black Americans in the medical field. Understanding the struggles Black doctors and nurses faced, he founded Provident Hospital in Chicago, the first Black-owned and -operated hospital in the United States. His goal was to provide a space where Black medical professionals could train, practice, and serve their communities without facing racial discrimination. In 1893, he performed one of the first successful open-heart surgeries, an operation that was considered nearly impossible at the time. He saved a man who had been stabbed in the chest by carefully suturing his wound, all without modern antibiotics or advanced surgical tools. This achievement proved that Black excellence in medicine could rival and even surpass that of white doctors. Beyond surgery, Williams was committed to medical education and training the next generation of Black healthcare professionals. He mentored Black doctors and nurses when most medical schools refused to admit them. His leadership led to him becoming the first Black member of the American College of Surgeons, breaking yet another racial barrier. His legacy is built on skill, perseverance, and an unwavering work ethic. Dr. Williams didn't just practice medicine; he built institutions and set a standard that Black medical professionals continue to follow today. His story is a testament to the power of determination and proves that when Black men refuse to be denied, they don't just succeed; they change history.

GARRETT MORGAN – Invented the traffic light and gas mask, innovations that saved countless lives.

Garrett Morgan was a Black American inventor, entrepreneur, and visionary problem-solver born in 1877 in Paris, Kentucky. Despite receiving only an elementary school education, he had a natural talent for mechanics and an unshakable drive to improve the world around him. From a young age, he displayed a relentless work ethic and a passion for solving problems that others ignored. One of his most revolutionary inventions was the modern three-position traffic signal, patented in 1923. Before Morgan's innovation, traffic signals only had two settings: "*stop*" and "*go,*" causing frequent collisions at busy intersections. His design introduced a warning phase, allowing vehicles to slow down before the light changed, significantly improving road safety. This crucial adjustment laid the foundation for the traffic lights still in use today. Despite this achievement, his contributions to transportation safety remain largely unrecognized in mainstream discussions. However, his brilliance extended beyond traffic innovation. In 1912, he developed the "*safety hood,*" a precursor to the gas mask, designed to protect workers from smoke and toxic fumes. The effectiveness of his invention was proven in 1916 when he personally used it to rescue workers trapped in a tunnel explosion under Lake Erie. Yet, despite its life-saving potential, many white buyers refused to purchase the device once they discovered it was created by a Black man. To navigate this racial bias, Morgan hired white salesmen to demonstrate the product, ensuring its widespread adoption. His design was later adapted by the U.S. military for use in World War I, saving countless soldiers from chemical attacks. Beyond his inventions, Morgan was also a successful businessman and advocate for Black progress. He founded the *"Cleveland Call"* newspaper to support Black communities and fight for civil rights. His wealth and influence were not just for personal gain; he used them to uplift others and create opportunities where none existed. Garrett Morgan's legacy is a testament to the brilliance, resilience, and industrious spirit of Black American men. Despite the systemic racism and limited opportunities he faced, he refused to be confined by society's expectations. His life's work continues to shape modern technology, proving that true innovation is not defined by race but by determination, intelligence, and vision.

ELIJAH MCCOY – Developed automatic lubrication for steam engines, improving efficiency in industrial machinery.

Elijah McCoy was a brilliant Black American inventor and engineer born in 1844 in Ontario, Canada, to parents who had escaped slavery in the United States. Determined to excel, he traveled to Scotland to study mechanical engineering, but upon returning to America, racial discrimination denied him opportunities in his field. Forced to work as a railroad fireman, McCoy refused to let obstacles define him and used his knowledge to innovate. In 1872, he patented the automatic lubrication system for steam engines, a groundbreaking invention that transformed the railroad and manufacturing industries. His device was so effective that companies specifically requested *"the real McCoy,"* a phrase that became a symbol of authenticity and high quality. Throughout his lifetime, McCoy secured over 50 patents, primarily focused on lubrication systems and mechanical devices. Despite facing systemic racism, his work ethic and ingenuity never wavered, proving that talent and determination could break through barriers. His contributions not only improved industrial efficiency but also set a standard for Black excellence in engineering. Elijah McCoy's legacy remains a testament to the power of perseverance and innovation in the face of adversity.

LEWIS LATIMER – Enhanced Thomas Edison's light bulb with a longer-lasting carbon filament, making electric lighting more practical.

Lewis Latimer was a Black American inventor and engineer born in 1848 in Chelsea, Massachusetts, to formerly enslaved parents. Despite having little formal education, he taught himself mechanical drawing while working at a patent law firm, where he quickly gained recognition for his drafting skills. His expertise led him to work with Alexander Graham Bell, helping to draft the patent for the telephone in 1876. However, his most significant contributions came in the field of electric lighting, where he developed a longer-lasting carbon filament for light bulbs, making Thomas Edison's invention more practical and commercially viable. Despite Latimer's crucial role in improving electric lighting, Edison is widely credited as the sole inventor of the light bulb, overshadowing Latimer's work. This is a prime example of how Black American innovators have had their contributions erased or minimized while others took the credit. As the saying goes, *"The only thing the white supremacist built was the patent office,"* highlighting how Black ingenuity was often exploited for profit while the true creators were denied recognition. Latimer didn't just improve Edison's design; he also wrote *Incandescent Electric Lighting: A Practical Description of the Edison System*, helping to standardize and expand the use of electric light. Despite facing racism and exclusion from many scientific circles, Latimer continued his work, securing multiple patents and mentoring other Black engineers and inventors. His contributions went beyond the technical; he was a founding member of the Edison Pioneers, the elite group of innovators in the early electrical industry, yet even within that group, his name remains less known. Latimer's legacy serves as a testament to the brilliance and perseverance of Black American men in the face of systemic erasure. Without his work, modern electrical lighting would not have been as efficient, yet history largely credits Edison while Latimer's impact remains underappreciated.

GRANVILLE T. Woods – Known as *"The Black Edison,"* he invented railway telegraphy, improving train communication and safety.

Granville T. Woods was a Black American inventor and electrical engineer born in 1856 in Columbus, Ohio. Largely self-taught, he studied mechanical and electrical engineering while working in the railroad and steel industries, eventually becoming one of the most prolific Black inventors of his time. Woods held over 60 patents, many of which revolutionized railway communication and electrical systems. One of his most significant inventions was the *"telegraphony,"* a device that allowed voice communication over telegraph lines, which improved long-distance communication and helped lay the foundation for modern telephone systems. His invention was so groundbreaking that Alexander Graham Bell's company, which held a monopoly over telephone technology, attempted to claim it as its own. Woods was forced into a legal battle against one of the most powerful companies of the time. However, in a rare victory for a Black inventor against white industrialists, he successfully defended his patent in court and proved that he was the true creator of the telegraphony. This victory not only protected his work but also set a precedent for Black inventors fighting against intellectual theft. Despite this triumph, Woods still faced constant challenges in securing funding and recognition for his work. Unlike Thomas Edison or Bell, who had financial backers and institutional support, Woods often had to sell his patents to larger corporations just to continue his research. Edison, recognizing Woods's brilliance, repeatedly tried to hire him, but Woods refused, preferring to maintain his independence. Woods's contributions to railway safety and electrical engineering were invaluable; his inventions, such as the induction telegraph and improved third-rail system, made train travel safer and more efficient. His work played a crucial role in the development of modern transportation, yet he remains largely unrecognized compared to white inventors of his era. His legal battle against Bell and his refusal to be controlled by Edison are testaments to his intelligence, resilience, and determination to be credited for his own genius. Woods's legacy stands as proof that Black American inventors were not only innovators but also warriors in the fight for recognition and ownership of their intellectual contributions.

FREDERICK MCKINLEY JONES — created refrigeration technology for trucks, revolutionizing the food industry.

Frederick McKinley Jones was a Black American inventor and entrepreneur born in 1893 in Cincinnati, Ohio. Largely self-taught, he developed a deep understanding of mechanics and engineering through hands-on experience. His most significant invention was the automatic refrigeration system for trucks, trains, and ships, revolutionizing the transportation of perishable goods. Before his innovation, food and medical supplies had to be transported using unreliable ice-based cooling methods. His invention led to the creation of the Thermo King Corporation, which became a leader in refrigeration technology. Jones secured over 60 patents, including designs for air conditioning units and portable X-ray machines used in World War II. Despite his groundbreaking contributions, his name is often overlooked in discussions of refrigeration and modern logistics. His work made fresh food and medicine more accessible worldwide, proving essential to industries like agriculture and healthcare. Jones' relentless work ethic and ingenuity demonstrate the lasting impact of Black American inventors on global advancements in technology.

OTIS BOYKIN — The man who improve the *"pacemaker,"* helping those with heart conditions worldwide.

Otis Boykin was a Black American inventor and electrical engineer born in 1920 in Dallas, Texas. A brilliant mind in electronics, he studied at Fisk University before working on military and consumer technology. Boykin is best known for improving the resistor, a crucial component in electrical circuits, which made devices more reliable and affordable. His resistors were used in radios, televisions, and even guided missile systems, showcasing his impact on both everyday life and national defense. One of his most significant contributions was developing a control unit for the pacemaker, a life-saving device that regulates heartbeats. His innovations in electrical resistance technology made pacemakers more effective and accessible, saving countless lives. Throughout his career, Boykin secured 26 patents, constantly improving electronic components. Despite facing racial barriers in the engineering field, he never stopped refining his inventions. His work continues to influence modern electronics, proving that Black American ingenuity has been at the heart of technological progress.

DAVID CROSTHWAIT JR. – Mastermind Behind Modern Heating and Ventilation Systems.

David Crosthwait Jr., born in 1898 in Nashville, Tennessee, was a Black American mechanical and electrical engineer who broke new ground in the field of heating, ventilation, and air conditioning (HVAC). He earned over 39 patents for his work in temperature and climate control, with his designs powering major landmarks like Radio City Music Hall and Rockefeller

Center. Crosthwait didn't just build systems—he set the standard, writing technical manuals that engineers still follow today. Despite facing the heavy hand of racism, he pushed through and became a recognized authority in his field, earning honorary degrees along the way. His unmatched work ethic and skill helped shape the modern HVAC industry and stand as a lasting testament to Black American excellence and innovation.

JOHN STANDARD –Innovator in Modern Refrigeration.

John Standard was a Black American inventor born in 1868 who made significant contributions to the improvement of refrigeration technology. In 1891, he patented an improved refrigerator design that enhanced cooling efficiency, making food preservation more effective. His invention came at a time when refrigeration relied on unreliable and inefficient methods, helping to pave the way for modern kitchen appliances. Standard also patented an improved oil stove, making cooking safer and more efficient for households. Despite facing racial barriers that limited recognition for Black inventors, he remained dedicated to innovation and problem-solving. His work ethic and commitment to excellence reflect the long-standing tradition of Black American ingenuity in shaping everyday life.

Elijah McCoy, Granville T. Woods, Lewis Latimer, and David Crosthwait Jr. didn't just work hard they redefined what work ethic looks like. Together, these Black men racked up 209 patents, laying the foundation for industries we still depend on today. Their inventions didn't just change technology; they changed the course of history yet their names are too often buried beneath the lies of omission. Most were born into chains or into a country still dripping with the blood of slavery, but they refused to let oppression suffocate their brilliance. While America tried to deny them recognition, they outworked, out-thought, and outlasted those who sought to erase them. Their genius wasn't missing, it was shackled by a system designed to keep it hidden. But when the chains broke, their impact was undeniable and permanent. Black excellence has always been here, building, inventing, and leading whether history wants to admit it or not.

Black Men and Politics After Slavery

Following emancipation, Black men didn't waste time claiming their rightful place in leadership and governance. Despite facing fierce opposition, they became congressmen, senators, and mayors during Reconstruction. Men like Hiram Revels, the first Black U.S. senator, and Robert Smalls, a former slave turned congressman, exemplified how Black men seized opportunities and led with integrity. However, this progress was met with violent resistance. Systemic efforts such as Jim Crow laws, voter suppression, and lynchings were designed to strip Black men of their political power. Yet, they continued to fight, setting the foundation for future generations to reclaim their rightful place in leadership.

HIRAM RHODES REVELS (1827–1901) – The first Black U.S. senator.

Hiram Rhodes Revels was the first Black American to serve in the U.S. Senate, representing Mississippi in 1870 during Reconstruction. His election was a monumental achievement, proving that Black men were capable of leadership at the highest levels despite systemic racism. Revels wanted to challenge the perception that formerly enslaved people were unfit for political office. His presence in the Senate was a direct rebuttal to white supremacist narratives, showcasing the resilience and intellect of Black American men in governance. Hiram Rhodes Revels was born free in 1827 in Fayetteville, North Carolina, at a time when most Black Americans were enslaved. He pursued education and became a minister in the African Methodist Episcopal Church, using his platform to advocate for the rights of freedmen. During the Civil War, he helped organize Black regiments for the Union Army and worked to improve conditions for freed people. In 1870, during Reconstruction, he made history by becoming the first Black American to serve in the U.S. Senate, representing Mississippi. As a senator, Revels fought for racial equality, education, and amnesty for former Confederates who supported integration. After leaving politics, he continued his work in education, serving as president of Alcorn State University. His legacy represents the political strides Black men made after slavery and the fight to secure their rightful place in American leadership.

ROBERT SMALLS (1839–1915) – From Enslaved Man to Congressman

Robert Smalls was born into slavery in South Carolina but made history in 1862 when he commandeered a Confederate ship and delivered it to Union forces, securing freedom for himself and others. After the Civil War, he became a politician, serving in the U.S. House of Representatives for South Carolina. Smalls was a champion of Black civil rights, public education, and economic independence for freedmen. His rise from enslaved laborer to lawmaker exemplifies how Black American men, despite unimaginable obstacles, worked tirelessly to shape the political landscape of a nation built on their oppression.

BLANCHE K. BRUCE (1841–1898) – The first Black man to serve a full Senate term.

Blanche K. Bruce was born a slave in Virginia, yet he fought his way to become a landowner and a political force in Mississippi. In 1875, he shattered barriers as the first Black American to serve a full term in the U.S. Senate. Bruce stood his ground for Black voting rights, education, and economic freedom, even as white supremacist forces worked overtime to drag the country backwards with Jim Crow laws. His rise marked the peak of Black political power during Reconstruction, before the system regrouped and launched a full-scale attack to erase everything Black men had built. Even after leaving the Senate, Bruce kept fighting, holding major federal roles like *"Register of the Treasury."* His legacy isn't just about titles, it's about resilience, leadership, and proof that Black American men, when given even the smallest chance, could out-lead, out-govern, and out-build anyone. Bruce's life exposes the lie America told about Black capability and shows the truth they worked so hard to bury.

The Systematic Destruction of Black Towns

After slavery, Black Americans built thriving communities across the country, many of which were systematically targeted and destroyed. The book *Sundown Towns* by James W. Loewen exposes how entire cities were violently purged of Black residents through intimidation, economic sabotage, and outright massacres. Some of the most well-known Black-built cities that were destroyed include:

Tᴜʟsᴀ, **Oklahoma (Black Wall Street, 1921)** – One of the most prominent Black communities in America was burned to the ground by white mobs, erasing generations of economic progress. Greenwood, also known as *"Black Wall Street,"* was one of the most prosperous Black communities in the United States, located in Tulsa, Oklahoma. Founded in the early 20th century, it became a hub for Black entrepreneurs, featuring banks, hotels, theaters, grocery stores, and schools, all Black-owned and operated. The community thrived due to strong economic circulation within the Black population, creating a level of self-sufficiency that rivaled white communities. However, in June 1921, white mobs, supported by local law enforcement, launched a violent attack, burning the entire district to the ground. Over 300 Black residents were killed, thousands were left homeless, and more than 1,200 homes and businesses were destroyed in one of the worst acts of racial terrorism in American history. The attack began under the false pretense that a Black man had assaulted a white woman, but its true motive was economic jealousy and white supremacist fear of Black prosperity. Survivors were placed in internment camps, and insurance companies refused to pay claims for damages. No one was held accountable, and the city actively suppressed records of the massacre for decades. The destruction of Black Wall Street represents a deliberate effort to cripple Black economic advancement and erase a model of Black success.

ROSEWOOD, Florida (1923) – A thriving Black town was obliterated after false accusations led to a violent massacre. Rosewood was a small, predominantly Black town in Florida that thrived in the early 20th century, with Black residents owning land, businesses, and homes. Many Black families in Rosewood were self-sufficient, growing their own food and operating a sawmill industry that provided economic stability. In January 1923, a white woman falsely claimed that a Black man had assaulted her, sparking days of white mob violence. Armed groups of white men from neighboring towns burned Rosewood to the ground, slaughtering Black residents and forcing survivors to flee. Those who attempted to defend themselves were killed, and the town was erased from official records for decades. The Black families who lost their homes and businesses were never compensated, and Rosewood was abandoned as a Black settlement. In 1994, Florida became the first state to issue reparations to the surviving families, acknowledging the massacre as a racial atrocity. However, the destruction of Rosewood highlights the pattern of economic and racial violence used to strip Black Americans of land and opportunity. This massacre, like many others, served as a warning to Black communities across the South that economic independence could be met with deadly consequences. In *"Like Judgment Day: The Ruin and Redemption of a Town Called Rosewood,"* Michael D'Orso chronicles the 1923 massacre, detailing how a prosperous Black

American town was destroyed under the guise of a false accusation against a Black man—an all-too-common tactic used to justify violence against Black communities for over a century and a half. This tragedy serves as yet another example of how systemic racism has consistently sought to dismantle the progress, self-sufficiency, and economic independence of Black American men, even when they exemplify the highest standards of work ethic, integrity, and responsibility. Through survivor testimonies and extensive historical research, D'Orso not only captures the horror of the event but also the resilience of those who refused to be erased. Decades later, their unwavering fight for justice led to Florida's unprecedented decision to provide reparations, one of the few times the government formally acknowledged its role in racial violence. Rosewood's story is a testament to the principle that a Black man stands by his community, fights for justice, and refuses to let oppression define his legacy.

ELAINE, **Arkansas (1919)** – Black sharecroppers organizing for fair wages were met with deadly white supremacist attacks. Elaine, Arkansas, was home to a significant Black sharecropping population who worked on white-owned plantations under unfair and exploitative conditions. In September 1919, Black sharecroppers, many of them World War I veterans, met to discuss forming a union to demand fair wages.

Their efforts for economic justice were seen as a threat, and white mobs, along with federal troops, carried out one of the deadliest racial massacres in U.S. history. Between 200 and 300 Black men, women, and children were murdered as white mobs attacked Black neighborhoods, burning homes and killing indiscriminately. The massacre was falsely justified by claims that Black sharecroppers were planning an uprising against white landowners. Following the violence, hundreds of Black men were arrested, and twelve were sentenced to death in sham trials. The massacre successfully crushed Black economic and political aspirations in the region, reinforcing a system of racial subjugation. Elaine's destruction serves as a tragic example of how Black communities attempting to assert their rights were met with brutal force to maintain white economic control. The legacy of Elaine is rarely taught in American history, yet it remains a clear example of how systemic racial violence targeted Black economic progress.

Forsyth County, Georgia (1912) – Hundreds of Black families were forcibly removed, leaving behind land and wealth that were stolen by white settlers. Forsyth County, Georgia, was once home to a thriving Black community in the early 1900s, with Black farmers, business owners, and laborers contributing to the county's economy. However, in 1912, a campaign of racial terror erupted after the alleged assault of a white woman. White mobs lynched several Black men and terrorized the entire Black population, leading to the forced expulsion of over 1,100 Black residents. Black homes, churches, and businesses were burned or seized, and their land was stolen, leaving an all-white county behind. This violent purge of Black residents ensured that Forsyth County remained nearly 100% white for most of the 20th century. Decades later, descendants of the displaced Black families were never compensated for their stolen land or generational wealth lost. This event became a symbol of how systemic violence and economic theft were used to erase Black communities. Forsyth County's racial cleansing was so effective that, even in the 1980s, civil rights marches through the county were met with hostility. It remains one of the most striking examples of how Black Americans were driven from land they rightfully owned, setting back generations of economic progress. These attacks were deliberate and had lasting consequences. The destruction of Black towns robbed Black families of generational wealth and economic stability, contributing to the disparities seen in Black communities today. Instead of being allowed to thrive, Black men were repeatedly forced to rebuild from scratch while facing systemic obstacles at every turn.

Some not-so-well-known cities that Black Americans built.

Boley, Oklahoma founded 1903 — Boley was one of the most successful Black towns in Oklahoma and became a thriving economic hub for Black Americans. Unlike many other Black towns that struggled under systemic oppression, Boley flourished with Black-owned businesses, banks, schools, and even its own electric company. Booker T. Washington once praised Boley as a model for Black self-sufficiency. The town's success was a testament to the work ethic and resilience of its founders, though its prosperity declined due to economic hardships and racist policies.

Mound Bayou, Mississippi founded 1887 — Founded by former slaves led by Isaiah T. Montgomery, Mound Bayou was one of the most prominent Black settlements in the South. It was a self-sustaining community where Black residents owned businesses, farms, and institutions, providing a safe haven from racial violence. Unlike many other Black towns, Mound Bayou remained predominantly Black for over a century and played a crucial role during the Civil Rights Movement by providing a base for activism and resistance.

ALLENSWORTH, **California, founded 1908** — Founded by Colonel Allen Allensworth, a former slave and Union soldier, this town was the first in California to be founded, financed, and governed entirely by Black Americans. It was envisioned as a self-sufficient community where Black people could escape discrimination and thrive. Allensworth had schools, a library, a church, and successful agricultural development. However, due to water supply issues and systemic racism, the town eventually declined. Today, it is preserved as a state historic park.

DEARFIELD, **Colorado, was founded in 1910** — Founded by Oliver Toussaint Jackson, Dearfield was a Black farming colony that grew rapidly during the early 20th century. Residents built homes, schools, and businesses, turning barren land into productive farms. At its peak, Dearfield had hundreds of residents and was a symbol of Black economic independence. However, the Great Depression and declining agricultural conditions led to its downfall.

BLACKDOM, **New Mexico, founded 1903** — Blackdom was established by Francis Marion Boyer, a Black homesteader, as a self-sustaining Black community in the arid lands of New Mexico. It was the first all-Black settlement in the state, providing an escape from Jim

Crow oppression. The town had a school, a post office, and a thriving agricultural economy, but a lack of water and economic hardship led to its decline by the 1920s.

These towns, though not as widely known as Tulsa's Black Wall Street, are powerful examples of Black American resilience, innovation, and self-reliance. They also highlight how systemic racism and targeted attacks played a role in the destruction or decline of many Black-founded communities. These towns stood as powerful examples of Black self-sufficiency, innovation, and economic success. They prove that when left alone, Black Americans have been able to thrive and prosper, building schools, businesses, infrastructure, and entire communities without outside interference. However, history has shown that white supremacist forces often targeted these communities, using systemic racism, violence, and economic sabotage to disrupt their progress. Despite these efforts, the resilience and work ethic of Black Americans have continually demonstrated that when given the opportunity to build freely, we not only succeed but also set the standard for excellence.

Black American Men in the Military: Work Ethic in Action

Black American men have proven, time and again, that their work ethic, courage, and discipline are second to none—especially on the battlefield. Even while being disrespected at home, they showed up and showed out. The Tuskegee Airmen are living proof. These men flew critical escort missions in World War II and did what no one else could—they protected every bomber under their watch without losing a single one. Not once. That level of precision and excellence has never been matched in military history. Their success wasn't an accident—it was the result of brutal training, strict discipline, and a refusal to be anything less than great. The Tuskegee Airmen didn't just fly planes—they destroyed every lie that said Black men couldn't lead, couldn't fight, or couldn't master high-level strategy. And they weren't the only ones. Black American men have carried this nation on their backs in every war it has fought—earning honor in a country that too often tried to deny them even basic humanity. Here are a few notable Black officers who exemplified work ethic and leadership:

COLONEL CHARLES YOUNG — The first Black American to reach the rank of colonel in the U.S. Army—a legacy of excellence and resilience.

Colonel Charles Young was a pioneering Black American military officer whose career exemplified perseverance, intelligence, and an unbreakable work ethic. Born into slavery in 1864 in Mays Lick, Kentucky, Young's early years were shaped by the struggles and triumphs of the Reconstruction era. His father, Gabriel Young, escaped slavery and enlisted in the Union Army during the Civil War, setting an example of courage and service that would influence Young's path. From a young age, Charles displayed remarkable academic ability and determination, which led him to pursue an education despite the racial barriers of the time. In 1889, Young made history as only the third Black American to graduate from the United States Military Academy at West Point. His time at West Point was marked by severe racism and isolation; he endured relentless hostility from white cadets and instructors who sought to break his spirit. Despite these obstacles, Young refused to falter, graduating and earning a commission as a second lieutenant. His perseverance during these years is what *"The 14 Codes"* is all about, particularly the principles of integrity, work ethic, and character. Young's military career was defined by excellence and leadership. He served in the 9th and 10th Cavalry Regiments, also known as the Buffalo Soldiers, where he quickly gained a reputation for his intelligence, discipline, and ability to lead men under challenging circumstances. His assignments took him across the country and beyond, including service in the Philippines, Mexico, and Haiti. He also became the first Black American to serve as a national park superintendent, overseeing Sequoia National Park in 1903, where he and his men built essential infrastructure that remains in use today.

Despite his achievements, Young faced institutional racism at every turn. When World War I began, he was the highest-ranking Black officer in the U.S. Army and a prime candidate for a general's commission. However, the military establishment, unwilling to see a Black man rise to such a prominent position, declared him medically unfit for duty and forced him into retirement. Unwilling to accept this injustice, Young undertook a grueling horseback ride from Ohio to Washington, D.C., to prove his fitness for service. This act of resilience and defiance is a testament to his solid commitment to duty and excellence. Although Young was reinstated and promoted posthumously, the racism he endured underscores the systemic barriers that Black men have historically faced, even when they exhibit unparalleled dedication and capability. His life serves as a reminder that Black American men have always had to work twice as hard to receive half the recognition, a reality that continues to this day. Yet, Young's story is not just one of struggle but of triumph, showing how a Black man, through perseverance and integrity, can shape history despite the odds. Colonel Charles Young's legacy lives on through the generations of Black American servicemen who followed in his footsteps. His story aligns with code #2; he never let anyone question his work ethic, stood by his responsibilities, and understood that his integrity and perseverance defined him as a man. His contributions laid the groundwork for the success of future Black military officers and proved that *"excellence cannot be denied, only delayed."*

GENERAL BENJAMIN O. DAVIS SR.– The first Black general in the U.S. Army, breaking barriers in military leadership.

General Benjamin O. Davis Sr. was a trailblazing military leader who became the first Black American general in the U.S. Army. Born in 1877 in Washington, D.C., Davis grew up in an era of intense racial segregation and discrimination. Despite these challenges, he was determined to pursue a career in the military at a time when opportunities for Black men in the armed forces were severely limited. Davis enlisted in the U.S. Army in 1898 during the Spanish-American War and quickly demonstrated exceptional leadership and discipline. His dedication and competence earned him a commission as a second lieutenant in 1901. Over the next several decades, he steadily rose through the ranks, serving with the 9th and 10th Cavalry Regiments, also known as the *"Buffalo Soldiers."* Despite his qualifications, he was repeatedly denied opportunities for advancement due to the military's racist policies.

Throughout his career, Davis was often assigned to administrative and training roles rather than combat positions. The Army leadership deliberately kept Black officers from commanding white troops, limiting Davis's ability to take on key leadership roles. Nonetheless, he used these assignments to mentor and train the next generation of Black American soldiers, ensuring that they were prepared for greater opportunities in the future. In 1940, after more than 40 years of service, Davis was promoted to brigadier general by President Franklin D. Roosevelt, making him the first Black American to achieve this rank. His promotion was largely symbolic, intended to address criticism of racial discrimination in the military, but Davis used his position to advocate for better treatment of Black soldiers. He fought against segregation in the armed forces and worked to expand opportunities for Black servicemen during World War II.

Davis's legacy paved the way for future Black military leaders, including his son, General Benjamin O. Davis Jr., who commanded the legendary Tuskegee Airmen. His perseverance and commitment to excellence exemplify the Codes, particularly the principles of work ethic, integrity, and holding one's peers accountable. He never allowed systemic racism to define his contributions and worked tirelessly to ensure that Black American men in the military were given the respect and opportunities they deserved. General Benjamin O. Davis Sr. proved that Black American men, when given the chance, could excel in leadership, strategy, and service. His career set a precedent for generations to come, showing that dedication, resilience, and an unbreakable spirit could break through even the most rigid barriers of white supremacy.

GENERAL BENJAMIN O. Davis Jr. –Commander of the Tuskegee Airmen and later the first Black general in the U.S. Air Force.

Leading the Tuskegee Airmen to Excellence. General Benjamin O. Davis Jr. was a pioneering military leader who shattered racial barriers in the U.S. Air Force. Born in 1912 in Washington, D.C., he was the son of General Benjamin O. Davis Sr., the first Black American general in the U.S. Army. Growing up in a segregated America, Davis Jr. was determined to follow in his father's footsteps and serve his country, despite the obstacles placed before him. In 1932, he became the first Black American to be admitted to the U.S. Military Academy at West Point in the 20th century. During his time at the academy, he faced extreme racism and isolation; his white classmates refused to speak to him unless absolutely necessary. Despite this, he endured the silent treatment and graduated in 1936 as only the fourth Black cadet to ever complete the program.

When Davis joined the Army Air Corps, he was immediately met with resistance, as the military did not believe Black men were capable of flying or commanding aircraft. However, with the formation of the Tuskegee Airmen in 1941, Davis was given the opportunity to prove them wrong. He became the commander of the 99th Pursuit Squadron and later the 332nd Fighter Group, leading his men with discipline and precision. Under his leadership, the Tuskegee Airmen became one of the most successful fighter groups of World War II. They flew more than 1,500 combat missions and never lost a single bomber under their escort, an unparalleled record in military aviation. Davis's strict training standards and relentless work ethic ensured that his men were among the best pilots in the U.S. Air Force, directly disproving the racist notion that Black American men lacked the discipline or skill to serve as elite aviators. After the war, Davis continued to break barriers, becoming the first Black American general in the U.S. Air Force in 1954. He played a key role in the desegregation of the military, advising the government on race relations and advocating for equal opportunities for Black servicemen. His leadership and firm commitment to excellence laid the groundwork for future generations of Black officers.

SERGEANT WILLIAM H. Carney -A former enslaved man who became the first Black American to receive the Medal of Honor during the Civil War.

Sergeant William H. Carney was a Black American soldier who became a symbol of bravery and resilience during the Civil War. Born into slavery in Norfolk, Virginia, in 1840, he later gained his freedom and joined the 54th Massachusetts Infantry Regiment, one of the first Black units in the Union Army. Carney's defining moment came during the Battle of Fort Wagner in 1863 when he risked his life to save the American flag after the color bearer was shot. Despite being wounded multiple times, he carried the flag forward, ensuring it never touched the ground, and famously declared, *"Boys, I only did my duty; the old flag never touched the ground!"* His unbendable commitment to duty and courage under fire made him a legend. Nearly four decades later, in 1900, Carney became the first Black American to receive the Medal of Honor for his heroics during the battle.

The legacy of Black American men is built on an unshakable foundation of work ethic, perseverance, and excellence. From the plantations where our ancestors were forced to labor, to the patent offices where their innovations changed the world, to the battlefields where they fought with valor, Black men have always shown up and delivered. The narrative that Black men are lazy is not only false but intentionally misleading, designed to erase the very contributions that built this nation. The principles outlined in the 14 Codes reinforce the necessity of work ethic as a defining characteristic of manhood. A Black man takes pride in his labor, ensuring that his work speaks for itself. He does not seek validation but commands respect through action. Whether in business, politics, science, or the military, Black American men have consistently proven their dedication to excellence. The challenge for future generations is to uphold this standard, refusing to let anyone question their commitment to hard work and responsibility. True work ethic is about more than just effort; it is about impact. A Black man understands that what he builds today must serve as a foundation for those who come after him. The legacy of our ancestors demands that we continue pushing forward, creating, innovating, and striving for greatness. No matter the obstacles, our work will define us, and we will never allow anyone to question our integrity, our contributions, or our place in history.

30 Black American Inventors & Their Patents:

- **Lewis Latimer** – Improved carbon filament for the light bulb (U.S. Patent No. 252,386, 1881)
- **Granville T. Woods** – *"Induction Telegraph System for Trains"* (U.S. Patent No. 373,915, 1887)
- **Garrett Morgan** – Three-Way Traffic Signal (U.S. Patent No. 1,475,024, 1923)
- **Elijah McCoy** – Automatic lubrication system for steam engines (U.S. Patent No. 129,843, 1872)
- **David Crosthwait Jr.** – Heating and cooling systems (U.S. Patent No. 1,392,629, 1921)

- **Frederick McKinley Jones** – Refrigerated transport system (U.S. Patent No. 2,303,857, 1940)
- **Otis Boykin** – Improved electrical resistor used in pacemakers (U.S. Patent No. 2,972,726, 1961)
- **John Standard** – Improvements to the Refrigerator (U.S. Patent No. 455,891, 1891)
- **Norbert Rillieux** – Multiple-effect evaporator for sugar refining (U.S. Patent No. 4,845, 1843)
- **Madison Washington** – Steam engine improvements (patent unknown, early 1800s)
- **Henry Blair** – Seed planter and cotton planter (U.S. Patent 8,447X, 1834)
- **Thomas L. Jennings** – *"Dry Cleaning Process"* (U.S. Patent 3,306, 1821)
- **Benjamin Banneker** – Wooden clock & almanacs (self-made, 1750s)
- **Jan Ernst Matzeliger** – Shoe-lasting machine (U.S. Patent No. 274,207, 1883)
- **James E. West** – Electret Microphone (U.S. Patent No. 3,118,022, 1964)
- **Alexander Miles** – Automatic elevator doors (U.S. Patent No. 371,207, 1887)
- **George Washington Carver** – Agricultural innovations (no patents, focused on public domain research)

- **Valerie Thomas** – Illusion transmitter used in 3D imaging (U.S. Patent No. 4,229,761, 1980)
- **Lonnie Johnson** – Super Soaker water gun (U.S. Patent No. 4,591,071, 1986)
- **Andrew J. Beard** – Automatic railroad coupler (U.S. Patent No. 594,059, 1897)
- **Charles Drew** – Blood plasma preservation methods (research, no patent)
- **Joseph Winters** – Wagon-mounted fire escape ladder (U.S. Patent No. 203,517, 1878)
- **Dr. Daniel Hale Williams** – Open-heart surgery pioneer (medical procedure, no patent)
- **Philip Emeagwali** – *"Parallel Processing in Supercomputers"* (U.S. Patent No. 5,835,913, 1999)
- **Albert C. Richardson** – *"Butter Churn Improvement"* (U.S. Patent No. 303,087, 1884)
- **Hugh G. Robinson** – Military bridge-building innovations (*Various Patents, U.S. Army Engineer*)
- **Benjamin Thornton** – multi-functional hospital bed (U.S. Patent No. 3,810,304, 1974)
- **Henry Sampson** – Gamma-electric cell used in early mobile phone technology (U.S. Patent No. 3,591,860, 1971)

- **Paul E. Williams** – Early computer microprocessor design (patent information unknown)
- **Victor Lawrence** – Advances in fiber-optic communication (multiple patents, 1990s–2000s)

These inventors are the definition of Code #2—real work ethic, unstoppable drive, and razor-sharp creativity. A lot of them came out of slavery or lived under brutal segregation, but that didn't kill their fire. They still pushed forward, innovated, and left their mark, even while fighting against a system built to hold them back. Their impact is still felt today, shaping the world we live in. Black American men have always been pioneers in science, technology, and industry working twice as hard just to get a fraction of the recognition they deserved.

CODE NO. 3

A BLACK MAN HAS EMOTIONS. HE IS NOT EMOTIONAL

Gang culture is one of the most vicious predators of emotional weakness. Gangs don't want thinkers; they want reactors. They thrive on young Black men who act first and think never—who see violence as the only answer to disrespect, and retaliation as a way of life. A gang leader doesn't recruit soldiers with discipline; he hunts for emotional time bombs. Whisper a word about *"disrespect"* in an undisciplined man's ear, and he's ready to kill. Tell him to prove his loyalty, and he'll throw his life away without a second thought.

But it's bigger than the streets. Across every level of society, Black men have lost everything because they couldn't control their emotions. Some explode and destroy careers they spent years building. Others drown themselves in addiction or depression. Many are dead or locked in cages because they made one emotional decision in a weak moment—one moment they can never get back. The truth is brutal but simple: the emotionally unstable Black man is one of the greatest threats to the Black community. He's a loaded weapon with no target discipline, ready to be aimed at his own people by anyone who knows how to push the right button. History shows us this pattern over and over—empires falling not by enemy hands, but by the emotional recklessness of their own men. Our community is no different.

A major reason for this crisis is the collapse of masculine leadership in our homes. Over 70% of Black households today are run by single mothers. Black women have fought hard and done the best they could under brutal conditions, but nature is what it is: women and men are built differently. Women resolve conflict through communication and emotional expression. Men are wired for strategy, structure, and discipline. A boy raised only by women often learns feminine emotional patterns quick to argue, quick to gossip, quick to retaliate. But unlike women, a boy becomes a man, and when that emotional instability meets male aggression, it turns deadly. You see it every day: boys in grown bodies arguing like women, gossiping like women, and retaliating like wounded women, but now with fists, guns, and lives on the line. Gangs know this. That's why they target young boys without fathers, boys craving guidance but poisoned by emotional impulsiveness. Without a masculine hand to teach discipline, these boys confuse emotional reaction with strength and they die because of it.

Throughout history, the downfall of many great Black men has been tied to their inability to master their emotions. In this chapter, we will examine three powerful examples that drive this point home: Tupac Shakur: a brilliant and gifted Black man, destroyed because he couldn't separate passion from discipline. His emotional reactions made him a legend—but they also made him a target. Robert "Yummy" Sandifer: an 11-year-old child soldier, exploited and abandoned by a gang system that weaponized his broken emotional state. Malcolm X: the blueprint of transformation—a street hustler who once lived recklessly, who then sharpened himself into one of the most feared and respected Black leaders in American history through pure emotional discipline. These aren't just stories from the past. These are blueprints. Lessons. Proof. Control your emotions or be controlled by them. Master your reactions or be mastered by those who want you dead or locked away. If a Black man does not rule over his emotions, someone else will. And when that happens, he's no longer a man. He's a pawn.

TUPAC SHAKUR — The Rise and Fall of an *"Emotional Thug"*

Tupac Amaru Shakur was a man of extremes. He

was both revolutionary and reckless, intelligent and impulsive, compassionate and confrontational. His life, as chronicled in *Tupac Shakur: The Life and Times of an American Icon* by Tayannah Lee McQuillar and Fred L. Johnson III, was shaped by his deep love for Black people and his inability to control the emotions that often put him in dangerous situations. While Tupac had the mind of a leader, he lacked the discipline to channel his emotions productively, which ultimately led to his downfall. His story is a cautionary tale of what happens when a Black man allows his emotions to be manipulated by forces greater than himself.

Tupac's emotional volatility was evident in both his music and his personal life. His lyrics, often poetic and profound, reflected a deep understanding of the struggles of Black America; yet they also revealed an internal conflict, a battle between his revolutionary ideals and the street mentality he had absorbed. He could record *"Keep Ya Head Up,"* a heartfelt anthem uplifting Black women, and then turn around and release *"Hit 'Em Up,"* one of the most aggressive and inflammatory diss tracks in hip-hop history. This duality made him one of the most compelling figures of his time, but it also made him unpredictable and susceptible to manipulation. His association with Suge Knight and Death Row Records only amplified his more destructive tendencies, pulling him further into a lifestyle that thrived on impulse and retaliation.

At his core, Tupac was an artist, a thinker, and a

man who wanted to see Black people rise above their circumstances. However, his inability to master his emotions made him an easy target for those who sought to exploit his passion for their own agendas. Whether it was the East Coast-West Coast rivalry or the dangerous alliances he formed in the streets, Tupac often reacted instead of strategizing, allowing his emotions to dictate his actions rather than using them as a tool for leadership. As McQuillar and Johnson III highlight in their book, his tragic death at just 25 years old was not just the result of a single moment of violence but a culmination of years of emotional impulsivity. His story is a powerful lesson on why emotional discipline is essential for Black men, because without it, even the most brilliant minds can be led to self-destruction. Tupac was born into a revolutionary family. His mother, Afeni Shakur, was a member of the Black Panther Party and instilled in him a deep sense of political awareness. As *"Holler If You Hear Me: Searching for Tupac Shakur"* by Michael Eric Dyson explains, Tupac saw himself as more than just a rapper; he was a voice for the voiceless, a bridge between the streets and the movement. However, Tupac was also an actor, both literally and figuratively. He attended the Baltimore School for the Arts, where he trained in theater and ballet. This background gave him the ability to perform not just on stage but also in his public persona. As Dyson notes, Tupac often played into the expectations placed on him, whether that meant embodying the *"thug"* image or the revolutionary. But the more he leaned into the role of the aggressive, street-oriented rapper, the harder it became to separate the act from reality. His early career reflected this duality. His debut album, *2Pacalypse Now*, was filled with social commentary and messages about systemic oppression. Songs like *"Brenda's Got a Baby"* and *"Trapped"* showcased his concern for the Black community. But as he gained fame, his emotions—specifically his need for validation, his paranoia, and his deep-seated anger—became his greatest weaknesses. Tupac's need for validation stemmed from a childhood filled with instability. As *"Holler If You Hear Me"* explains, his early years were marked by poverty, frequent moves, and the struggles of a single mother battling addiction. Without a stable father figure, Tupac sought guidance from the strong women in his life, particularly his mother, Afeni. While she instilled in him a deep sense of Black pride and revolutionary thought, she also embodied the struggle of many single Black mothers, raising a son without the masculine presence necessary to temper his emotional responses. As a result, Tupac, like many young Black men raised in similar environments, expressed his emotions in ways that mirrored feminine patterns: passionate, reactive, and at times volatile. This lack of masculine emotional discipline would later manifest in his personal and professional conflicts, making him a prime target for manipulation.

As Tupac's career progressed, his emotional turmoil

became more visible. By the time he released "*Strictly 4 My N.I.G.G.A.Z.,*" his frustrations with systemic oppression and the pressures of fame had begun to show in both his music and public persona. He was increasingly confrontational with the media, law enforcement, and even fellow artists. His shooting of two off-duty police officers in Atlanta (a case in which he was ultimately acquitted) reflected both his revolutionary spirit and his impulsiveness; he acted without fully considering the consequences, reacting emotionally to a situation where a more calculated response may have served him better. While this incident made him a hero to many, it also reinforced the idea that Tupac was unpredictable and dangerous, painting a target on his back. His legal troubles only escalated from there. In 1995, Tupac was convicted of sexual abuse, a charge he vehemently denied. This moment was pivotal, not just because it sent him to prison but because it deepened his paranoia and sense of betrayal. He believed the people around him, including his friend The Notorious B.I.G., had failed him. The quad studio shooting in New York, where Tupac was ambushed and shot multiple times, only reinforced this paranoia. Instead of stepping back and assessing the situation logically, he allowed his emotions to dictate his next moves. As Dyson points out, Tupac's inability to separate personal emotions from strategic decision-making led him deeper into conflict, particularly with the East Coast rap scene.

His decision to align with Suge Knight and Death

Row Records was another emotionally driven move. Fresh out of prison, Tupac was hungry for revenge, validation, and power. Suge, a master manipulator, provided all three, at a cost. Under Death Row, Tupac fully embraced the *"Thug Life"* image, pushing aside the revolutionary intellect in favor of the street soldier persona. His music became more aggressive, his feuds more public, and his emotional instability more pronounced. The release of *"Hit 'Em Up"* was a perfect example of this. Instead of engaging in a calculated attack against his rivals, Tupac used the song to air out personal grievances, escalating tensions that would eventually turn deadly. This was no longer just entertainment; Tupac had blurred the line between performance and reality, and it would cost him his life. Despite these self-destructive choices, Tupac still showed moments of deep reflection and a desire for something greater. In his final interviews, he spoke about wanting to start a new movement and elevate Black consciousness. There were also rumors he wanted to leave Death Row. He recognized the cycle he had been trapped in, but by then, it was too late. The momentum of his emotional decisions had set him on an irreversible path. His murder in Las Vegas in 1996 was not just the result of a single altercation but a culmination of years of emotional reactivity, making enemies in powerful places, and allowing others to control his emotions. Tupac's story is one of immense talent and potential, undone by an inability to master his own emotions. His life serves as a cautionary tale for Black men, proving that intelligence, charisma, and talent mean nothing without emotional discipline. Had Tupac learned to control his impulses and think strategically rather than emotionally, he could have been one of the greatest leaders of his time. Instead, he became another young Black man lost to violence, leaving behind a legacy of both brilliance and tragedy.

One of the defining moments in Tupac's life came when he joined Death Row Records under Suge Knight. *Tupac Shakur: The Authorized Biography* by Staci Robinson highlights how this move changed everything. Before Death Row, Tupac had already been in legal trouble, but there was still a sense that he was an artist trying to uplift his people. Death Row placed him in an environment where aggression, retaliation, and unchecked emotional responses were not only encouraged but expected. Suge Knight, a known gang affiliate, operated Death Row with an iron fist. He thrived on emotional manipulation, pitting artists against each other, fueling conflicts, and rewarding those who responded violently. As *Have Gun, Will Travel: The Spectacular Rise and Violent Fall of Death Row Records* by Ronin Ro details, Suge created a culture where men who controlled their emotions were seen as weak, and those who reacted with anger and violence were rewarded with loyalty and protection. Tupac, who had always been sensitive and reactive, played right into this dynamic. His rivalry with The Notorious

B.I.G. escalated beyond a musical competition into an all-out war because he allowed his emotions to be easily provoked. His infamous diss track, *"Hit 'Em Up,"* was pure emotional release, an unfiltered, rage-filled response that did nothing but increase tension. In one of his last interviews, featured in *Tupac: Resurrection*, he admitted that he often felt trapped by his own persona. He wanted to help his people, but he also couldn't escape the expectations placed on him to be a gangsta, a warrior, and a man who responded with aggression rather than strategy.

On September 7, 1996, Tupac let his emotions lead him into the most consequential mistake of his life. After a Mike Tyson fight at the MGM Grand in Las Vegas, Tupac and his entourage, including Suge Knight, spotted Orlando Anderson, a known Crip member who was suspected of robbing a Death Row affiliate. Without hesitation, Tupac attacked Anderson, setting off a chain of events that led to his assassination later that night. As McQuillar and Johnson explain in *Tupac Shakur: The Life and Times of an American Icon*, this was a classic example of an emotional decision with permanent consequences. Tupac didn't need to fight Anderson. He didn't need to prove anything. But because he was trapped in a world where respect was everything and disrespect had to be answered with violence, he reacted instead of responding. Six days later, he died from the gunshot wounds he sustained in the drive-by shooting that night.

Tupac's fatal mistake was not just engaging in the fight but failing to recognize the larger forces at play. The streets had always been filled with tension, but by aligning himself so closely with Suge Knight and Death Row, Tupac had unknowingly placed himself in the middle of a much deeper conflict. The battle between the Bloods and Crips, the tension between East and West Coast rap, and the personal vendettas that had been brewing for years all converged in that single moment at the MGM Grand. As McQuillar and Johnson highlight, this was more than just an impulsive act; it was the culmination of years of emotional reactions, unchecked anger, and an environment that rewarded aggression over wisdom. Tupac was a man who spoke often about breaking free from the cycle of violence, yet he ultimately fell victim to it because he could not control his emotions in the most crucial moment of his life.

His death was a tragedy not only because of the loss of an immense talent but also because of what he represented. Tupac was a young Black man with the potential to bridge the gap between the streets and revolutionary thought, between hip-hop and political activism. However, his inability to channel his emotions into something constructive rather than destructive cut his life short before he could fulfill that potential. His story serves as a warning for Black men: no matter how intelligent, charismatic, or influential you are, a single emotional decision can end everything.

His legacy lives on, but so does the lesson: a Black man who cannot master his emotions will always be vulnerable to forces greater than himself. Tupac's story is a painful reminder that brilliance, talent, and good intentions mean nothing if a man cannot control his emotions. He had the potential to be one of the greatest Black leaders of his generation. He understood systemic oppression, the struggles of Black America, and the need for change. But because he allowed his emotions to dictate his decisions, he became easy to manipulate—by the industry, by Suge Knight, and ultimately by the streets. His story forces Black men to ask themselves a difficult question: Do you want to be powerful, or do you want to be controlled? A powerful man masters his emotions and uses them to build, strategize, and lead. A controlled man reacts impulsively, destroys relationships, and plays right into the hands of those who seek to exploit him.

Tupac's tragic end was not just a personal loss; it was a loss for the entire Black community. It showed how quickly a promising Black man could be taken down by his own inability to control his emotions. And this brings us to another tragic example, one that happened even earlier in life. If Tupac's story was a case of a man's emotions leading to his downfall, then the story of Yummy Sandifer is what happens when a Black boy is never even given the chance to learn emotional control in the first place. Tupac's story illustrates how a lack of emotional control can derail even the most gifted and charismatic Black men. But what happens when that lack of control is exploited before a boy even has the chance to become a man? Robert "Yummy" Sandifer's life answers that question in the most tragic way possible. Unlike Tupac, Yummy never had the opportunity to grow into his potential; he was swallowed by the streets before he could even understand the world around him. His short life was not just a personal tragedy but a reflection of a system that grooms emotionally unstable Black boys into tools of destruction. Yummy's story serves as a chilling reminder of what happens when young Black boys are denied discipline, protection, and guidance. If Tupac's downfall was a cautionary tale, Yummy's fate is a stark warning: without emotional control and strong male leadership, Black boys are left vulnerable to forces that see them as nothing more than disposable soldiers in a deadly game.

The Tragedy of Robert "Yummy" Sandifer

Robert "Yummy" Sandifer was not a monster. He was an 11-year-old boy whose life was shaped by neglect, abuse, and the unforgiving streets of Chicago. His story is not just one of personal failure but of a system that preys on Black boys who lack emotional guidance and stability. Unlike Tupac, who at least had a foundation of revolutionary thought and artistic expression, Yummy had nothing: no strong male figures, no structure, no path toward anything but destruction. He was both a product and a victim of the gang culture that exploits emotionally reactive boys, turning them into tools of violence before they even understand the consequences of their actions. Yummy's life was doomed from the start. Born in 1983 into extreme poverty, he was raised in a household marked by chaos. His mother was a drug addict, and his father was absent, spending most of his life in and out of prison. The Illinois Department of Children and Family Services (DCFS) had been called to investigate his living conditions nearly 50 times, but nothing changed. Yummy, like so many other young Black boys, was left to raise himself in an environment where survival was the only priority.

By the time he was a toddler, Yummy had already developed a reputation for violent outbursts. Without structure, discipline, or proper emotional development, he learned early on that aggression was his only defense mechanism. By age 8, he was committing petty crimes. By age 10, he was running with the Black Disciples, one of the most notorious gangs in Chicago. In the absence of male role models to guide him toward manhood, the streets provided their own twisted version of mentorship. To the gang, Yummy's youth was not a weakness; it was an asset. According to Natasha M. Tarpley's book, *Girl in the Mirror: Three Generations of Black Women in Motion*, Yummy's small size and age made him the perfect recruit for the Black Disciples. He could carry weapons, commit crimes, and even kill without facing the same legal consequences as an adult. The gang knew this, and they used his emotional instability to their advantage, feeding his need for acceptance and belonging in exchange for acts of violence.

That need for belonging is what led Yummy to make the decision that would seal his fate. On August 28, 1994, he was given a mission: to prove himself to the gang by shooting a rival. Armed with a 9mm pistol, he opened fire on a group of people. But in his reckless, uncontrolled attack, he struck and killed Shavon Dean, a 14-year-old girl who had nothing to do with the conflict. The murder of Shavon Dean sparked national outrage. Suddenly, Yummy was not just another nameless street kid; he was a symbol of everything wrong with inner-city violence, gang culture, and the lost Black youth of America. His face, a haunting mugshot of a child hardened beyond his years, was plastered across newspapers and television screens. In a cover story titled *"The Short, Violent Life of Robert 'Yummy' Sandifer,"* **TIME** magazine asked how an 11-year-old could become a killer. But the real question was: Who failed Yummy? The Black Disciples understood the attention Yummy was bringing to their operation, and they knew they had to get rid of him. Just days after Shavon's murder, the same gang that had once called him *"family"* decided he was a liability. Two older gang members, the same people who had encouraged his recklessness, were ordered to silence him. On

September 1, 1994, Yummy was lured into an underpass by two fellow Black Disciples, Craig and Derrick Hardaway, who were only teenagers themselves. There, he was executed with two bullets to the back of the head. The streets had used him, and when he was no longer useful, they discarded him like trash. Yummy's story is not just a tragedy; it's a systemic failure. It is what happens when young Black boys are left without strong male leadership, emotional discipline, or guidance toward something greater than survival. If Tupac's story is a warning about the dangers of emotional impulsivity, Yummy's is a reminder of what happens when Black boys never even get the chance to learn control. He never had the opportunity to become a man. Instead, he was molded into a weapon and disposed of before he even reached adolescence.

His death should have been a turning point, a wake-up call for Black America to step in and save the next generation before the streets claim them. Instead, his story has been repeated time and time again. The cycle continues, and unless Black men take responsibility for leading, teaching, and protecting their own, there will always be another "Yummy," another lost boy swallowed by a world that only values his ability to self-destruct. The tragic story of Robert "Yummy" Sandifer is not an isolated case; it is the direct result of a predatory gang culture that preys on young Black boys who lack emotional discipline and strong male leadership. The same forces that consumed Yummy continue to operate today, recruiting emotionally unstable boys, weaponizing their pain, and discarding them when they are no longer useful. His fate is a grim reminder of why Black men must reclaim their roles as leaders, mentors, and protectors in the community. The 14 Codes outline a blueprint for Black manhood, and Yummy's story exposes what happens when those principles are absent.

Yummy, like so many other young boys, was never taught the difference. He acted out of impulse, reacting to his environment with aggression and violence instead of thoughtfulness and control. The streets took advantage of this lack of discipline, channeling his raw emotion into destruction rather than purpose. Gang culture intentionally seeks out Black boys who lack emotional control because they are easier to manipulate. The Black Disciples saw Yummy's pain, his desperation for acceptance, and his reckless nature as assets. They molded him into a soldier who would follow orders without question, never pausing to consider the consequences of his actions. Yummy, like many young boys without guidance, was never given the chance to develop proactive thinking. Instead, he was raised in survival mode, reacting to every threat, every slight, and every demand from the streets. Without control over his emotions, he was controlled by the streets. Yummy never had peers who held him to a higher standard. Instead, he was surrounded by people who encouraged his worst instincts. The gang members who recruited him did not see him as a child who needed guidance; they saw him as a tool, someone they could send to do their dirty work. This is the result of fatherlessness and the absence of real Black male leadership. Without men enforcing discipline, setting expectations, and demonstrating emotional control, Black boys seek authority figures elsewhere. The gangs become their fathers, the streets become their home, and the only lessons they learn are those of violence and self-destruction. Gangs make false promises of brotherhood, loyalty, and protection, but in reality, they treat Black boys as disposable resources. Yummy believed he was earning respect, proving himself to be valuable to his gang. Instead, when he became a liability, the same people who called him *"family"* executed him without hesitation. Yummy's story proves that when Black men do not step up to lead, the streets will lead in their place. Gang culture understands that the easiest men to control are those without discipline. But the streets do not teach Black boys how to command respect through character, integrity, or self-control. Instead, they teach that respect is earned through fear, violence, and emotional outbursts. Yummy followed that model. When ordered to prove himself, he reacted without thinking, killing an innocent girl in the process. The gang culture enforces this idea in the worst possible way: if you are not bringing in money, bodies, or influence, you are worthless. Once Yummy became a liability, his life was deemed expendable.

"Yummy" was not born a killer; he was made into one by a system that preyed on his lack of emotional control. His story should not just serve as a cautionary tale but as a wake-up call for Black men. The responsibility to guide, teach, and protect young Black boys cannot be ignored. If Black men do not step up as leaders, the gangs will continue to step in. Yummy's story is not just about one lost boy; it is about a pattern that will continue until Black men take back control over the development of the next generation. If we do not enforce the 14 Codes in our communities, the streets will enforce their own. And the streets have only one rule: destroy or be destroyed.

Malcolm X: The Power of Emotional Discipline

Yummy Sandifer's story illustrates the tragic consequences of a life dictated by unchecked emotions. He was a child soldier in a war he didn't understand, manipulated by men who saw his emotional instability as a weapon. But what happens when a Black man masters his emotions instead of being ruled by them? This is where Malcolm X's story provides a stark contrast. Like Yummy, Malcolm was once consumed by his environment, reacting impulsively and recklessly to the streets. However, unlike Yummy, Malcolm found the discipline to transform himself from an emotionally volatile hustler into one of the most disciplined and intellectually sharp Black leaders in history. His life stands as the ultimate example of how a Black man can evolve when he controls his emotions instead of letting them control him. In the next section, we will examine Malcolm X's journey, from his chaotic youth to his disciplined leadership, and how his mastery of emotional control made him a force to be reckoned with. His transformation is a blueprint for how Black men can rise above emotional manipulation and reclaim their power.

Malcolm X's life is the ultimate example of how a Black man can reclaim his power through discipline, accountability, and emotional control, all principles found in *The 14 Codes.* His transformation from a reckless, emotional street hustler to a disciplined, self-mastered leader embodies what happens when a Black man controls his emotions instead of being controlled by them.. *The Autobiography of Malcolm X* by Alex Haley, *Malcolm X: A Life of Reinvention* by Manning Marable, and Malcolm's own speeches will break down how his mastery of emotion and adherence to these principles allowed him to become the Black man that the system fears most: a man who cannot be controlled.

Before Malcolm X became one of the most disciplined leaders of the 20th century, he was a hustler named Detroit Red, lost in the streets of Harlem. He was intelligent, charismatic, and bold, but his lack of emotional control made him reckless. As he recounts in *The Autobiography of Malcolm X*, he lived for pleasure, fast money, and status. He was a gambler, a drug dealer, and a pimp. He wanted respect, but like many young Black men today, he believed respect came through intimidation, violence, and material possessions However, he was trying to command respect without first mastering himself, which is impossible. His downfall was inevitable. In 1946, at the age of 20, he was sentenced to 10 years in prison for burglary. He had been playing by the streets' rules, and the streets had no loyalty to him. But unlike so many Black men who are consumed by the system, Malcolm did something different, he transformed himself.

Prison was supposed to break Malcolm, but instead, it became the place where he reclaimed himself. At first, he resisted the structure of incarceration, seeing it as another system designed to control him. But soon, he realized that the real prison wasn't just the walls around him; it was his own undisciplined mind. He had spent years chasing temporary power through the streets, but in reality, he had been powerless all along. Through the influence of his siblings, particularly his brother Reginald, Malcolm was introduced to the teachings of the Nation of Islam (NOI) and Elijah Muhammad. These teachings forced him to look at himself differently. He had always been quick to blame white supremacy, but now he was forced to take personal accountability, starting with himself. He had been his own worst enemy, and only he could change that. Malcolm's prison years were his period of rebirth. As detailed in *The Autobiography of Malcolm X*, he was introduced to Elijah Muhammad and the Nation of Islam, who taught him about self-discipline, self-respect, and the power of the Black man. However, Malcolm's real transformation wasn't just about religion; it was about self-mastery.

Instead of wasting time in prison like most inmates, Malcolm studied relentlessly. He read books on philosophy, history, and language. He copied entire dictionaries to build his vocabulary. He turned his mind into a weapon sharper than any gun he had ever carried in the streets. Most importantly, he learned how to control his emotions. Instead of reacting impulsively to disrespect or anger, he learned patience, strategy, and discipline. He understood that real power does not come from emotional outbursts but from controlled, calculated action. By the time he left prison in 1952, Detroit Red was dead. Malcolm X was born. Once Malcolm understood that true power comes from knowledge, not intimidation, he made reading his new hustle. He trained his mind the way a warrior trains his body, sharpening his intellect until he could debate anyone on any subject. Unlike his past life, where his energy was spent chasing distractions, Malcolm now focused. He committed to self-improvement with the same intensity he once committed to the streets. And as he mastered his mind, something even more powerful happened: he began to master his emotions. No longer did he let anger, frustration, or pride dictate his actions. He learned that discipline over emotions is the key to true strength.

By the time Malcolm was released from prison in 1952, he was no longer a pawn in the white man's game or the street's game. He had elevated himself from a reckless hustler to a self-possessed man. He had once been driven by impulse and survival, but now he operated from a place of intention and strategy. This transformation made him dangerous to the system. The government had always feared angry Black men, but they feared disciplined Black men even more. A man who cannot be emotionally manipulated, distracted, or bought is a man who cannot be controlled. Malcolm X was now that man. As Malcolm rose through the ranks of the Nation of Islam, his discipline and work ethic became legendary. He was the embodiment of not requesting respect; he commanded it. He didn't demand loyalty; he earned it through his actions, his consistency, and his example. When he spoke, people listened, not because he was loud, but because he was undeniable. His words carried weight because they were backed by discipline. He never allowed himself to be seen as weak, and he never let his emotions control him in public. His ability to stay composed, even in the face of racist journalists, government informants, and internal betrayal, showed the strength of a man who had mastered himself.

As a minister of the Nation of Islam, Malcolm X became a powerful speaker, inspiring thousands with his uncompromising stance on Black self-sufficiency, self-defense, and accountability When Malcolm spoke, people believed him because he never wavered in his truth. However, his greatest strength was his discipline. Unlike many Black leaders who allowed emotions to cloud their judgment, Malcolm was calculated and deliberate. He never let his enemies bait him into reckless action This discipline made him dangerous. He could not be manipulated, he could not be bought, and he could not be distracted. While white America feared Martin Luther King Jr.'s peaceful protests, they feared Malcolm X's self-controlled militancy even more. Malcolm's transformation from a reckless hustler to a strategic revolutionary is the clearest example of why Black men must control their emotions to control their destiny. It wasn't just white America that feared Malcolm; it was the entire system. Unlike other leaders who could be swayed, bribed, or emotionally provoked into mistakes, Malcolm was too disciplined to be manipulated. He understood how power worked, and he refused to play by their rules. This made him a threat. The FBI's COINTELPRO program labeled him *the most dangerous man in America,"* not because he advocated for violence, but because he advocated for self-sufficiency, self-defense, and Black unity under discipline. When Malcolm spoke, his people believed him. That belief was more powerful than any bullet or law that could be used against him.

Malcolm X's greatest challenge came in 1964 when

he broke away from the Nation of Islam. Despite dedicating over a decade of his life to Elijah Muhammad, Malcolm discovered corruption within the leadership. Rather than reacting emotionally and destroying himself in anger, he did what few Black men are willing to do: he walked away and rebuilt himself. Malcolm's pilgrimage to Mecca in 1964 was more than a religious journey; it was a transformation of thought. For years, he had preached a doctrine of strict racial separation under the Nation of Islam, but in Mecca, he saw Muslims of all colors worshiping together as equals. This revelation deepened his understanding of global Black unity and redefined his mission. Rather than allowing his past ideology to trap him, he evolved. He could have remained bitter and blamed the NOI for misleading him, but instead, he used the experience as fuel to sharpen his perspective and expand his vision. This shift made Malcolm even more dangerous to his enemies. Now, he wasn't just speaking for Black Americans; he was building international coalitions, connecting the struggles of Black people in the U.S. with those in Africa, the Caribbean, and beyond. He refused to waste time dwelling on the past; instead, he focused on creating something new. Malcolm X wasn't just about fighting oppression, he was about building a world where Black people controlled their own future. He moved with focus and purpose, not anger or bitterness, and that discipline is what made his legacy untouchable. His assassination on February 21, 1965, at the Audubon Ballroom in Harlem was the brutal end of a life shaped by struggle, betrayal, and political growth. By the time of his death, Malcolm had become one of the most feared Black leaders in America, not just by white supremacists and the U.S. government but also by his former allies in the Nation of Islam. His break from the NOI, along with his public exposure of Elijah Muhammad's indiscretions, made him a marked man. Death threats became frequent, his home was fire-bombed just a week before his murder, and he knew he was being watched by both government agencies and his former organization. Despite these dangers, Malcolm refused to let fear dictate his actions

On the day of his assassination, Malcolm stood before a packed crowd of over 400 people, prepared to deliver a speech on the future of Black liberation. Before he could begin, a commotion broke out in the audience, distracting his security team. At that moment, three shooters rushed forward and opened fire. Malcolm was struck multiple times in the chest, arms, and legs. According to Les Payne's *The Dead Are Arising: The Life of Malcolm X*, the first shotgun blast was so powerful that it lifted him off the ground. As he fell, more bullets followed. In just seconds, one of the most disciplined, intelligent, and courageous Black men of the 20th century lay dying on the stage, his life cut short at the age of 39. The aftermath of his murder was filled with speculation and controversy. Many pointed to the Nation of Islam as the direct orchestrator, with

Talmadge Hayer (also known as Thomas Hagan), Norman Butler (later known as Muhammad Abdul Aziz), and Thomas Johnson (later known as Khalil Islam) being arrested and convicted. However, in later years, evidence surfaced that at least two of the men convicted were likely innocent, while the real perpetrators remained free. The FBI's COINTELPRO program, which had actively sought to sow division between Malcolm and the NOI, also played a significant role in fueling the environment that led to his death. As *"Malcolm X: A Life of Reinvention"* by Manning Marable details, government surveillance and infiltration made it nearly impossible for Malcolm to escape the forces working against him. He was not just a threat to the NOI but to the entire U.S. system of racial oppression.

Malcolm's death was a devastating loss, but his assassination also reinforced the importance of Code #8: A Black MAN will die for his Responsibilities. Even in the face of death, Malcolm never wavered in his commitment to Black liberation. His murder was intended to silence him, but instead, it immortalized him. His words, his discipline, and his transformation from a reckless street hustler to a principled revolutionary became a blueprint for generations of Black men seeking strength, integrity, and purpose. The system may have taken his life, but it could never erase his impact.

Malcolm X was one of the rare Black men who mastered every aspect of the 14 Codes, making him one of the greatest Black American leaders in history. He upheld his integrity (Code #1) by never compromising his beliefs, even when it cost him everything. His tireless work ethic (Code #2) was evident in his transformation from a street hustler to a disciplined leader who studied relentlessly and dedicated himself to uplifting others. Malcolm controlled his emotions (Code #3) with precision, never allowing anger, fear, or betrayal to dictate his actions. He responded strategically, not impulsively. His character (Code #4) was defined by his ability to follow through on his promises, whether in his dedication to the Nation of Islam or his commitment to Pan-Africanism. He refused to gossip (Code #5). One of Malcolm X's defining traits was his refusal to engage in gossip or petty disputes. Even when he became aware of Elijah Muhammad's indiscretions, he did not initially expose them to the public. Instead, he addressed them privately and sought clarity, hoping the leader he once revered would hold himself accountable. As detailed in *The Autobiography of Malcolm X*, it was only when Malcolm saw that the corruption within the Nation of Islam was harming the movement that he spoke out; but even then, he did so with facts, not speculation. He never indulged in personal attacks or slander; he simply told the truth. This discipline and restraint reinforced his credibility, making his words even more powerful. Malcolm understood that engaging in gossip or emotional outbursts would only weaken his cause, so he always chose integrity over petty distractions.

He focused on facts rather than petty disputes and commanded respect (Code #6) through his intelligence, confidence, and unwavering discipline. Unlike men who seek validation from women, Malcolm understood that women do not define a man (Code #7); instead, he set the standard, and his wife reflected his strength and purpose. Malcolm's relationship with his wife, Betty Shabazz, was a reflection of his growth as a man. Unlike many men who allow their relationships to define them, Malcolm knew that his purpose came first. As his speeches and letters reveal, he deeply respected Betty, but he did not seek validation from her; he led with purpose, and she supported his mission. His leadership in the household mirrored his leadership in the movement; he was firm, disciplined, and focused, setting the tone for his family rather than being swayed by emotions or external pressures. Betty, in turn, was a strong, intelligent, and devoted partner who reflected the values Malcolm embodied. Their marriage demonstrated that a man's strength is not determined by the woman he chooses but by the foundation he builds for himself. Malcolm's commitment to his principles ensured that his relationship was a partnership, not a dependency.

Malcolm X was willing to die for his responsibilities (Code #8), knowing that his mission was bigger than himself. His word was his bond (Code #9), making him one of the most trusted voices in the fight for Black liberation. He gave reason, not excuses (Code #10), constantly seeking solutions rather than complaining about oppression. He was proactive, not reactive (Code #11), always thinking several steps ahead of his enemies. Malcolm knew that if he could not produce "*Code #12*," he would be useless to his people, so he dedicated his life to educating and mobilizing Black men and women. He held his peers accountable ("*Code #13*"), challenging the hypocrisy within the Nation of Islam and demanding excellence from Black leadership. Finally, Malcolm understood the power of discipline over desire ("*Code #14*"), never allowing lust or distractions to weaken his mission. Malcolm X lived by discipline, not just in public, but behind closed doors. When it came to women, he stood firm. While Elijah Muhammad's actions with women exposed cracks in the Nation of Islam, Malcolm stayed loyal to his wife and never let temptation or weakness make a clown out of him. He understood: a man who can't master his own flesh is already a slave.

As *The Dead Are Arising* by Les Payne details, Malcolm saw sexual discipline as a crucial part of self-control. He understood that many great men had fallen because they allowed their desires to dictate their decisions, weakening their power and credibility. This level of restraint set Malcolm apart from other leaders, whose lack of discipline made them vulnerable to scandals and manipulation. By maintaining control over his own desires, Malcolm ensured that his legacy would not be tainted by personal failings. His ability to master himself in all aspects of life, mentally, emotionally, and physically, solidified his status as a true example of Black manhood.

Because Malcolm X embodied all 14 Codes, his legacy remains one of strength, integrity, and transformation. He was not a perfect man, but he was a man who continuously evolved, never allowing his past mistakes to define his future. His ability to master himself made him immune to the traps that have destroyed so many Black men, ensuring that his impact would live on far beyond his lifetime. Even in death, Malcolm X stands as the blueprint for what a Black man can and should be. His life is proof that when a Black man follows the 14 Codes, he commands respect, builds a lasting legacy, and leaves behind a foundation for future generations to follow. Malcolm X was not just a revolutionary; he was the embodiment of Black manhood at its highest level.

Malcolm X's embodiment of all 14 Codes made him the biggest threat to the system of oppression that sought to control Black America. His unwavering integrity, discipline, and commitment to Black liberation set a powerful example for Black men everywhere, showing them how to take control of their emotions, build self-discipline, and demand respect without compromise. His voice and actions resonated deeply, challenging the status quo and inspiring Black men to reject victimhood and embrace power, purpose, and accountability. As he gained influence, his message became a call for Black men to rise up and take charge of their destinies, making him a direct challenge to the entrenched systems of white supremacy. Because of this, the establishment saw him as a dangerous figure who could mobilize a generation of Black men to resist and reclaim their power. In the end, Malcolm X's assassination was not just about silencing him, but about eliminating the example he set for Black men who could have followed his lead and changed the course of history. His example proved that Black men did not have to conform to destructive stereotypes; they could reclaim their power by following the *"Codes."* However, as history shows, merely following the *"Codes"* does not protect you from being targeted; in fact, it makes you a more prominent target for those who wish to maintain control. Malcolm's assassination was a calculated move by those threatened by his influence, a reminder that even the most righteous of leaders are vulnerable when they challenge the status quo.

Master the Storm: Feel It but Don't Fold to It

The stories of Tupac Shakur, Robert "Yummy" Sandifer, and Malcolm X all serve as powerful illustrations of the importance of emotional control and how the lack thereof can have devastating consequences. Tupac's life was marked by the tension between his revolutionary ideals and his inability to master his emotions, which led him down a path of self-destruction. Yummy Sandifer, on the other hand, never had the opportunity to develop emotional control, with his environment preying on his emotional instability, which ultimately led to his tragic end. In contrast, Malcolm X's journey showed the immense power of emotional discipline, as he not only overcame his early recklessness but also became a strategic, self-controlled leader who had a profound impact on Black America. These examples reflect Code #3: *"A Black MAN has Emotion, but he is not Emotional."* A Black man who can master his emotions is capable of shaping his own destiny, whereas one who allows his emotions to dictate his actions becomes susceptible to forces beyond his control.

The failure to develop emotional control, especially in a community where trauma is prevalent, is often magnified in Black men raised in single-mother households. Without the presence of a strong male figure to model discipline, many Black boys grow up mimicking feminine behavior, lacking the tools to channel their emotions effectively. This gap in emotional education often leads to reactive behavior, such as the violent impulsiveness that we see in Tupac's and Yummy's stories. In contrast, Malcolm X was able to transcend this limitation, partially due to his exposure to strong, disciplined male mentors during his incarceration and later in his leadership roles. The absence of emotional control is a societal and familial issue that needs to be addressed in order to prevent the systemic destruction of Black men. Without the guidance of a consistent role model, many young Black men fall victim to circumstances, perpetuating cycles of violence, and fueling the broader issues that plague the community.

Malcolm X's ability to display emotional control and apply it to his strategic thinking ultimately made him a model for Black manhood. By adhering to Code #3, he transformed from a hustler caught up in the dangerous cycle of street life to a disciplined leader who commanded respect through his wisdom and foresight. Unlike Tupac, who allowed his emotions to lead him into irreversible mistakes, Malcolm channeled his feelings of anger and frustration into something productive: a movement for the empowerment of Black people. He set a standard not just for Black men but for men of all backgrounds, showing that emotional control is a key element of leadership and survival in a world designed to break one down. His legacy proves that a Black man who controls his emotions is not only capable of achieving greatness but can also inspire generations to follow suit.

These lessons are a critical reminder that emotional control, especially in a world that constantly seeks to undermine Black men, is not a luxury; it is a necessity. As we continue to face challenges as a community, it's imperative that Black men learn to control their emotions, even in the face of adversity. By doing so, they can avoid the pitfalls of impulsiveness and violence that have claimed far too many lives and instead build legacies of strength, dignity, and impact. The examples set by figures like Tupac, Yummy, and Malcolm X show us that emotional control is the difference between destruction and triumph, and it is the cornerstone of becoming the kind of man who commands respect and leads with integrity.

DISCIPLINE

A man without discipline is a man without control, and a man without control is at the mercy of the world. Discipline is the foundation of self-mastery; how you think, move, and operate daily determines your success. It's about setting standards for yourself and refusing to deviate from them, no matter the distractions or temptations. Whether it's maintaining your physical health, controlling your emotions, or sticking to your goals, discipline is what separates men who build from men who beg.

CODE NO. 4

A BLACK MAN SHOWS CHARACTER: THE ABILITY TO FOLLOW THROUGH

Character is one of the cornerstones of the foundation of a Black man's identity. It is not just about how others perceive him, but about his ability to follow through on his word, commitments, and responsibilities. A man's true worth is not measured by what he says he will do but by what he actually does. In a world where many talk but few act, character separates the weak from the strong. Without character, a man is unreliable, his word is meaningless, and his presence holds no weight. A Black man understands that his character is his signature, and it determines how he will be remembered. Character is not something a man is born with; it is something he builds over time through discipline and action. Every decision he makes, every promise he keeps or breaks, shapes his character. A Black man does not blame circumstances for his failures; he takes full ownership of his actions and follows through, no matter the difficulty. Weak men look for excuses, but men of character find a way to get things done. Whether it is in his work, his family, or his community, a Black man's commitment to follow-through defines his value. His consistency becomes his legacy.

In today's world, too many men are satisfied with looking the part instead of being the part. Social media has created a culture of performative masculinity, where men post about their ambitions but never execute them. Words without action are nothing but noise. A Black man does not seek validation from others; his validation comes from his ability to complete what he starts. When he speaks, people listen, not because of his words, but because of his track record. He knows that only through action does a man prove his worth. A Black man's character is tested in times of adversity, not when things are easy. Anyone can be disciplined when life is going well, but true character is revealed when obstacles arise. Does he break under pressure, or does he rise to the challenge? A man of character does not fold when life gets tough; he adapts, he overcomes, and he finds a way forward. The struggle is where men are forged, and the Black man understands that his response to hardship determines his greatness. His ability to follow through, even in the face of difficulty, is what makes him a "*MAN*."

Throughout history, the greatest Black men have been those who demonstrated unwavering character.

They were men who did what they said they would do, regardless of the cost. Whether it was leading revolutions, building businesses, or protecting their families, these men proved that character is the foundation of power. A Black man honors their legacy by upholding this standard in his own life. He understands that his actions today will shape the future of his family and community. To be a man is to be accountable, reliable, and disciplined; without that, he is just another male. Character is the one thing a man cannot fake. A man may lie to others, but he cannot lie to himself about whether he follows through or not. If his word means nothing, then he is nothing. If his commitments are empty, then so is his future. A Black man does not tolerate weakness within himself; he holds himself to a higher standard. His character is his contract with the world, and he ensures that when he gives his word, it stands firm. Without character, a Black man is just another talker, and the world does not respect talkers; it respects doers.

JOHN PARKER: The Power of Character and the Fear of a Free Black Man

John Parker exemplified Code #4, "*A Black MAN shows Character; Character is defined as the ability to follow through,*" through his undeniable commitment to both his people and his principles. Born into slavery, Parker refused to accept his condition and worked tirelessly to buy his own freedom, an act that, in itself, demonstrated immense character. But what set him apart was what he did afterward. Instead of seeking safety and comfort, he risked everything to help others escape bondage, becoming one of the most daring conductors on the Underground Railroad. One powerful example from his autobiography, *His Promised Land: The Autobiography of John P. Parker, Former Slave and Conductor on the Underground Railroad,* is how he repeatedly risked his life to free enslaved people in Kentucky. Unlike many conductors who only provided shelter, Parker took action by sneaking onto plantations, evading slave catchers, and guiding people across the Ohio River to freedom. He made promises to those who sought his help and never wavered in fulfilling them.

His character was also evident in business. After securing his freedom, he became a successful iron molder and inventor in Ripley, Ohio. Even when facing racial discrimination and economic challenges, Parker never quit; he built a thriving business and continued his work as an abolitionistHis ability to follow through on his principles made him a true Black man, proving that character is not about words but about consistent, fearless action. Parker's character was a direct threat to white supremacy because it shattered the myth of Black inferiority. In the eyes of the white power structure, a Black man who was intelligent, resourceful, and capable of independent action was dangerous. He not only freed himself but also used his skills and courage to liberate others, proving that enslaved people were not content or helpless; they were actively resisting. His work defied the slaveholding South's belief that Black people were incapable of self-determination. The fact that Parker went from being property to becoming a successful businessman and inventor after the Civil War made him even more of a threat. He didn't just break free, he thrived, showing that Black men, when given the opportunity, could outwork and outthink their oppressors.

White supremacy depends on Black men lacking character, on them being passive, afraid, and unwilling to take risks for the greater good. Parker's actions directly opposed that narrative because he embodied everything a Black man is supposed to be: proactive, responsible, and committed to his word. His ability to follow through, even when faced with the real possibility of death, made him an enemy of the system. Slaveholders feared men like him because they represented an alternative future, one where Black men led their own communities, built wealth, and operated without fear. Parker proved that character, when put into action, is not just a personal virtue but a revolutionary weapon. His legacy teaches an important lesson: white supremacy is only sustained when Black men fail to follow through. When Black men embrace character and stand by their principles, they become forces of change. Parker's life serves as a model for how a Black man should move, with discipline, strategy, and an unshakable commitment to his values. His story is proof that when a Black man commits to a purpose greater than himself, he not only uplifts his people but strikes fear into the systems that seek to keep them weak. True character, the ability to follow through, is not just about self-respect; it is an act of defiance against those who believe Black men should remain powerless.

John Parker's ability to follow through on his commitments aligns with the themes explored in *"The Underground Railroad Records"* by William Still. This book documents firsthand accounts of enslaved people who risked everything for freedom, emphasizing the role of conductors like Parker, who demonstrated unshakable character. Parker's actions mirrored the stories in Still's work, proving that true leadership comes from action, not rhetoric. Unlike those who hesitated out of fear, Parker took direct action, fully understanding the consequences if he failed. His courage was not reckless; it was calculated, methodical, and rooted in the belief that Black people had the right to shape their own destinies. His commitment to the cause showed that character is about persistence, especially when the stakes are life and death.

Parker's defiance also aligns with W.E.B. Du Bois's analysis of Black leadership in *Black Reconstruction in America*. Du Bois argued that Black men who demonstrated intelligence, discipline, and self-sufficiency were systematically targeted because they disrupted the racial hierarchy. Parker embodied this threat by proving that a Black man could outthink and outmaneuver his oppressors, making him a living contradiction to white supremacist ideology. His story reinforces the argument that the destruction of Black character, through oppression, fear, and systemic barriers, is necessary for white supremacy to function. But Parker's life also proves that character is stronger than any system designed to break it. His ability to follow through, both as a freedom fighter and later as a successful businessman, demonstrates that a Black man with character is not just dangerous to white supremacy; he is the blueprint for liberation.

CLYDE KENNARD: The Price of a Black Man's Unshakable Character.

The fight for Black manhood did not end with Parker's era. It evolved, as new struggles arose in the form of Jim Crow laws and racial segregation, which aimed to suppress Black advancement through barriers like restricted access to education. In this new battle, Clyde Kennard emerged as a symbol of resistance, fighting to break down the walls that kept Black people from accessing education and self-determination.

Born in 1927 in Hattiesburg, Mississippi, Clyde Kennard grew up in a state infamous for its violent enforcement of segregation. Unlike many of his contemporaries, Kennard refused to accept the racial limitations imposed by society. His military service during the Korean War shaped his strong sense of duty and perseverance, and after returning home, he made it clear that he would not be content with the status quo. Kennard initially pursued his studies at the University of Chicago before returning to Mississippi to be with his family. However, upon his return, he found that his home state was not a place where educated and ambitious Black men were welcomed. Despite the hostile environment, Kennard remained determined to continue his education and set his sights on Mississippi Southern College, an all-white institution where he would challenge the barriers of racial segregation head-on.

At the time, Mississippi Southern College was an institution that enforced strict segregation policies, barring Black students from enrollment. White officials feared that integrating the school would disrupt the social hierarchy they had meticulously maintained. Undeterred, Kennard believed that education was a right, not a privilege, and he repeatedly attempted to apply to the college, only to be met with rejection, intimidation, and bureaucratic roadblocks. But Kennard's character was defined by his refusal to back down in the face of injustice. His repeated attempts to gain admission to the university, despite the immense personal risk, exemplified Code #4 of *"The 14 Codes."* Kennard did not just dream of a better life; he actively pursued it, becoming a living embodiment of Black manhood: resolute, focused, and unwavering.

Kennard's pursuit of education directly challenged the white supremacy of his time, exposing the greatest fear of segregationists: a Black man who would not be silenced or intimidated. His education and discipline made him a direct threat to the existing racial power structure. White supremacists knew that a Black man who committed to his education and principles could dismantle the very systems that oppressed Black people. As a result, Kennard became a target of Mississippi's racist power structure. The Mississippi State Sovereignty Commission, a state agency dedicated to preserving segregation, began to monitor Kennard, seeking ways to discredit him and halt his efforts. Despite their intimidation tactics, Kennard refused to retreat from his cause, continuing to push forward with unyielding determination. But when intimidation failed, white supremacists resorted to legal manipulation, ultimately falsely accusing him of stealing $25 worth of chicken feed. This baseless charge resulted in his conviction by an all-white jury and a seven-year prison sentence. His imprisonment was not about justice; it was about sending a message to other Black men that they, too, could be punished for challenging the status quo. Yet, even behind bars, Kennard's resilience remained unbroken.

Clyde Kennard's wrongful imprisonment was yet another example of how America has always tried to criminalize Black men for their ambition and refusal to bow down. His story isn't unique; it's part of a pattern stretching from Black Reconstruction all the way to today's prison system, as outlined in *The New Jim Crow* by Michelle Alexander. Kennard wasn't locked up because he did anything wrong; he was punished for representing everything white supremacy fears: education, discipline, and self-determination. The system's goal was clear: destroy his name and break his spirit so he wouldn't inspire other Black men to rise. Even as his health deteriorated due to the state's deliberate neglect, Kennard refused to let them break him. They could lock his body away, but they couldn't erase his impact. His suffering became a testament to his strength, and his legacy became a rallying cry in the fight against racial oppression, helping to push Mississippi toward desegregation. Kennard's story is a direct threat to white supremacy because it exposes its biggest weakness: it only works if Black men surrender their power. But he didn't. He showed that real strength isn't about avoiding struggle; it's about standing firm in the face of it. He didn't ask for permission to claim what was rightfully his; he took his stand, knowing full well the consequences. Kennard's story proves that for a Black man, character isn't just a foundation; it's a weapon. His refusal to fold, his commitment to principle, and his unwillingness to live on his knees made him a force that couldn't be ignored. His example still sets the standard for what it means to be a Black man today.

GABRIEL PROSSER: The Man Before the Revolt

Gabriel Prosser was born into slavery in 1776 on a tobacco plantation in Virginia. Unlike many enslaved people of his time, Gabriel was taught to read and write, which exposed him to revolutionary ideas that were spreading throughout the young United States. He was a skilled blacksmith, a trade that gave him a certain level of mobility and access to conversations with both free and enslaved Black people across the region. His physical stature was also commanding, standing well over six feet tall, which added to his aura as a leader among his people. Gabriel was not just another enslaved man; he was a thinker, a strategist, and a man determined to shape his own destiny.

Gabriel's exposure to the rhetoric of the American Revolution, which emphasized liberty and resistance against tyranny, made him deeply question the hypocrisy of white Americans who fought against British oppression while keeping Black people in chains. He was heavily influenced by the Haitian Revolution, where enslaved Africans successfully overthrew their French masters and established their own republic. Gabriel believed that a similar uprising was possible in America, particularly in Virginia, where enslaved people outnumbered whites in many areas. His vision was not just for freedom but for a Black-led government in which the formerly enslaved would rule over their former oppressors.

By 1799, Gabriel had begun organizing enslaved

men across multiple plantations. He recruited warriors from the skilled labor ranks, including blacksmiths, carpenters, and artisans, who had access to tools that could be turned into weapons. Gabriel's ability to inspire loyalty was a testament to his natural leadership and his ability to make men believe in his vision. He crafted a meticulous plan to seize control of Richmond, take weapons from the armory, and kill any whites who resisted. He even had plans to hold the governor hostage to negotiate the freedom of all enslaved people in Virginia. Gabriel was not just a dreamer; he was a man of action, determined to follow through on his mission. However, Gabriel was also aware of the dangers posed by traitors among his own people. He operated in secrecy, only revealing the full plan to those he deemed absolutely loyal. But even the most cautious leader cannot fully control human nature, especially when fear becomes a factor. Gabriel's growing army, which some estimate reached over a thousand men, was proof of his ability to inspire. But one thing he failed to account for was the weakness of those who lacked the courage to see the mission through to the end.

DENMARK VESEY: The Road to Rebellion

Denmark Vesey was born around 1767 in the Caribbean, possibly on the island of St. Thomas. As a child, he was sold into slavery and ended up in the hands of a Charleston slave trader named Joseph Vesey.

Unlike many enslaved people, Denmark was able to travel extensively with his master, gaining exposure to different cultures and languages. This exposure sharpened his intellect and widened his perspective on the injustices of slavery. His opportunity for freedom came in 1799 when he won a local lottery and purchased his own emancipation for $600. From that moment forward, Denmark Vesey was a free Black man, but he never forgot those who were still in bondage. After gaining his freedom, Vesey became a respected carpenter in Charleston, South Carolina, a city where free Black people lived alongside the enslaved in a tense and uneasy coexistence. He joined the African Methodist Episcopal Church, a place where many free and enslaved Black people gathered to worship and discuss their struggles. He used the church as a means of spreading revolutionary ideas, often referencing the Bible to justify resistance against oppression. Vesey was especially drawn to the story of the Israelites, seeing clear parallels between their escape from ancient Kemet and the plight of enslaved Black people in America. Vesey's disdain for slavery grew as he saw the brutal treatment of his enslaved brethren, many of whom worked on the plantations surrounding Charleston. Despite his own freedom, he knew that his fate was still tied to the condition of his people. He could have chosen to live quietly, avoiding trouble, but instead, he took on the dangerous task of organizing one of the most ambitious slave revolts in American history. He began recruiting both enslaved and free Black men, building a network that spanned plantations, churches, and city streets. By 1822, Vesey had developed a plan to take over Charleston, kill the white enslavers, and escape to Haiti, where Black people had successfully overthrown their oppressors. His plan was detailed, including coordinated attacks on armories and the strategic use of fire to create chaos. He recruited over 9,000 people—a staggering number that showed just how deep the desire for freedom ran. But, as in Gabriel Prosser's case, Vesey's downfall would come not from external forces but from within.

Both Gabriel Prosser and Denmark Vesey had the character, vision, and determination to follow through on their missions. They were men of action, not just words. But their revolts were ultimately undone by those who lacked character—fearful and weak-minded men who chose self-preservation over the liberation of their people. In Gabriel's case, two enslaved men betrayed the plan to white authorities, leading to mass arrests and executions before a single strike could be made. A torrential rainstorm had already delayed the attack, but it was the traitors who truly sealed the fate of the revolt. Denmark Vesey's fate was even worse. He had managed to keep his plan a secret for years, but as the day of the uprising neared, fearful enslaved men leaked the plan to their masters. One of the most controversial figures in this betrayal was Morris Brown, a prominent church leader who was rumored to have given white authorities key information about the rebellion. The irony is that Morris Brown was later honored by having a college named after him, a symbolic reward for his loyalty to white supremacy. This mirrors how the system continues to uplift those who betray Black progress while punishing those who fight for true liberation.

The betrayal of these revolts is a lesson that a leader can have all the character in the world, but if those around him do not share that same drive, the mission will fail. It also highlights the danger of what we call *"Sambos"* or *"Coons,"* those who actively work against the interests of their people for personal safety or favor from the oppressor. Kanye West once controversially said, *"Slavery was a choice."* While that statement ignored the brutal reality of chattel slavery, there is some truth in the fact that many revolts were thwarted not by white power alone, but by the choices of scared Negroes who refused to fight. Throughout history, there were countless revolts that never even made it to the battlefield because of betrayal. Fear, cowardice, and self-preservation have always been the tools used to keep Black people in bondage. The story of Gabriel Prosser and Denmark Vesey should serve as a warning that, while having strong character is essential, vetting those around you is just as critical. A revolution cannot be built on weak foundations, and freedom is never won through compromise. It demonstrates that character is the defining trait of a true Black man, one who does not just speak of change but brings it into reality. His relentless pursuit of freedom, both for himself and others, proved that words without action mean nothing. His story exemplifies the principle that a Black man's value lies in his ability to follow through, even in the face of immense danger. Parker's legacy is a direct challenge to those who believe Black men are incapable of self-determination and leadership. His life stands as proof that character is not just a personal virtue but a revolutionary weapon against oppression. A Black MAN with character does not wait for permission, he creates his own path and forces the world to respect his actions.

Parker's unwavering commitment to his word exposes the weakness in men who hesitate, make excuses, or shrink in the face of adversity. His ability to outmaneuver his oppressors was not just a matter of courage, but of discipline, intelligence, and relentless execution. Today, too many Black men are conditioned to talk about change without taking the necessary steps to create it. Parker's life proves that true manhood requires action, not just rhetoric. A Black man must embrace responsibility, execute his plans, and ensure that his commitments hold weight. Character is not built in comfort; it is forged in struggle, and only those willing to endure will leave a lasting impact. The men who turned on Gabriel Prosser and Denmark Vesey stand in stark contrast to this principle. Their betrayal was not just an act of self-preservation but a failure of character. They exemplified the weakness of words without conviction, of men who feared consequence more than they valued freedom. Their actions highlight why character is the defining trait of a true Black man; it separates those who simply dream of change from those who make it a reality. Had they upheld the same unwavering commitment to their word as Parker did, history might have turned in a different direction.

The lesson from Parker's life is clear: a Black man's legacy is defined by what he does, not by what he claims he will do. Just as he defied the expectations of white supremacy, modern Black men must reject mediocrity and embrace a higher standard of discipline and accountability. A Black man must be a producer, not a spectator; one who takes control of his destiny rather than allowing external forces to dictate his fate. Whether in business, family, or community, his consistency in action determines his value. The respect a Black man commands comes not from his words, but from the undeniable proof of his follow-through. Without character, he is just another voice lost in the noise of weak men. John Parker's story is more than history; it is a blueprint for Black men today. He proved that character is not just about individual success but about uplifting the entire race. His ability to follow through made him a direct threat to the system designed to keep Black men passive and powerless. If Black men today embrace the same principles of discipline, execution, and responsibility, they will not only strengthen themselves but also dismantle the very structures that seek to keep them weak. The world does not fear Black men who talk; it fears those who act. And a Black man with unwavering character is the most dangerous force of all.

CODE NO. 5

A BLACK MAN DOESN'T GOSSIP

In a time when social media and mainstream culture thrive on sensationalism, a Black MAN must stand apart by refusing to engage in gossip. Gossip is a form of idle talk that serves no productive purpose, spreading rumors, misinformation, and negativity. It is the behavior of those who lack discipline, direction, and the ability to focus on what truly matters. A Black man understands that his words carry weight, and he refuses to waste them on discussions that do not build, uplift, or advance his mission. Gossip is a direct contradiction to masculinity because it is rooted in emotional impulsiveness rather than logic and action. When men engage in gossip, they reveal insecurity, weakness, and a lack of self-control—traits that diminish their respect and credibility among other men. A Black MAN who avoids gossip maintains a sense of mystery and power, as he refuses to indulge in petty conversations that can be used against him. Instead of discussing another man's business, he focuses on his own, keeping his energy on his responsibilities, goals, and purpose.

Historically, gossip has been a tool of destruction within the Black community, used to divide and weaken the collective. The *"Poison Pill Letters"* are a great example of this. In the 1960s and 1970s, tensions between the U.S. government, the Maulana Karenga-led US Organization, and the Black Panther Party (BPP) reached a boiling point. As both groups fought for the liberation and empowerment of Black Americans, the government used tactics like infiltration, surveillance, and manipulation to sow division. A notable example of this was the *"poison pill"* letters sent by the FBI's COINTELPRO program, designed to incite conflict between Black organizations by feeding false information. The letters fueled distrust and paranoia, creating internal conflict within the Black power movement. Maulana Karenga's US Organization and the Black Panther Party, once potential allies, became bitter enemies, largely due to these fabricated messages.

The rivalry between the US Organization and the BPP ultimately contributed to the tragic death of Bunchy Carter, a member of the Black Panther Party. In 1969, Carter was gunned down on the UCLA campus during a meeting with fellow Panther members, an event that became a symbol of the destructive consequences of internal divisions. The poisoning of the relationships between Black organizations, particularly through COINTELPRO, set the stage for violence, mistrust, and, ultimately, loss of life. Carter's murder was the direct result of this discord, proving the devastating effects of not adhering to Code #5 of the 14 Codes: a Black man does not gossip.

The Black Panther Party's response to the rise of the US Organization turned into bloody conflict, fueled by lies planted by outside forces. Instead of building unity and fighting for a common cause, both sides fell into petty, destructive competition. The government played them against each other on purpose, knowing division would kill the movement. That infighting and payback drowned out the real mission of Black liberation and left the people bleeding instead of building. The murder of Bunchy Carter serves as a stark reminder of how the violation of Code #5 can have catastrophic consequences. The poisoned letters that sowed distrust between powerful Black organizations illustrate the destructive nature of hearsay and misinformation. By falling prey to these tactics, the Black Power movement not only lost one of its dedicated members but also weakened its ability to unite for the greater good of the Black community. The legacy of Carter's death underscores the importance of remaining focused on the cause, resisting internal division, and protecting the integrity of one's mission.

Enslaved Black people were often manipulated through the spread of rumors, turning them against one another to prevent unity and rebellion. In modern times, the same tactics are at play through the media, which highlights scandals, drama, and personal failures of Black men while ignoring their successes. When a Black MAN refuses to engage in gossip, he protects himself from becoming a pawn in a system designed to keep him distracted and ineffective. One of the greatest examples of a Black MAN who rejected gossip and stood on principle was Malcolm X. He refused to entertain slander, personal attacks, or trivial matters, instead keeping his focus on the larger mission of Black liberation. Even when others tried to bait him into speaking on irrelevant issues, he remained disciplined, understanding that engaging in gossip would weaken his stance and distract from his purpose. His ability to remain above petty conversations is one of the reasons he remains one of the most respected Black men in history.

A Black MAN who does not gossip also commands a higher level of respect among women. Women respect men who are focused, disciplined, and secure in their identity—traits that are diminished when a man indulges in gossip. A man who spends his time talking about other people instead of making moves signals to women that he lacks ambition and leadership. The strongest men are those who control their tongues, knowing that their words should be used to build, not to destroy. Ultimately, Code #5 reinforces that a Black MAN values his time, his energy, and his reputation. He understands that gossip is a sign of weakness and refuses to participate in conversations that do not serve a greater purpose. By rejecting gossip, he positions himself as a leader, a man of integrity, and someone who is worthy of respect. In a world that thrives on distractions, a true Black MAN remains focused on what matters most: his mission, his responsibilities, and his legacy.

Social media is pushing Black men in the wrong direction, turning them into gossipers instead of leaders. Platforms like Twitter aka X, Instagram, and YouTube encourage men to talk instead of act, rewarding meaningless engagement with likes and comments. Too many Black men are caught up in online drama, seeking attention and debating trivial matters when they should be using these platforms to build wealth, create opportunities, and uplift their communities. Instead of being productive, they waste valuable time discussing celebrity gossip and trending topics that have no real impact on their lives. Gossip is a sign of deficiency. A man who spends his time talking about others without purpose is unfocused, undisciplined, and wasting time that could be used to build his legacy. Too many Black men have turned into online entertainers, seeking validation instead of leading with intention. Instead of using their voices to teach, strategize, or inspire, they speak just to be heard, chasing approval from strangers who have no investment in their success. This is not leadership. This is not strength. Furthermore, this behavior is changing how

Black women perceive Black men. Women naturally respect strength, discipline, and direction. When men engage in gossip and online disputes, they blur the line between masculinity and femininity. They lose their position as leaders and begin to appear emotional, unstable, and unproductive. This shift contributes to the growing disconnect between Black men and women because when men fail to lead, the balance in relationships is disrupted. If men behave like women, women will feel the need to take on the leadership role, and this imbalance weakens the entire structure of the community.

The long-term consequences of this are serious. Black masculinity is being diluted, and leadership is being lost. Every moment spent arguing online is a moment wasted in the real world, where a man's worth is determined by what he builds and accomplishes, not by what he says. A Black MAN is defined by action, discipline, and results. Gossip does not create wealth, strengthen character, or earn respect. The solution is clear: eliminate distractions, reject gossip culture, and embrace true manhood. Time wasted on meaningless debates is time lost in reality, where a man's legacy is shaped by his work, not his words. If Black men do not make this shift, they risk losing respect not just from women, but from other men who still uphold traditional masculinity. A Black MAN controls his own path; he does not allow social media to dictate his actions. It is time to step away from meaningless distractions and focus on building, leading, and producing. Because ultimately, real men do not gossip. They take action.

In today's world, where social media dominates discourse, Black men are being pressured to engage in emotionally charged discussions and trivial gossip instead of focusing on what truly matters. This shift undermines their role as leaders and providers. Black women, naturally inclined toward nurturing and guidance, often express frustration at the absence of strong male leadership. Rather than finding support, direction, and reliability, they encounter men just as consumed by the noise of social media as they are. This dynamic fosters a cycle of disrespect; when men indulge in gossip, they are perceived as weak and incapable of fulfilling the responsibilities historically assigned to them. Social media has redefined masculinity, shifting expectations of what it means to be a man in the Black community. To restore balance and regain respect, Black men must reject these distractions and reclaim their purpose. The constant need for attention erodes the foundation of Black manhood, reducing men to mere participants in a system that prioritizes spectacle over substance. Gossiping weakens credibility and authority. A man who fuels online drama or engages in meaningless debates is not leading, he is performing. Rather than building, strategizing, and inspiring, he seeks validation from strangers who have no stake in his success.

This behavior does not command respect; it diminishes it.

Historically, gossip has been used as a tool of betrayal. During slavery, some enslaved men, especially those in privileged positions, would inform on their peers to gain favor or avoid punishment. This act of gossiping to the oppressor did not just harm individuals; it undermined collective resistance. Even after slavery, this culture of betrayal persisted in various forms, weakening unity within the Black community. Today, the problem has evolved. Social media has given rise to a culture where people no longer just gossip about others; they openly betray themselves. From criminals incriminating themselves online to individuals exposing personal business for attention, the loss of discretion has reached new heights. What was once private is now public, and in this climate of self-exposure, the principles of silence, restraint, and accountability are disappearing. A Black MAN must understand that his word carries weight. Gossip erodes trust, undermines self-respect, and weakens the foundation of leadership. Whether it's spreading rumors or airing personal struggles online, engaging in gossip is a betrayal, not only of others but of oneself. A man who prioritizes gossip over discipline and action lacks focus, wasting time and energy on fleeting distractions rather than lasting achievements.

The true strength of a Black MAN lies in his discipline, his purpose, and his ability to move in silence when necessary. He does not waste his voice on meaningless chatter; he speaks with intent and commands respect through action. Social media has created a false narrative where attention is mistaken for influence. But real power, real leadership, comes not from seeking validation but from embodying integrity and discipline. Violating Code #5: is not just a minor flaw; it is a fundamental weakness. A man who gossips loses not only respect but control over his own narrative. To uphold this Code, a Black MAN must reject gossip in all its forms, focus on his mission, and ensure that his words and actions carry purpose. A disciplined man does not engage in distractions. He builds. He leads. He produces. That is the true mark of manhood.

The Black church has historically been a pillar of the community, shaping both its moral foundation and social structure. It has served as a sanctuary for spiritual growth, a refuge from racial oppression, and a space for organizing resistance. However, the church has also played a complex role in the spread of gossip. Many preachers, entrusted with the private struggles of their congregations, became the first to hear and sometimes share sensitive information. This blurred the line between spiritual leadership and social entertainment, allowing gossip to take root and erode trust within the community. Yet, the church was more than just a place where personal matters circulated; it was also a center for rebellion and progress. During times of racial injustice, Black churches became meeting grounds for organizing resistance. Under the guise of religious services, leaders strategized civil rights movements and mobilized their communities to challenge oppression. The pulpit was not only a place for preaching faith but also for inspiring action. However, the church's influence was a double-edged sword. While it provided guidance and protection, it also became a space of harsh judgment. Preachers, wielding both moral and social authority, often imposed their own views on personal behavior, reinforcing rigid standards of acceptable conduct. This tension between uplifting the community and controlling it created an environment where both empowerment and restraint coexisted. The church could foster unity and resilience; yet, it could also breed division and fear.

Despite its contradictions, the Black church remained a vital institution. It reflected the community's struggles, offering both hope and scrutiny, resistance and conformity. The influence of the pulpit extended beyond spiritual matters, shaping social norms and political action alike. While some preachers fueled gossip, others used their platform to challenge injustice and inspire change. The Black church, like the community it serves, embodies both strength and imperfection. Its legacy is one of survival and adaptation, balancing its flaws with its indispensable role in Black life. It has been both a tool of control and a force for liberation, proving that even within its contradictions, it remains a cornerstone of Black resilience and progress.

Today, too many Black men are talking just to be heard instead of talking to create real change. Social media platforms have turned conversation into a game where the goal is to get likes, retweets, and clout instead of building something that actually matters. Instead of focusing on action, brothers are wasting time chasing validation, debating nonsense, and gossiping about celebrities like it's a full-time job. Every second spent on that foolishness is a second stolen from building legacy, wealth, and real power. That's where Code #5 comes in, A Black MAN doesn't gossip. His words should be weapons of influence and blueprints for action, not entertainment for a mindless crowd.

Social media has turned gossip into a sport, and too many Black men have fallen into the trap of performing instead of leading. It's a dangerous game because it taps into feminine energy always seeking emotional validation instead of demanding respect through action. The more Black men post, argue, and seek attention, the more they lose their position as protectors and builders. Women are biologically wired to follow strength, not emotional instability. When men act like gossiping teenagers, women naturally lose respect, and the entire dynamic of man and woman shifts. Now you have women leading, and men sitting in the passenger seat, confused about why they feel powerless.

The feminization of Black men through social

media is no accident it's engineered. Social media rewards emotional reactions, vanity, and public displays of weakness, all traits that pull Black men away from their natural position of strength. Black men are being conditioned to think that emotional outbursts, thirst traps, and constant attention-seeking are normal masculine behavior. But all it does is strip them of their leadership spirit and dull their warrior mentality. Real Black masculinity is about strategy, production, and silent power not performance for strangers who don't care. Every time a Black man trades purpose for popularity, he steps closer to being a caricature instead of a king.

This new digital environment has also broken the social skills of young Black men. Instead of learning how to build genuine, face-to-face relationships with women, they hide behind likes, DMs, and OnlyFans subscriptions. They treat women like digital trophies instead of human beings who respond to real strength and charisma. Social media has made it too easy to chase fantasy instead of mastering reality. A Black MAN who lives by The 14 Codes knows that real experiences, not virtual ones, shape your manhood. To get back what was lost, Black men must log off the nonsense, step outside, sharpen their minds, strengthen their bodies, and lead their communities by example , not by likes.

CODE NO. 6

A BLACK MAN DOES NOT REQUEST RESPECT, HE COMMANDS IT

Respect isn't something a Black man asks for; it's something he takes. From the moment he steps into a room, his energy should tell people who he is. The way he walks, the way he talks, and the way he moves should demand respect without him having to beg for it. Too many Black men think respect comes from being liked or going along to get along. That's not how it works. A man who looks for approval will always be chasing it, and people will play with him because they know he needs it. But a man who commands respect? People move differently around him because they know he will not accept anything less.

A Black man's presence should be felt, not just seen. The world will test you, try to shrink you, and make you feel like you need permission to take up space. That's a lie. The moment you start dimming your light to make others comfortable, you've already lost.

Respect is about standing on what you believe in, no matter who's watching. It's about making decisions based on principle, not public opinion. A man who moves like that forces people to adjust to him, not the other way around. A man who commands respect knows that being liked is a weak man's goal. When you spend your time trying to please everybody, you end up pleasing nobody, including yourself. A Black man has to understand that respect and likability don't always go hand in hand. Some people will hate you simply because they can't control you. Others will admire you because they wish they had your strength. Either way, that isn't your concern. Your focus is standing firm, because a man without respect is just another lost soul in the crowd.

This applies to every part of life: family, business, friendships, and relationships. In the home, a man who commands respect leads his family with authority, not fear, and they follow because they trust his judgment. In business, a man who won't let himself be disrespected earns more because people know he won't be lowballed or played. In friendships, a man who holds his ground is surrounded by loyalty, not leeches. And in relationships, a man who doesn't beg for a woman's validation attracts the kind of woman who actually respects him. Too many Black men have been trained to be agreeable, to keep their heads down, and to avoid confrontation. That conditioning started in slavery, and it still exists today. But history proves that the Black men who made the biggest impact never asked permission to be great. They moved how they moved, and the world had no choice but to adjust. Jack Johnson walked with an arrogance that shook white society to its core. Muhammad Ali's mouth made him enemies, but it also made him a legend. They didn't wait for anyone to give them respect; they took it.

The other side of this is what happens when a Black man violates the code. A man who tries to please everybody ends up losing himself completely. He bends, he folds, and eventually, he breaks under the weight of trying to fit in. History is littered with Black men who lost their souls and everything they built because they cared more about being liked than being respected. They played it safe, ducked conflict, smiled when they should've stood tall and when it was all said and done, they were forgotten and disrespected. No real Black MAN wants to go out like that. Respect is the only real currency we got. Money will fade, fame is temporary, and women come and go, but if you built your name on strength and principle, that name echoes long after you're gone. The only way to earn that kind of respect is by standing firm, setting the tone, and refusing to fold for anybody.

JACK JOHNSON — The Heavyweight Who Refused to Be Humble

When you talk about a Black man who commanded

respect, you have to start with Jack Johnson. This wasn't a man who asked for permission, played by the rules, or worried about who liked him. He carried himself like a king at a time when white America wanted Black men to bow. He didn't just fight in the ring; he fought in life, and he never backed down. Jack Johnson wasn't just the first Black heavyweight champion; he was the first Black man that white America was scared to death of because he wouldn't submit. He didn't walk around trying to make people comfortable. He lived life how he wanted, without apology. He understood something that too many Black men today forget: when you move like a man who respects himself, others have no choice but to follow. The world tried to break him. They tried to humble him. White society wasn't mad just because he was winning fights; they were mad because he was winning his way. He talked his talk. He smiled in their faces. He dated and married white women, knowing full well the danger. He didn't care. He wasn't waiting for anyone's approval. He was a Black man who dared to live free, and that's why they hated him.

See, Jack Johnson understood what a lot of Black men today don't: respect is taken, not requested. If he had been quiet, humble, and *"grateful"* for his success, maybe they would've let him breathe. Maybe they would've let him exist peacefully. But he knew that wasn't real respect. That's tolerance. A Black man who bows his head gets tolerated. A Black man who stands on business gets feared. He never begged for respect, and he damn sure never softened himself to be accepted. He knew his value and demanded the world see it too. That's why he flaunted his wealth. That's why he carried himself with confidence. It wasn't arrogance; it was ownership of his own image. He understood that a Black man has to move like a boss if he ever wants to be treated like one.

Jack Johnson proved that a Black man's power isn't just in his fists; it's in how he carries himself. White society wasn't just mad that he was knocking out their best fighters. They were mad that he was walking around like he was better than them. He wasn't playing the humble servant. He wasn't lowering his head. He wasn't seeking acceptance. He was setting the tone. They threw everything they had at him. The *"Great White Hope"* campaign was created just to stop him. They were desperate to find a white fighter who could shut him up and knock him down. But every time they tried, Jack sent them home embarrassed. He didn't just beat them; he humiliated them. He showed the world that a Black man could dominate.

Even after they robbed him of his title, he still never begged to get it back. He went on the run. He lived his life. He never came back asking for forgiveness. He knew that a Black man who bows down loses everything. They didn't take his pride. They didn't take his confidence. Because when you truly command respect, it's not just about winning; it's about standing firm. See, when a Black man tries too hard to be liked, he ends up weak. That's where so many fall short today. They think if they just play nice, if they just talk the right way, if they just smile enough, the world will respect them. It never works that way. A Black man must make people respect him through his actions, his presence, and his discipline, not by begging for approval.

Look at Jack Johnson's life. He lived on his own terms. He didn't care if white America liked him or not. He wasn't here for their approval. He wasn't here to make them comfortable. And because of that, even though they hated him, they feared him. And when a Black man is feared, he is respected. That's the lesson right there. If Jack Johnson had been humble, if he had played the *"good Negro,"* they might've let him exist. But because he commanded respect, they had to work overtime to stop him. They had to rewrite the rules. They had to lie, cheat, and steal because a Black man who stands firm is a threat to the whole system. Jack Johnson showed that respect is the foundation of power. If a Black man doesn't demand respect in his daily life, he'll get walked over. He'll get ignored. He'll be used by everyone around him. But when a Black man makes it clear that he will not accept disrespect, suddenly, people start treating him differently. This applies everywhere. If you don't demand respect in your family, your kids and your woman won't take you seriously. If you don't demand respect in business, people will try to play you. If you don't demand respect in the streets, you will be a target. A Black man must make sure that every room he walks into understands who he is.

Jack Johnson's story is a blueprint. He showed us what happens when a Black man stands tall. But too many of us today are trying to please everybody. We're too worried about how people feel instead of making them respect us. And that's why so many Black men are struggling. You can't be respected if you're too afraid to stand firm. The worst thing a Black man can do is shrink himself just to make others comfortable. The moment you do that, you've already lost. When you ask for respect, you're already beneath the person you're asking. That's why a Black man should never request respect; he should move in a way that forces people to give it to him.

Jack Johnson understood that. He understood that people might hate you when you stand firm, but they will still respect you. And that's more important than being liked. Because a liked man can still be disrespected. But a respected man? He holds weight wherever he goes. This isn't just about history; this is about right now. Every Black man walking this earth today needs to understand what Jack Johnson showed us. If you don't command respect, you'll be walked over. If you don't stand on business, you'll be overlooked. And if you don't move with strength, the world will treat you like you're weak. Jack Johnson didn't just fight for himself; he fought for the idea of a Black man who refused to bow. He set the standard. He showed us the way. The question now is, are you going to live by that standard, or are you going to shrink yourself for approval? Because one path leads to power, and the other leads to being forgotten.

Jack Johnson laid the blueprint, proving that a Black man who refuses to bow will always be a threat to the system. Decades later, Muhammad Ali took that same defiant spirit, sharpened it, and used it to shake the world on an even bigger stage. Muhammad Ali wasn't just a boxer; he was a force of nature. From the moment he stepped onto the stage, he made it clear that he wasn't asking for respect; he was taking it. He didn't wait for white America to acknowledge him, and he damn sure didn't beg for approval. He called himself *"The Greatest"* before anyone else did, and he backed it up every single time. That's what it means to command respect: you tell the world who you are, and you make them believe it.

"I AM THE GREATEST" – Ali's Unmatched Confidence and Command of Respect

Ali understood that respect wasn't about being liked; it was about standing firm. He knew white America would never truly accept him, so he stopped caring. When they tried to humble him, he doubled down. He talked his talk, walked his walk, and never folded under pressure. A Black man who commands respect doesn't bow to anybody, especially not to a system designed to break him. The Vietnam War proved that Ali wasn't just about words. He was willing to lose everything, his title, his money, even his freedom, to stand on principle. That's what a man does. He refused to fight a war that had nothing to do with him while America was waging war on Black people at home. That wasn't just bravery; that was manhood in its purest form. They stripped him of his heavy weight title, thinking it would break him. But Ali knew something most men don't, respect isn't about what you have, it's about who you are. When a man commands respect, they can take everything from him, and he's still standing. That's why, when he came back, he wasn't just a fighter, he was a legend.

Ali never begged for his spot back. He took it. He trained, fought his way back, and reclaimed the throne like he never left. A Black man who knows his worth doesn't ask for opportunities; he creates them. He doesn't whine about what's been taken; he focuses on what he can take back. That's what separates men from males. The way Ali carried himself made it impossible to ignore him. His confidence wasn't arrogant; it was power. A Black man who believes in himself at an unshakable level forces the world to respect him. Even his haters have to acknowledge him. That's what happens when a man commands respect; whether they love you or hate you, they can't deny you. He understood that respect is rooted in consistency. Every time

Ali spoke, he meant what he said, and he stood by it. That's why people listened. A man who changes his stance to please others is weak. But a man who holds the line, no matter the cost, earns the respect of real men and real women.

Even outside the ring, Ali's presence was unmatched. He walked into a room, and people felt it. That's because respect isn't just about words; it's about energy. When a Black man moves with certainty, speaks with conviction, and refuses to shrink himself, people respond. You don't have to demand respect when you naturally command it. Ali knew how to control a room without trying. He didn't have to be aggressive or violent; his words, his confidence, and his reputation did all the work. That's another lesson Black men need to understand. You don't need to beg for respect, and you don't need to force it. When you carry yourself like a man, respect follows. He also understood that you don't have to be nice to be respected. Too many Black men think being agreeable will get them somewhere. Ali showed that standing firm, even if people don't like it, is the real key. Respect isn't about being liked; it's about being valued.

Ali had women all over him, not because he was rich or famous, but because he commanded respect. Women follow men who move with confidence and certainty. They're drawn to men who don't chase validation. When a Black man holds his ground, women fall in line naturally. That's something a lot of brothas need to relearn. When you look at Ali's career, he never apologized for being who he was. That's a major lesson. Too many Black men today are scared to take up space, scared to offend, scared to be seen as *"too much."* Ali never played small. He didn't ask if he was too loud, too bold, too Black; he just was. That's why he outlasted his enemies. The same people who hated him ended up praising him. But here's the thing: he didn't change for them. They had to change how they saw him. That's what happens when a man commands respect. The world adjusts to you; you don't adjust to it.

His impact wasn't just about boxing. He gave Black men a blueprint on how to carry themselves. He showed that being unapologetically yourself is the most powerful thing you can do. Ali didn't just fight in the ring; he fought in life. And he won because he refused to bend. Even when he got older and his body started to fail, the respect never left. That's because respect isn't about how strong you are physically; it's about what you stand for. A man with principles will be respected long after his prime, but a man who chases approval will be forgotten the second he loses value. Ali's whole life was proof that if you try to please everyone, you'll end up pleasing no one. If he had spent his time trying to make white America comfortable, he wouldn't be the legend he is today. Respect isn't about pleasing people; it's about making them acknowledge your presence, whether they like it or not.

That's a lesson every Black man needs to learn. You

can't live your life trying to be liked. You can't water yourself down hoping people will accept you. The second you start doing that, you lose respect. And once you lose respect, you're done. A Black man's focus should always be on respect first. When you move with integrity, when you stand firm, when you refuse to fold, people have no choice but to respect you. From your family to your friends to your business, respect is the currency that makes everything work. Without respect, nothing else matters. A man who isn't respected is useless. You can have money, status, and women, but if people don't respect you, none of it means anything. Ali had all of that, but what made him legendary was the respect he commanded from the world.

Respect is earned through action. It's built through how you carry yourself, how you handle conflict, and how you stand by your word. Ali never let anyone question his stance, and that's why he stood the test of time. He didn't ask for respect; he was respect. That's the lesson of Muhammad Ali and the 14 Codes. A Black man doesn't request respect; he commands it. And when you do that, the world bends to you, not the other way around.

But what happens when a Black man does the opposite, when he begs for respect instead of commanding it? That's where we see the failure of men like Terry Crews. Instead of standing firm, he let himself be humiliated and then ran to the system, asking for permission to be a man. That's not strength; that's submission. And submission in the face of disrespect doesn't just weaken one man; it sends a message that all Black men can be *"Buck Broken."* Terry Crews became the perfect example of what happens when a man forfeits his dignity, proving that respect isn't given to those who plead for it, it's only given to those who demand it through action.

"*Buck Broken in Broad Daylight*" — Terry Crews and the Emasculation of Black Men

Terry Crews was a walking, talking embarrassment to Black manhood. This dude let a white man grab his manhood in front of his wife and didn't do a damn thing about it. Instead of handling business like a man, he went to the government, begging for permission to defend himself. That's modern-day *"buck breaking"* at its finest—emasculating a grown Black man in front of the world so that all Black men get the message: *"Sit down, shut up, and take it."* And what did he do? He played right into the game, making excuses, talking about how he *"couldn't react"* because he was afraid of what would happen. That's the exact energy white supremacy loves: a big, strong Black man who's mentally weak and submissive. See, this isn't just about Terry Crews; it's about a long history of breaking Black men in front of our women and children. Back in slavery, they would take the strongest Black man, tie him up, beat him, and sometimes even rape him in front of the whole plantation. That wasn't just about hurting that one man; it was about sending a message to the rest of us: *"If we can do this to him, what do you think we'll do to you?"* Fast forward to today, and they don't need whips and chains; they use the media, the law, and psychological warfare. Terry Crews didn't just embarrass himself; he embarrassed Black men as a whole by showing that even the biggest, most muscular among us can be neutered like a damn pet. That's why they love putting guys like him on a pedestal, because he's the perfect representation of what they want Black men to be.

Hollywood and the media play a huge role in all this. They make sure to put weak Black men on the biggest platforms, while strong, uncompromising Black men get silenced or villainized. Think about it: when was the last time you saw a powerful, masculine, intelligent Black man being pushed in mainstream media? Instead, they prop up soft, goofy, or outright compromised Black men to represent all of us. Terry Crews fits the bill perfectly. They let him be big and muscular, but mentally, he was as soft as a wet paper bag. That's exactly what they want: a man who looks strong but is completely under their control. It's the same reason they love making sure our best athletes and entertainers stay out of politics or social issues unless they're pushing a soft, submissive message. The worst part is, Terry doubled down on it. Instead of realizing his mistake, he went on TV and social media defending his cowardice. He even said straight up that Black men need to learn to *"control themselves"* and *"not be toxic,"* basically reinforcing every stereotype that white supremacy loves. He let Viola Davis, a Black woman, speak out against racism and discrimination in Hollywood while he sat there silent, only speaking up to say he had never experienced racism. So not only did he fail himself, but he failed Black women and the community as a whole. How are you going to be a grown-ass man, a whole 6'3 and built like a damn tank, but act like a neutered house pet when it's time to stand up? That's why they keep him around, because he represents exactly what they want Black men to be.

We also can talk about how this all ties into the bigger agenda. White supremacy doesn't just want to weaken Black men; it wants to redefine what Black masculinity even looks like. They know they can't physically enslave us anymore, so now they use psychological chains. They put weak men like Terry Crews on display as *"role models,"* while strong Black men who stand up for themselves and their community get demonized. They want us either docile or dysfunctional, nothing in between. If you're not a clown, an entertainer, or completely submissive, then you're labeled aggressive, dangerous, or toxic. This is why we have to reject these fake role models and start upholding real Black manhood again. Terry Crews failed us, but we don't have to follow his example. This is why *"The 14 Codes"* exist. A Black man does not request respect; he commands it. A Black man has character, which means following through and handling his responsibilities. A Black man doesn't make excuses for cowardice. Terry Crews violated all of these codes and showed the world what happens when you let fear control you. He was so worried about what white Hollywood would think of him that he threw away his dignity. And the worst part? They don't even respect him for it. The system will use you, prop you up as an example of a *"good, non-threatening Black man,"* and then toss you away when you're no longer useful. That's exactly what's happening to him now; he played the game, but he still lost.

The truth is, white supremacy has always had two types of Black men they love: the big, strong but obedient one, and the weak, effeminate one. They'll let a Black man be physically intimidating as long as he's mentally submissive, just like they did during slavery. That's why you see so many athletes, bodybuilders, and action stars who look like warriors but act like servants when it comes to real-life issues. They love a big Black man who won't fight back, who smiles and shucks and jives when it's time to stand up. And that's why Terry Crews keeps getting work, because he's the perfect example of that. He made it clear that he'd rather be accepted by white Hollywood than respected by his own people. Terry Crews didn't just fail himself; he failed Black men everywhere. He showed our women that even the biggest among us can be broken, that we won't even fight for our own dignity. He showed our children that when a man is disrespected, he's supposed to go beg the government for protection instead of handling his own. That's not just weakness; that's betrayal. And the saddest part is, he really thinks he did the right thing. He truly believes that his inaction makes him a better man when all it really did was confirm to white supremacy that their tactics still work. He let fear, money, and the desire for white approval turn him into a modern-day *"buck-broken"* slave. This is why we must be on code. We cannot afford to have men like Terry Crews representing us. We need men who stand on integrity, who don't bow down, who don't let fear dictate their manhood. Because as long as we let the media pick our leaders, they're going to keep giving us men like him—big in stature, small in spirit. And if we don't reject that narrative, the next generation is going to grow up thinking that's what a Black man is supposed to be. We owe it to ourselves, our ancestors, and our future to make sure that never happens.

A Black man who knows his worth never asks for respect; he commands it. That's a fundamental truth in *"The 14 Codes."* Respect isn't something to beg for; it's something you establish through your presence, actions, and principles. When you carry yourself with integrity and unwavering confidence, the world has no choice but to acknowledge your value. In a society designed to belittle Black men, commanding respect is an act of defiance. White supremacy thrives on keeping

Black men in a place of submission, but when a Black man walks into a room with undeniable confidence, he disrupts that system. His reputation, work ethic, and his discipline speak for themselves, forcing people to recognize his worth without him ever having to plead for it. When you demand respect, you set the tone for how people treat you. You also set a standard for how Black men treat each other. White supremacy benefits from division within our community, but when Black men respect themselves and one another, we become an unshakable force. Holding each other accountable ensures that we all rise together. This principle extends to every aspect of life, whether in business, relationships, or everyday interactions. A Black man who commands respect in his professional life ensures that he's compensated fairly and that his contributions aren't overlooked. He refuses to be exploited or shortchanged because he knows his value.

That same mindset applies to his personal life, ensuring that he isn't disrespected by peers, family, or even romantic partners. Great Black men throughout history have embodied this principle. Jack Johnson, Muhammad Ali—these were men who commanded respect through their actions, their words, and their defiance of an unjust system. They didn't shrink themselves to make others comfortable. They stood tall, knowing their worth and refusing to be treated as less than. On the other hand, Terry Crews is a prime example of a man who violated Code #6. Instead of commanding respect, he allowed himself to be humiliated and then sought validation from the very system that disrespected him. When he was publicly violated, rather than standing firm and demanding justice on his own terms, he chose to play the victim, looking for sympathy instead of demanding accountability. That's not how a Black man operates. A Black man doesn't let disrespect slide, nor does he run to the same people who disrespected him for acceptance. Crews' actions sent the wrong message, one that directly contradicts what it means to be a man of respect. Commanding respect isn't about arrogance or intimidation; it's about self-assurance. It's about knowing who you are and refusing to compromise that for anyone. When you command respect, you shape your own narrative. You dictate how the world treats you instead of allowing it to dictate your worth. A Black man doesn't ask for permission to be respected; he walks in his power and takes it. That's how you create a legacy, and that's how you ensure that your presence is always felt, no matter where you stand.

INTEGRITY

Your name and reputation should be worth more than gold. Integrity is about standing on truth, even when it's inconvenient. It means keeping your word, doing right when no one is watching, and refusing to compromise your principles for temporary gain. In a world full of deception and shortcuts, a man with integrity is rare, respected, and trusted. When people know you stand on something solid, they will follow, support, and uplift you.

CODE NO. 7

A BLACK MAN UNDERSTANDS THAT A WOMAN DOESN'T MAKE HIM; SHE IS ONLY A REFLECTION OF THE MALE THAT HE IS

Society has fed men a lie—that a woman will complete you, fix you, or turn you into a better man. But the truth is, a woman does not make a man. She only reflects the man that he already is. If you're weak, she will mirror that weakness. If you're strong, she will amplify that strength. The idea that a woman can mold a man into greatness is a dangerous myth that keeps too many men stagnant. A man who waits for a woman to give him purpose will always be lost. A woman can inspire, support, and encourage, but the foundation of who you are must already be solid. Aset could only restore Asur because he had already built himself into a ruler. If he had been weak, directionless, or without value, there would have been nothing for her to rebuild. This is why men without discipline and vision find themselves in relationships that reflect their chaos. They attract women who mirror their instability, feeding their weaknesses instead of strengthening their strengths. A man who stands for nothing will fall for anything, and the women in his life will expose that instability. *"If you want a woman of substance, you must first be a man of substance."*

History proves this over and over. The strongest women have always stood beside men of purpose, not men waiting to be made whole. A woman does not create your character; she amplifies it. If you lack direction, she will either mirror that confusion or move on to someone who knows where he's going. This is why the relationship between a Black man and a Black woman has always been under attack. White supremacy understands that a strong Black man leading a strong Black family is a threat. It knows that if Black men reclaim their leadership, discipline, and purpose, Black families will rebuild. That is why the system has spent centuries trying to convince Black men that they need women to define them, instead of the other way around. Look at the women great men choose. Their choices reveal everything about them. Coretta Scott King and Betty Shabazz stood beside two of the most disciplined, focused Black men in history—Martin Luther King Jr. and Malcolm X. They didn't just happen to be there; they were chosen by men with purpose, and they reflected that purpose in the way they carried themselves. Raymond Parks supported Rosa Parks before the world knew her name. She was already a woman with a strong sense of justice, and he recognized that. He didn't suppress her passion or make her smaller; he encouraged it. He stood beside her not as a man threatened by her strength, but as a man who saw her as a reflection of his own values. The same goes for Ferdinand Lee Barnett, husband of Ida B. Wells-Barnett. Barnett was a lawyer, journalist, and activist, yet he had no issue standing beside a woman whose voice was just as strong as his. Ida B. Wells fearlessly exposed the horrors of lynching when others were too afraid to speak. Barnett didn't shrink in her presence; he embraced it. He understood that a strong man does not fear a strong woman. He knew that her fight was his fight, and together, they became an even greater force.

These men weren't passive figures in their wives' legacies. They were men of principle who knew that a woman doesn't weaken a man; she reveals him. A weak man will see a powerful woman as a threat; a strong man will see her as an ally. Raymond Parks and Ferdinand Barnett weren't just lucky to have women like Rosa Parks and Ida B. Wells-Barnett; they attracted them because they were built with the same discipline, purpose, and unwavering commitment to justice. This is why white supremacy has always sought to disrupt the bond between Black men and Black women, turning us against each other and making us see each other as adversaries instead of allies. When Black men lack purpose, they become weak. When they become weak, they either neglect or resent the women who should be their strongest allies. This is by design. A man without direction can be controlled. A man without a solid foundation can be manipulated. And when the bond between Black men and Black women is broken, the entire community suffers.

A man must understand that the woman he chooses is a reflection of him. She is not his builder or his savior. She can support him, but she cannot create him. If he is weak, his choice in women will expose that weakness. If he is strong, his choice in women will reflect that strength. A man who truly embodies this code won't just choose wisely; he will be wise enough to be the kind of man a great woman would want to stand beside. The lesson is simple: build yourself first. A woman can only rebuild what's already there. If you want a woman of integrity, purpose, and value, you must embody those qualities yourself. Otherwise, you will either push good women away or attract those who feed into your weaknesses. The relationship between a Black man and a Black woman is one of the greatest threats to white supremacy. The stronger we are together, the harder we are to break. Great men don't choose weak, lost women. They choose reflections of themselves: strong, disciplined, and focused women. On the other hand, look at weak men. They attract chaos, dysfunction, and women who drain them. A man who lacks discipline will pick a woman who reinforces his lack of control. A man who moves with purpose will attract a woman who strengthens his mission.

CORETTA SCOTT KING — The Strength to Preserve a Legacy and Lead the Fight

Coretta Scott King was more than just the wife of Dr. Martin Luther King Jr.; she was a warrior in her own right. Before she ever became Mrs. King, she was a woman of strength, discipline, and purpose. She was an educated woman, a classically trained singer, and an activist long before she stood beside Martin. She didn't just marry a great man; she married a mission, a fight, and a responsibility. From the moment she became Dr. King's wife, she understood that her role wasn't just to support him, it was to stand beside him in the struggle for Black liberation.

When Dr. King was assassinated in 1968, many expected Coretta to fade into the background, to grieve quietly and let the Civil Rights Movement move on without her. But she refused. Instead, she stepped forward, holding his torch high, ensuring that his message and sacrifice would not be buried with him. Just four days after his death, she led a march in Memphis for the sanitation workers' strike that Dr. King had been organizing before he was killed. She made it clear that this wasn't just Martin's fight; it was hers too. She had been in the trenches with him from the beginning, and she wasn't about to let the movement die with him. The U.S. government, particularly the FBI, wanted Dr. King's legacy destroyed, even in death. They spread rumors, lies, and propaganda in an attempt to discredit him, hoping to tarnish his name in the eyes of the public and his own family. But Coretta never wavered. She had seen the man behind closed doors, and she knew who he truly was. No whisper campaign could shake her faith in her husband or his mission. In public, she remained composed, always presenting a united front, making sure the world knew that Martin Luther King Jr. was not just a man but a movement, and that movement would not be broken.

Coretta didn't just defend her husband's honor; she went after the very system that took his life. Unlike many widows who would have accepted the official government narrative, she dug deeper. She fought to expose the truth that the U.S. government had a hand in Dr. King's assassination. She pushed for investigations, gathered evidence, and never let the world forget that Martin's death was not just the act of a lone gunman but a calculated move to silence a revolutionary. And in 1999, after years of fighting, a civil trial found that there was indeed a conspiracy to kill Dr. King, something Coretta had known all along. Her strength wasn't just in her fight for justice; it was in how she carried herself through it all. She never let them see her break, never let them see her bitter. She understood the power of dignity and grace, even when she had every reason to lash out. She moved with strategy, not emotion. That kind of discipline is rare, but it's what kept Dr. King's legacy alive and made sure his name would never be erased from history. She turned her pain into power, using her platform to continue the work they started together, ensuring that their children and future generations knew the truth.

Coretta didn't just preserve Dr. King's memory; she expanded his impact. She founded the King Center, an institution dedicated to his teachings and the fight for justice. She continued to push for civil rights, human rights, and economic justice, knowing that the struggle was far from over. Even after losing the love of her life, she never lost sight of the bigger picture. She met with world leaders, spoke at protests, and continued to challenge the system that had tried to break her. Where many would have retreated into mourning, she transformed herself into a living symbol of resilience. She also took on battles that Martin himself never got the chance to fight. While Dr. King was focused on racial justice, Coretta expanded the mission to include women's rights and global human rights issues. She understood that oppression didn't just come in one form. She used her voice to advocate for those who were still struggling, recognizing that liberation was not just about Black people but about all people who suffered under systems of inequality. She didn't just protect Martin's legacy; she evolved it.

Despite all the attacks on her family, Coretta never backed down. She continued to challenge the government, demand justice, and keep Dr. King's name alive. The same system that feared Martin tried to silence her too, but she was unshakable. She was a prime example of what it means to stand by a man not just in life but in his mission, even in death. She understood that Martin was not just her husband; he was a symbol of something greater. And as his wife, she carried that burden with grace and power. Coretta Scott King's story is proof that the right woman can help a man's legacy live far beyond his years. She didn't let the system define who her husband was, and she didn't allow herself to be turned into a helpless widow. She remained strategic, relentless, and focused, never letting emotions dictate her moves. In a world that wanted Dr. King's memory erased, she made sure his impact only grew stronger. She was not just the wife of a great man; she was a force of her own.

Her commitment to her husband's mission shows what real partnership looks like. A weak woman would have crumbled under the pressure, let the system dictate the narrative, or sought comfort instead of justice. But Coretta stood firm, proving that the woman a man chooses is a reflection of the man himself. Dr. King chose a woman who could carry the weight of the fight, and in doing so, he ensured that his dream would not die with him. Coretta Scott King's life is a lesson in strength, loyalty, and purpose. She teaches us that the work doesn't stop when the man falls; it continues with those who have the discipline to carry it forward. Just as *"Isis"* restored *"Osiris"* in the ancient myth, Coretta restored and protected Dr. King's legacy, making sure his impact was never forgotten. She rebuilt his name, his mission, and his vision for the future, proving that a great woman does not make a man; she preserves the man that he was.

Every Black man must understand the importance of the woman he chooses. The right woman will carry his name with honor, protect his vision, and continue his mission even when he is no longer here. Coretta Scott King set the standard for what that looks like. A man's work is his own, but the woman he stands beside will determine how far that work reaches. If you want to be a man of value, choose a woman who understands what that truly means.

BETTY SHABAZZ — Strength, Loyalty, and the Unbreakable Bond of Revolution

Every Black man must understand that the woman he chooses is not just a companion but a reflection of his purpose and legacy. The right woman will not only stand by his side, but she will amplify his mission and continue the work when he is no longer able to. Coretta Scott King was the embodiment of this principle, proving that a woman's role in a man's life can shape the course of history. A man's success isn't solely determined by his work; it is determined by the strength and vision of the woman he chooses to walk alongside him. When you choose wisely, your vision grows, and your mission extends far beyond your lifetime. This is exactly what Betty Shabazz demonstrated in her partnership with Malcolm X; she wasn't just his wife; she was his equal, his co-laborer, and his undying supporter.

Betty Shabazz was the definition of a strong Black woman. She wasn't just Malcolm X's wife; she was his partner in every sense of the word. From the moment they came together, she understood the weight of the man she was standing beside. She didn't just marry Malcolm; she married his mission, his struggles, and the risks that came with them. She knew the kind of world they were up against, but she never wavered. Betty stood ten toes down for her husband, making sure that no matter what the world threw at them, their bond remained unshaken. When Malcolm was assassinated, many expected Betty to break. They thought that without him, she would fade into the background, left to mourn in silence while the world moved on. But they underestimated the kind of woman she was. Betty was built for war just like Malcolm was, and his death didn't stop the fight; it made her dig even deeper. She took his message and carried it forward, refusing to let his legacy die with him. Instead of crumbling under grief, she turned her pain into power, raising their six daughters while making sure the world never forgot the name *"Malcolm X."*

The FBI and other enemies of Malcolm X tried to

use his death to destroy everything he built. They spread rumors, planted lies, and tried to turn his own people against him. But Betty wasn't having it. She never let outside noise shake her belief in her husband or what he stood for. She knew the tactics of the system and refused to play into them. She made it clear that no matter what was said, Malcolm was her man, and she would stand by his name with her head held high. In public, Betty never showed weakness. She carried herself with grace, discipline, and an unshakable sense of purpose. She made sure that everyone knew that Malcolm's death did not mean the end of his mission. She continued speaking on his behalf, making sure his teachings were passed down, not just to their children but to the entire Black community. She understood that Malcolm wasn't just her husband; he was a symbol of resistance, and it was her duty to protect that symbol at all costs.

Her union with Malcolm came before anything, even her faith. When Malcolm left the Nation of Islam and converted to Sunni Islam, Betty didn't hesitate to follow. Not because she was a blind follower, but because she was a woman who understood that loyalty to her husband and their shared vision came first. She saw the changes he was making, the growth in his beliefs, and she trusted him. She knew that whatever direction he took, it was based on truth, and she was right there with him. Betty's loyalty to Malcolm wasn't just about love; it was about alignment. They were on the same page mentally, spiritually, and emotionally. She understood him in a way that most people never could. She wasn't just with him when things were good; she was with him when the world turned against him, when he was outnumbered, and when the pressure was at its highest. That's what made her different. She didn't just love Malcolm X; she understood Malcolm X, and that's why she never let his enemies define his legacy.

Even after Malcolm's assassination, Betty never let bitterness consume her. She had every reason to hate, to fall into despair, but she stayed focused. She understood that her husband was taken from her not just because of who he was, but because of what he represented. She made sure that her daughters grew up knowing the truth about their father, not the version that the media and the government tried to paint. She instilled in them the same strength, dignity, and resilience that she carried within herself. She went back to school and earned a doctorate, proving that education was another tool in the fight for Black liberation. She didn't just talk about empowerment; she lived it. Betty didn't rely on sympathy; she relied on action. She built herself into a powerhouse in her own right, making sure that her name carried just as much weight as Malcolm's. She was a leader in her own way, inspiring Black women to stand strong and carry on the fight, no matter what obstacles were placed in their path. Despite everything she endured, Betty never let her circumstances turn her into a victim. She carried her pain with pride, using it to fuel her purpose. She understood that Malcolm's work wasn't just his; it was theirs. And if he had to die for it, then she had to live for it. She wasn't just Malcolm X's wife; she was his extension, his living proof that his words and actions would never be erased. She took everything he poured into her and made sure it never went to waste. The system tried to break her by taking away the man she loved, but all they did was make her stronger. She never remarried, never sought another man to fill Malcolm's shoes, because she knew that their connection was deeper than just a marriage; it was destiny. She didn't need another man to validate her because she had already built a life alongside one of the greatest Black men in history. Her purpose was bigger than romance; it was about protecting a legacy. Betty understood the weight of her role and carried it with honor. She wasn't just a grieving widow; she was a warrior in her own right. She made sure that the world never forgot who Malcolm X was and what he stood for. Every speech she gave, every action she took, was a reminder that the fight was far from over. She knew that if she let Malcolm's message die, then everything he sacrificed would have been in vain. And she refused to let that happen.

She also played a critical role in shaping the next generation of activists. Through her work as an educator and mentor, she made sure that young Black men and women understood their history and their power. She taught them that strength wasn't just about fighting; it was about standing firm in their principles, even when the odds are against you. She made sure that Malcolm's teachings didn't just stay in the past but were carried into the future. Betty's story is one of resilience, loyalty, and purpose. She wasn't just Malcolm's wife; she was his partner in revolution. She understood that their love wasn't just personal; it was political. Their bond was a threat to the system because it showed what true unity between a Black man and a Black woman looked like. And that kind of unity has always been the most dangerous weapon against oppression. Her life serves as a lesson to all Black men and women. A strong woman does not replace a man's leadership, she reinforces it. And a strong man does not fear a woman's strength, he embraces it. Betty and Malcolm were proof of that balance. They moved as one, thought as one, and fought as one. And even in death, Betty made sure that unity never faded. She carried Malcolm X's name with pride until the day she died. She honored him, protected his legacy, and ensured that the world would never forget the man she loved. But most importantly, she proved that a strong Black woman is never just a shadow; she is a force in her own right. Betty Shabazz was more than just Malcolm X's wife. She was a pillar of Black strength, a blueprint for Black womanhood, and an eternal reminder that the fight for Black liberation never stops.

Betty Shabazz and Malcolm X's union showed the

world the power of a partnership where both individuals stood as equals, pushing each other toward greatness. Their relationship wasn't about competition or overshadowing one another; it was a mutual understanding that their shared vision for Black liberation was bigger than them. But when we turn our attention to Raymond Parks and his role with Rosa Parks or Ferdinand Lee Barnett and Ida B. Wells, we see a similar dynamic in a different light. While Rosa and Ida B. Wells were more widely recognized, their husbands played crucial roles in their successes, often operating behind the scenes but without ever seeking the spotlight for themselves. Raymond, much like the men behind these other powerful women, understood that true strength is in standing beside your wife, not trying to outshine them. And just like Betty, Coretta, and others, these women didn't just marry influential men; they were supported by men who knew that their contributions were just as important in the fight for justice, even if they remained unsung.

SILENT PILLARS — The Men Who Supported and Empowered Legendary Women

Raymond Parks, born in 1909 down in Wedowee, Alabama, was a real soldier in the Civil Rights Movement, even though he didn't get the spotlight like his wife, Rosa Parks. Before Rosa ever made history on that bus in 1955, Raymond was already out here fighting for our people, grinding quietly as a barber and active NAACP member. He wasn't flashy, but his strength was real steady, behind the scenes, making sure the fight stayed alive. Raymond was built on principles: justice, equality, and the belief that Black folks deserved better. He pushed and supported Rosa, not just emotionally but by helping her move smart, making sure she had the backup she needed to take her stand. His leadership wasn't loud, but it was solid, and it showed what a real Black MAN does support his woman while standing firm in his own purpose. Raymond's impact laid the foundation for the moves Rosa made, and he stayed true to the mission without ever chasing attention or glory.

Raymond Parks was a man who understood that behind every great woman is a man who knows his place. Before Rosa Parks became the face of the Civil Rights Movement, Raymond was the rock that stood beside her, supporting her vision of justice. He wasn't just her husband; he was her partner in every sense. Raymond saw the same inequality that Rosa saw, and he knew the importance of standing up for what was right. Long before she made history with her act of defiance, Raymond was in the trenches with her, fighting against systemic injustice. He encouraged Rosa, believed in her, and made sure she never felt alone in the battle for Black rights. Raymond Parks didn't seek attention or the spotlight; he didn't need it. He understood that his wife was a woman with a powerful destiny, and he respected that. But at the same time, Raymond was no bystander. He was a man of action, a man of conviction, and a man who supported his wife's efforts with everything he had. His role in the fight for justice was often overlooked, but Raymond's quiet strength was foundational to Rosa's success. The fact that he chose her as a wife, and that she chose him, spoke volumes about their mutual commitment to the cause. It was a partnership built on mutual respect, a shared vision, and unshakable loyalty. As a member of the NAACP, Raymond Parks didn't just stand by Rosa in her moments of triumph. He was there during the toughest of times, supporting her when the risks were real and the threats were personal. He was actively involved in the fight for Black rights long before Rosa's name became a symbol of defiance. Raymond's commitment to justice wasn't just theoretical; it was tangible. In the early 1930s, Raymond was one of the few Black men in Montgomery, AL, openly working against resistance to racial injustice. He was part of the local defense committee that raised money and awareness for the Scottsboro Boys, a case that highlighted the brutal injustice Black men faced in the legal system. Raymond's involvement in this fight showed that he was a man who wasn't afraid to stand up for what was right, even if it meant facing backlash. Raymond's work with the Scottsboro Boys is a testament to his character and his commitment to justice. He didn't just talk about change; he fought for it. By representing those falsely accused, Raymond stood on the frontlines of the battle for Black rights, proving that he was just as much a part of the movement as anyone else. His support for the Scottsboro Boys was a direct reflection of the man he was, a man who understood that true manhood is defined by action, not words. He didn't seek recognition or accolades; he did the work because it was the right thing to do. Raymond knew that justice didn't come without sacrifice, and he was more than willing to make that sacrifice.

When you look at the relationship between Raymond and Rosa Parks, you see the embodiment of "*The 14 Codes*" in action. Raymond was a man who understood the importance of integrity and work ethic, two codes that define a man's value. He didn't demand respect; he commanded it through his actions. His loyalty to Rosa wasn't just about love; it was about a shared purpose. Their union was built on mutual respect, and Raymond's steadfast support of Rosa showed that he was a man who didn't just stand for justice; he lived it. Every action Raymond took was a reflection of the man he was, and it showed in the woman he chose to marry. Rosa Parks is known worldwide for her courage, but Raymond was the man who stood behind her, making sure she had the support to do what needed to be done. The fact that he was married to a woman who would become one of the most well-known figures in the Civil Rights Movement reflects his understanding of who he was. Raymond wasn't intimidated by his wife's prominence; he was proud of her. He knew that his role wasn't to overshadow her but to support her mission, and that's exactly what he did. He didn't try to outshine Rosa; instead, he helped shine a light on her work. That's the mark of a true man, one who understands his place, honors his woman, and works together for a greater cause.

Raymond's support for Rosa was more than just a matter of standing by her; it was about partnership. He understood that a man doesn't have to be the loudest voice in the room to make a difference. Sometimes, it's about being the quiet strength that holds everything together. Raymond knew that while Rosa was the one who would be remembered for her act of defiance, their shared struggle would be remembered as well. Their union wasn't about individual glory; it was about collective action. Together, they made history, and Raymond's role in that history was just as vital as Rosa's. When a man chooses a woman, it's a reflection of who he is. Raymond Parks was a man of substance, a man of integrity, and a man who understood the value of loyalty and partnership. He didn't choose Rosa Parks because of her fame or potential; he chose her because she shared his commitment to justice. Their relationship was a partnership of equals, both fighting for the same cause and supporting each other in their respective roles. Raymond's role in the Civil Rights Movement may not have been as publicly celebrated as

Rosa's, but that didn't make it any less important. His quiet strength was just as necessary to the movement as her act of defiance.

Raymond Parks understood that real manhood is about supporting your woman's purpose, not competing with it. He didn't try to make himself the face of the movement; he understood that his wife's courage would be the spark that ignited the fight. But that didn't mean he wasn't equally involved in the struggle. He was a man who didn't need to be in the spotlight to be effective. His work behind the scenes, his legal efforts, and his support for his wife all showed that Raymond Parks was a man who understood his role in the fight for justice. He wasn't looking for credit; he was looking for change. The relationship between Raymond and Rosa Parks is a perfect example of *"The 14 Codes"* in action. Raymond understood that a true man supports his woman's growth and purpose. He didn't let ego or pride get in the way of their shared vision. He didn't need to be the one who received the accolades; he just needed to know that they were fighting the right fight. Raymond knew that the struggle for justice was bigger than any individual. It was about the community, and it was about creating a future where Black people could live freely and equally. He dedicated his life to that cause, alongside the woman he loved. Raymond's support for Rosa Parks wasn't just a matter of marriage; it was about a shared commitment. He believed in the cause, and he believed in her ability to bring change. He was a man who understood that his work in the movement was just as vital as hers. They were partners in every sense of the word, each playing their part in a larger struggle for equality. Raymond's involvement in the fight for justice, from the *"Scottsboro Boys"* to his support for Rosa, showed that real manhood is defined by action. It's about standing firm in your beliefs, even when the odds are stacked against you. Their marriage was a testament to the power of unity. Raymond and Rosa were not just fighting for their own lives; they were fighting for the lives of all Black people. They understood that the work of the movement was bigger than any one individual, and that's why their bond was unbreakable. Together, they were a force to be reckoned with. Raymond's support for Rosa allowed her to stand firm in her own fight, and together, they made a lasting impact on the Civil Rights Movement.

The story of Raymond and Rosa Parks serves as a reminder that real manhood is about supporting the people you love. Raymond Parks wasn't looking for recognition; he was looking to make a difference. His quiet support for Rosa, his legal efforts, and his dedication to justice all showed that he understood the deeper meaning of manhood. His legacy may not be as widely recognized as his wife's, but that doesn't make it any less important. Raymond's life was a perfect example of what it means to be a true partner, a true man, and a true ally in the fight for justice. Raymond Parks knew that real strength comes from the ability to support those around you. His dedication to Rosa, his involvement in the legal battles for Black rights, and his commitment to justice all reflected the qualities of a man who understood what it meant to be a Black man in America. He didn't need the spotlight; he just needed to know that the work they were doing was meaningful. His role in the movement may not have been as well-known as Rosa's, but it was just as vital. Raymond Parks was a man who understood his purpose, and he played his part in history with honor and integrity. Raymond Parks's quiet yet support for Rosa Parks set the tone for understanding real partnership in the fight for justice. His commitment to the cause was a testament to his strength, not in seeking accolades, but in making sure the work continued, no matter the risks. Just as Raymond supported Rosa, Ferdinand Lee Barnett stood alongside Ida B. Wells, sharing her vision and offering the same kind of steadfast dedication in the face of danger. Both men understood that true manhood is about being a supporter in every sense of the word: supporting the people you love and standing firm in the pursuit of justice, even when it's dangerous. In a time when both Rosa and Ida B. Wells were fighting against systemic oppression, these men didn't need to be in the spotlight; they knew their role was to support their wives and their missions. Like Raymond, Barnett exemplified the values of partnership and commitment to the cause, cementing their legacies as not just husbands, but powerful allies in the fight for equality.

Ferdinand Lee Barnett, born in 1854, was a man of great character and integrity, embodying many of the qualities that *The 14 Codes* calls for in Black men. In an era when lynchings of Black people were common, often happening twice a week, Barnett's actions proved his commitment to justice and equality. He was not just a passive supporter of his wife, Ida B. Wells, but an active force in her mission. Barnett knew the dangers of speaking out against the widespread racial violence of the time, yet he stood by his wife as she courageously fought for the rights of Black people, particularly through her work exposing lynching. He shared her vision of justice and stood with her even when it put both of their lives at risk. His loyalty to her mission, even in the face of peril, is a testament to the type of man he was—a man who would die for what he believed in. Ferdinand Barnett didn't just support Ida B. Wells in the background; he stood with her publicly, making sure the world saw their unity. He was a lawyer by trade, and while his legal expertise helped them navigate the challenges of their activism, his true strength came from his character. He understood that his work as a lawyer and editor of the *Chicago Defender* was important, but he also understood that his role as Ida's husband was of equal importance. Their partnership was more than just a marriage; it was a shared commitment to fighting against injustice.

Barnett encouraged Ida to pursue her career, often working alongside her to ensure that her work reached a wider audience. They worked as a unit, each supporting the other in ways that allowed them to thrive in their respective battles.

Even though Barnett was not as well known as Ida B. Wells, his choice to marry her speaks volumes about the kind of man he was. He chose to stand beside one of the most iconic figures in the fight against racial injustice. His decision to marry Ida was not one of convenience or status; it was a decision rooted in shared purpose and mutual respect. This is what Code #7 teaches us: a man's worth is reflected not just in his work but in the woman he chooses. He didn't see himself as secondary to her, but as a man who would support her in every way possible. By choosing Ida B. Wells, Barnett demonstrated his own sense of purpose and his understanding of the kind of legacy they could build together. Barnett's career as an editor of the *Chicago Defender* helped shape public opinion about race relations and provided a platform for Black voices, including his own and Ida's. The Defender was one of the most influential Black newspapers in the country, and Barnett used his position to advocate for justice and equality. But despite his role in the media, he never sought the spotlight for himself. His quiet support for Ida's work was more significant than any individual recognition he could have received. He understood that true greatness was not about seeking fame but about making a difference in the lives of others, and he did that by empowering his wife to speak truth to power. This quiet strength and dedication to a cause bigger than himself are key qualities that every Black man should embody.

As a lawyer, Barnett had the knowledge and resources to fight the oppressive legal systems that were designed to keep Black people down. He didn't just use his education for personal gain; he used it to further the fight for justice alongside his wife. His understanding of the law and the way it was wielded against Black people made him an invaluable ally in Ida's campaign against lynching. He wasn't just a man of words; he was a man of action, using his legal expertise to challenge the system that sought to destroy Black lives. His work as a lawyer and as an editor showed that being a man of purpose requires more than just intention; it requires practical steps and action. Barnett's story is also one of sacrifice. He knew that by standing with Ida B. Wells, he was putting himself in danger, but he did it anyway. The threats against their lives were very real, especially given Ida's outspoken opposition to lynching and her efforts to expose the horrors of white supremacy. Yet, Barnett didn't shy away from the risk. Instead, he leaned into it, showing that he understood the gravity of their cause. Barnett didn't just talk the talk, he walked it, standing firm in the face of imminent danger to support the woman he loved and the cause they both fought for.

Even though Barnett wasn't as famous as his wife, he still made significant contributions to the movement, using his position to support the fight for justice. The work that Ida B. Wells did would not have been possible without the steadfast support of Ferdinand Barnett. While she was the public face of the anti-lynching campaign, he was the quiet strength behind the scenes, providing her with the resources, encouragement, and love she needed to keep fighting. His actions reflect the wisdom in Code #7: a Black man's worth is not determined by how much attention he receives but by the strength of his character and his vow to the people and causes that matter most. Barnett's relationship with Ida B. Wells was built on trust, respect, and a shared commitment to justice. He didn't try to overshadow her; instead, he worked alongside her to amplify her message. In a time when the Black community was under constant threat, Barnett's steady presence and support helped ensure that Ida's voice was heard loud and clear. Together, they formed a partnership that was greater than the sum of its parts, showing the power of unity in the face of adversity. Their marriage was not just about love; it was about building a legacy of resistance and resilience—one that continues to inspire us today.

As we look at Ferdinand Barnett and Ida B. Wells, we are reminded of the critical importance of partnership in the fight for justice. A Black man's choices, especially the woman he chooses to stand with, are a reflection of the man he is. Barnett's support for Ida showed that a true man of purpose understands the importance of choosing a woman who will not only walk beside him but will also strengthen and challenge him along the way. His role in their partnership reflects the power of *"The 14 Codes,"* where a man's worth is determined by his actions, his integrity, and his ability to stand firm in his beliefs, no matter the cost. Ferdinand Barnett, like other great men of his time, understood the vital role of women in the fight for Black liberation. His commitment to Ida B. Wells and the fight against racial violence is a testament to his understanding of the deep connection between the strength of the Black community and the strength of its women. He didn't view himself as secondary to her but as a necessary ally in the cause. His actions reflect the power of unity between Black men and women, a partnership that has always been essential in the struggle for justice. Their union was a blueprint for what it means to be a Black man of purpose, one who chooses not just a woman, but a woman who will stand by his side, challenge him, and help carry his legacy.

In many ways, Ferdinand Barnett's story is a reminder of the value of choosing a woman who shares your vision and your fight. The woman you stand beside should be someone who not only understands your purpose but actively contributes to it. Barnett's life proves that a man's greatness is not just measured by his work, but by the partnerships he fosters and the people he chooses to support. By standing with Ida B. Well, he wasn't just supporting her; he was supporting the entire Black community in their fight for justice. This is the lesson every Black man should take from their story: understand the power of the woman you choose to stand with. Their legacy lives on as a reminder that every Black man must make choices that reflect his purpose and his values. Ferdinand Barnett's support for Ida B. Wells shows that true greatness comes from building a partnership that is based on a shared vision, respect, and an unshakable commitment to justice. His work as a lawyer and editor wasn't just about personal success; it was about using his position to uplift those around him and to fight for the greater good. In choosing Ida B. Wells, Ferdinand Lee Barnett chose a woman who reflected his own strength, purpose, and dedication to justice, and that choice continues to inspire generations.

THE STRATEGIC DIVIDE — How White Supremacy Has Targeted the Unity of Black Men and Women

White supremacy has always recognized the power of Black unity, particularly the strength of Black men and women together. A united Black family represents resistance, self-sufficiency, and autonomy—qualities that threaten the very foundation of white supremacy. For this reason, the system has spent centuries dismantling the connection between Black men and women, using every tool at its disposal to create division. From slavery to modern policies, this strategy has been intentional, aimed at preventing us from building strong, resilient families and communities. During slavery, the attack on Black families was blatant. Enslaved Black men were beaten, maimed, and murdered in front of their women to strip them of their dignity and power. This public humiliation was designed to make them appear weak, unworthy of their wives' respect or trust. Families were torn apart, leaving Black women without their natural protectors and Black men without the chance to be the providers and fathers they were meant to be. This attack wasn't just physical—it was psychological. The system's goal was to sow distrust and dependency between Black men and women. When Black men were seen as weak, it made it easier for Black women to rely on the system for survival instead of on their men.

The legacy of this strategy carried over into the 20th century. Welfare policies and mass incarceration played the same role in dividing Black families. Welfare programs, while advertised as help, came with stipulations that penalized Black families when a man was present in the home. This forced many Black women to rely on the state for support rather than their partners, creating a culture of dependency that eroded the stability Black men and women could have built together. Mass incarceration amplified the damage. With millions of Black men locked away, generations grew up without fathers in the home. Black women were forced to take on the roles of both providers and nurturers, not by choice but by design. This not only deprived children of male role models but also weakened the partnership and trust between Black men and women. Perhaps the most insidious form of division comes through media manipulation. For decades, Black men have been portrayed as irresponsible, dangerous, and incapable of leadership, while Black women are cast as aggressive, combative, and fiercely independent. This is not accidental. These stereotypes are carefully crafted to create a false narrative about Black relationships. The media encourages Black men and women to see each other as adversaries rather than allies. This narrative keeps us divided, ensuring that instead of uniting against the real enemy—the system designed to keep us disempowered—we remain caught up in conflict with one another.

This division is by design. People who are divided are easier to control. When Black men and women cannot trust each other, they cannot build together. When they cannot build together, they are less likely to challenge the status quo. A strong Black family is a direct threat to white supremacy. That's why the system has worked tirelessly to keep us apart. The destruction of the Black family is not incidental—it is a calculated strategy to prevent Black people from reaching their full potential. The long history of attacks on Black families, from slavery to the modern-day prison-industrial complex, was never about policy. It was about breaking down the core of Black strength. The Black family has always been the foundation of resistance. That is why it has been targeted for destruction. Today, we see the fallout of this strategy in our communities. Single-parent households, generational poverty, and a deep mistrust between Black men and women are direct results of policies designed to divide us. But as long as we remain divided, the system will continue to have power over us. The only way to break free is to rebuild the bonds that have been torn apart. The system understands this, which is why it works so hard to keep Black men and women separated. We must recognize this history, acknowledge the damage it has done, and commit to healing the divisions it has created.

Understanding Code #7—the importance of self-reliance and the reflection of a man's choices in his partner—has profound implications, not just for individuals but for the community at large. A man who understands this code does not enter relationships expecting his partner to make him into the man he wants to be. He knows it is his responsibility to build himself first. By doing so, he can choose a partner aligned with his values, purpose, and vision for the future. This clarity allows him to form relationships that enhance, rather than hinder, his growth. The act of choosing a partner wisely is an essential part of this code. A man who has developed discipline, purpose, and structure in his life will attract a woman who shares those same qualities. He won't settle for a woman who drags him down, nor will he look to her to fill the gaps he has neglected within himself. Instead, his choices will reflect his inner strength and determination. A man who is grounded in his self-worth attracts a woman who mirrors that self-assurance. Together, they create a foundation strong enough to withstand the pressures of life. This mutual respect is the bedrock of a relationship built on equality, support, and shared goals.

A man who understands this code knows that a woman cannot save him. Too many men believe that a woman will *"complete"* them, fix their brokenness, or bring them out of dysfunction. This is a lie. A woman can support and uplift a man, but she cannot be the source of his strength. A woman cannot give a man what he has not already developed within himself. The strength of a Black woman—her resilience, intellect, and beauty—is a reflection of her own self-reliance. She is not a crutch for a man who has failed to do the hard work of building himself. When both partners bring their own strength into the relationship, they create a dynamic that elevates them both. A strong Black man and a strong Black woman standing together form an unshakable force. When both individuals are focused on growth, when both partners are accountable to themselves and each other, they create a bond that cannot be broken by outside forces. White supremacy has always sought to weaken Black relationships, to divide Black families, and to reduce Black people to their lowest potential. But a man who understands this code will not allow his relationship to be dictated by those forces. Instead, he will build a partnership based on mutual respect, shared purpose, and the understanding that both individuals have their own personal strength. Together, they become a fortress, a representation of what can be achieved when Black people support one another.

The benefits of understanding this code extend beyond personal relationships. A man who builds himself first, who chooses wisely, and who knows that a woman does not complete him but complements him creates a solid foundation for future generations. His children will witness what a healthy, balanced, and purposeful partnership looks like. They will grow up knowing that they are responsible for building their own success and that the strength of their family comes from within. This understanding leads to a legacy of power. Too many Black families have been fractured by dysfunction, poor choices, and systemic oppression. By embracing this code, Black men and women can heal that dysfunction and break the cycles that have held them back. They can create families built on mutual respect, love, and shared responsibility. These families will become powerful units that contribute to the strength of the larger community. Strong families create strong communities, and strong communities build real, sustained power that cannot be easily broken. When a man chooses his partner wisely, he chooses a future. His decisions will have a lasting impact, not just on his life but on the generations that follow. This isn't just about romance; it's about building a partnership that withstands the test of time. Understanding this code ensures that his legacy will be one of power, not weakness. Strong men, strong women, and strong families—this is the legacy of Code #7.

CODE NO. 8

A BLACK MAN WILL DIE FOR HIS RESPONSIBILITIES

Responsibility, in the context of a Black man's duty, is more than just handling obligations; it's about being the foundation on which everything around him is built. A man's word, his actions, and his ability to follow through define his worth. Responsibility isn't just about providing or protecting; it's about standing firm in the face of pressure and never folding when the moment calls for leadership. Too many males exist without purpose, floating through life without a sense of duty to themselves or their people. A Black man who embraces responsibility understands that his choices don't just affect him; they impact his family, his community, and his legacy. To be responsible is to accept that everything you do has weight, and if you fail to carry it, you crumble under it. The *"14 Codes"* make it clear that a Black man's responsibility is tied to his character, discipline, and integrity. Integrity means doing what's right even when no one is watching, and responsibility is the action behind that principle. A man without responsibility is weak, easily swayed, and ultimately a liability to those around him. This is why Code #8 isn't about seeking death but about understanding that some things are bigger than yourself. *"Sacrifice"* is the price of true manhood, whether that means putting your life on the line for a cause or simply staying committed when it's easier to quit. Responsibility isn't just a burden; it's a badge of honor that separates men from males.

Throughout history, Black men who took responsibility for their people and their principles were the ones who left the greatest impact. Nat Turner didn't hesitate when he saw the weight of his people's suffering, and Fred Hampton didn't waver when it came to organizing for liberation. They knew that responsibility means putting the mission first, even when it costs everything. On the other hand, those who betray responsibility, like William O'Neal, show what happens when a man chooses fear over duty. A man who refuses to uphold his responsibilities is worse than a man who never had them to begin with because he had the power to stand but chose to kneel. Responsibility isn't just about what you do; it's about what you refuse to let happen on your watch. In today's world, responsibility is under attack, with too many men ducking accountability and blaming circumstances instead of owning their actions. A Black man who follows the 14 Codes understands that excuses are the language of the weak, while solutions are the mindset of the strong. He doesn't wait for someone to tell him what needs to be done; he sees a problem and handles it. Whether it's raising his children, building his business, or standing firm in his principles, he moves with purpose. A responsible man commands respect without demanding it because his actions speak for him. In the end, responsibility isn't about what a man has, it's about what he's willing to sacrifice to uphold his principles, his name, and his people.

A Black man dying for his responsibilities doesn't always mean taking his last breath. It means sacrificing comfort, ego, and even personal safety for something bigger than himself. Every great Black leader who lived by this principle didn't just risk death; they gave up normalcy, security, and sometimes their own family bonds to fulfill their duty. Malcolm X lost his name and religion before he lost his life. Fred Hampton gave up the illusion of safety the moment he chose to fight for the people. A real man understands that true responsibility comes with sacrifice, and some sacrifices are heavier than death itself. A weak man avoids responsibility because he fears what it will cost him. He won't stand on his principles if it means losing a job, respect, or even a relationship. But a Black man knows that if he bends to fear, he's already dead inside. Look at Nat Turner; he knew the odds, yet he still led a rebellion because his responsibility wasn't to survive; it was to free his people. Madison Washington refused to stay enslaved, even when it would have been easier to accept his fate. He proved that the greatest responsibility a man has is not to himself but to those who depend on him.

Ultimate sacrifice isn't about reckless martyrdom, it's about giving what's necessary to uphold your duty. Some men give their time, others give their freedom, and a few give their lives. The 14 Codes are built on this principle because without sacrifice, there is no legacy. Black men today aren't always called to fight with weapons, but they are called to fight for their families, communities, and self-respect. That fight might cost opportunities, friendships, or even peace of mind, but it's a price a real MAN pays without hesitation. The weak make excuses; the strong make sacrifices. Look at the ones who violate this code, and you'll see men who traded their responsibility for comfort. William O'Neal sold out Fred Hampton because he valued his own safety over his duty. The same applies to every Black man who betrays his own for money, clout, or fear of consequence. But there's always a cost, O'Neal may have lived, but he died as a coward. That's why a Black MAN understands that his responsibility defines him, and nothing, no money, no fear, no threat, can shake that. The difference between a MAN and a male is what he's willing to sacrifice.

Since the foundation of this country, Black men have fought for something bigger than themselves.

Whether it was Crispus Attucks standing up in the Boston Massacre or the countless Black soldiers who risked their lives in the Civil War, they knew their responsibility was to build a future they could own. These men didn't die for a flag; they died for freedom, for family, for the very land that rejected them. In the Revolution, they fought for a country that saw them as less than human, yet they gave everything for the hope of something greater. The fight didn't stop at the battlefields; it continued in every act of resistance, in every Black man who stood tall and said, *"I will die for my people."* Black men have always had a deeper understanding of responsibility, knowing their sacrifice was bigger than personal gain.

When we look at Nat Turner, we see a man who knew his duty went beyond survival. His rebellion wasn't just about freeing himself; it was about setting his people free, knowing the cost could be his life. Turner understood the weight of responsibility in a way that few could comprehend, and he carried it even when it meant facing the consequences head-on. He didn't fight for glory but for the future of his children and the generations that would come after. His actions weren't about dying in vain but rather about sending a message that Black men will never accept chains. He put his life on the line so others could live free, fulfilling his responsibility to his people.

Madison Washington, like Turner, understood that freedom was worth more than anything else. Leading the 1841 Creole Revolt, he risked everything to help his fellow enslaved men gain freedom, knowing full well that it could mean death for him. Washington's decision to take action wasn't one of rage but of responsibility, understanding that true liberty isn't given; it's taken. His sacrifice showed that sometimes the fight isn't about living but about ensuring the survival of others. He understood that his actions would inspire others to fight for what was right, knowing that the cause would outlive him. His revolt wasn't just a chance for freedom; it was a declaration that Black men would not accept being property any longer. Fred Hampton carried this torch in the twentieth century, embodying the ultimate responsibility that comes with leadership. As the head of the Illinois chapter of the Black Panther Party, he was charged with protecting his people and leading them toward liberation. Hampton's life wasn't about fighting for personal power but about uplifting his community and securing a future for his children. His death at the hands of the government was not just an assassination; it was a testament to the lengths the system would go to eliminate Black men who take responsibility for their people. Hampton's sacrifice, however, showed that responsibility is a burden many Black men have carried throughout history, one that sometimes costs them their lives. It proves that being a Black man in America means constantly putting your people above your own safety.

But with responsibility comes betrayal, and no story

illustrates this better than that of William O'Neal, the FBI informant who helped set Hampton up. O'Neal's responsibility as head of security was to protect Fred Hampton at all costs, but instead, he betrayed the very brotherhood he swore to serve. This violation of the code is a stark reminder that sometimes the ones closest to you are the ones most likely to let you down. O'Neal's actions were a direct contradiction of Code #8; his betrayal cost Hampton his life and proved that loyalty is often tested when the stakes are highest. The pain of this betrayal cuts deep, not just because of the life lost, but because it shows that true responsibility is about standing firm, even in the face of temptation or fear.

Black men have always understood that their fight isn't just for themselves but for their communities, their families, and their children's futures. Whether it's through taking up arms, organizing communities, or giving up their lives, it's about knowing that leadership requires sacrifice. A Black man's responsibility is a heavy mantle, one that requires him to be willing to give up his own comfort and sometimes his life to ensure the survival and success of those around him. The men who have lived by this principle have left a legacy that transcends their death, reminding us that real Black manhood is defined by what you're willing to give up for the good of others.

Crispus Attucks was the first man to take a bullet for what would become the United States, but his sacrifice wasn't just about breaking from British rule; it was proof that Black men have always been the first to step up, even when the country refused to step up for them. He had no rights, no guaranteed freedom, and no reason to fight for a system that saw him as less than a man, but he still stood on principle. Attucks didn't hesitate. He didn't wait for change; he forced it. Remember, respect isn't requested; it's taken. From the very beginning, Black men have been on the front lines of every war, conflict, and struggle in this country. Attucks set the tone, proving that a real man doesn't sit back while oppression runs unchecked; he meets it head-on. That's Code #8 in action. Whether it was the Revolutionary War, the Civil War, World Wars, or the fight for civil rights, Black men have always been willing to put their lives on the line, even when America gave them nothing in return. After every war, Black soldiers came home to second-class treatment, lynch mobs, and a system still built against them. But that never stopped them from fighting because the mission was bigger than America; it was about the future of our people. Attucks wasn't just a casualty; he was a warrior who made a choice. The same way Nat Turner, Madison Washington, and Fred Hampton did, men who understood that freedom doesn't come from asking; it comes from sacrifice. The weak let fear dictate their actions, but a Black man who stands on business knows that his legacy is built on what he's willing to fight for. America didn't make Attucks a man; his actions did. And that's the difference between just being male and being a *"MAN."*

From day one, Black men have fought and died for a country that never saw them as men. When war came, they were always on the frontlines, not because they owed America anything, but because they knew their sacrifice was about something bigger. The Civil War was no different. Black men saw it as their chance to fight for their own liberation. The Union Army didn't want them at first, but men like Frederick Douglass understood that respect isn't given; it's earned through action. He pushed for Black men to enlist, knowing that the only way to prove their worth was through responsibility and sacrifice. Enslaved men didn't wait for freedom; they ran from the plantations and took up arms, ready to die before staying in chains. They weren't just fighting for the Union; they were fighting for their own future, their families, and every generation that would come after them. The 54th Massachusetts Regiment embodied everything Code #8 stands for: Black men taking control of their own fate, even when the odds were against them. They knew they weren't seen as equals, but they still charged forward at Fort Wagner, proving their valor with blood. White officers questioned if Black men had the heart for war, but the 54th answered with sacrifice, forcing the Union to recognize their worth. By the end of the war, over 200,000 Black men had served, not just for America, but for their own dignity.

Black men have always understood that freedom isn't given; it's taken. From the Revolution to the Civil War, they didn't wait for permission; they stepped up because a man doesn't sit back while his people suffer. The 54th proved that no one could question a Black man's courage, work ethic, or willingness to sacrifice. These men set the standard for what it means to *"stand on business,"* and their legacy can't be erased. When Black soldiers went off to fight in World War I and II, they weren't just fighting for America; they were fighting for their self-respect. They believed that serving this country with honor would finally earn them the rights they had been denied. But when they came home, they were met with the same hatred, or worse. White mobs lynched Black soldiers in their uniforms, sending a clear message: no amount of service would make them equal. America wanted their labor, not their prosperity. They made sure these soldiers couldn't build wealth, locking them out of the benefits that white veterans received. The *"GI Bill"* was supposed to give veterans access to housing, education, and opportunity, but for Black men, those doors were slammed shut. Banks denied them loans, colleges refused them entry, and housing programs ensured they stayed locked out of homeownership. This wasn't just racism; it was economic sabotage.

Even in war, a Black man was expected to take orders but never to take command. Black units were given the most dangerous assignments with little recognition for their bravery. The Tuskegee Airmen, the 761st Tank Battalion, and the Harlem Hellfighters had to fight two battles: one against the enemy and one against their own military. A Black man had to be twice as good just to be seen as average. But despite everything, their work ethic was beyond question. They outperformed, even when the system tried to hold them back. The ultimate insult came when these veterans returned home and were treated as second-class citizens, or worse, as targets. White men who never left the country resented them for wearing the uniform, for daring to believe they had earned the right to be respected. America sent them overseas to fight tyranny but wouldn't protect them from lynch mobs in their own neighborhoods. But how do you command respect in a system designed to keep you powerless? The answer is simple: you build your own.

These betrayals forced Black veterans to take their fight to another battlefield: the fight for civil rights. Men like Medgar Evers, who fought in World War II, came back and dedicated their lives to justice. They knew America wasn't going to give them equality, so they had to demand it. Fighting for freedom abroad meant nothing if they weren't free at home. The truth is, America has always feared the disciplined, self-sufficient Black man. That's why they tried to strip these veterans of their benefits, their dignity, and their lives. They wanted Black men to stay dependent, to never rise above their conditions. But history proves that no system can break a man who lives by a code. The Vietnam War was another chapter in this same story: Black men putting their lives on the line for a country that never truly valued them. They made up a disproportionate number of combat troops, sent to the frontlines while white soldiers received safer assignments. They fought and bled in a war they didn't start, for a government that saw them as expendable. Many enlisted because they had no choice: either go to war, get drafted, or face prison. And when they came home, there was no honor waiting for them. No opportunities. No support. Just the same second-class treatment they had always known.

The trauma of Vietnam followed these men home, but the government didn't care. PTSD was rampant, but mental health care was nonexistent for Black veterans. Many turned to drugs to cope, and the same government that abandoned them made sure heroin and crack flooded their neighborhoods. With no jobs, no resources, and no way to heal, too many spiraled. This led to broken homes and fractured families, the beginning of what would later be called the *"fatherless household crisis."* But it wasn't because Black men didn't want to be fathers; it was because they were mentally, physically, and emotionally destroyed. The war took everything from them: their stability, their sense of purpose, and, in many cases, their lives. Some couldn't provide because they weren't given the chance. Others were removed from their homes through mass incarceration, another government-led effort to dismantle Black families. This was systematic, a direct attempt to break Black men so the next generation would grow up without strong male figures. That's why *"The 14 Codes"* exist: because responsibility is the foundation of manhood. A Black man is supposed to protect, provide, and lead, but Vietnam-era Black men were robbed of that opportunity. The system made them soldiers when it needed bodies for war, then discarded them when they came back. The long-term effects of this are still felt today. But a true Black man understands that even when the system works against him, he has to find a way to reclaim his responsibility and rebuild.

From the very beginning, Black men have fought and died for this country, not out of blind loyalty, but because they knew this land was just as much theirs as anyone else's. Stolen from their homelands and forced into labor, Black men built the foundation of America with their bare hands. Every road paved, every building raised, and every war fought carried the blood of Black men who knew they had a stake in this nation. They weren't just victims; they were architects of its wealth and power. So, when war came, whether it was the Revolution, the Civil War, or Vietnam, Black men stepped up. Not because they believed in America's promises, but because they understood that true ownership comes with responsibility. If they were going to be in this land, they were going to claim it, fight for it, and demand their place in it. Despite every betrayal, they never stopped standing on principle. That's why "*The 14 Codes*" exist, because a Black man's legacy is built on action, not words. A male complains about the game being rigged. A MAN finds a way to play and win. Black men knew America was never going to give them their due, so they took it, with blood, sweat, and sacrifice. That's the lesson: ownership isn't given; it's taken, defended, and passed down to the next generation. And a Black man who stands on business will always be remembered, while those who bow down will be forgotten.

NAT TURNER: The Duty to Liberate One's People

Nat Turner was more than just an enslaved man; he was a leader who understood that freedom was not something to request but something to take. Born into bondage in Southampton County, Virginia, Turner believed he was chosen by a higher power to lead his people out of slavery. Unlike many who accepted their condition, he saw himself as responsible for the liberation of those around him. This wasn't about personal survival; it was about duty. Turner knew that a Black man who failed to act when his people suffered was complicit in their oppression. His decision to lead the 1831 rebellion was not driven by emotion but by a deep sense of purpose, a core principle of what it means to be a man. A Black man's responsibility extends beyond himself; it's about what he's willing to stand for and, if necessary, die for. Turner understood that if he remained passive, he would be just another slave waiting for death on someone else's terms. Instead, he chose to command his own destiny and ignite a movement that sent shockwaves through the South. The rebellion he led was not just an act of defiance but a statement: a Black man who recognizes his responsibility will shake the very foundation of his oppressors. This aligns directly with *"The 14 Codes"*: a man doesn't run from his responsibilities, no matter the cost. Turner's actions forced the nation to see that enslaved men were not property but warriors. His leadership exemplified what it means to move with conviction and not fear consequences.

Every revolution requires sacrifice, and Turner knew his life would be the price. His uprising was brutally suppressed, and he was executed, but his legacy didn't die with him. His willingness to risk everything for the freedom of others set a precedent for future Black revolutionaries. Men like Denmark Vesey, Madison Washington, and eventually Fred Hampton all carried that same sense of ownership over our people's fate. Turner's rebellion made it clear that true responsibility comes with risk, something weak men avoid. His story is a lesson in action over words, in commitment over convenience, and in embracing the weight of leadership even when the outcome is uncertain.

The lesson from Turner's life is simple: A Black man who refuses to accept his chains will always be dangerous. Ownership isn't about paperwork or permission; it's about understanding that this land, this history, and this fight belong to us. Turner didn't live to see the end of slavery, but his actions fueled the fire that made it inevitable. His rebellion proved that no man can truly control another unless he allows it. Code #8 is about responsibility, and Turner's story is a reminder that a Black man's duty is not to simply exist but to lead, fight, and if necessary, lay it all on the line.

Nat Turner understood that being a Black man meant more than just existing; he had a responsibility to his people. Enslavement was not just a condition; it was an attack on the very essence of manhood, stripping Black men of their ability to protect, provide, and lead. Turner, a preacher, saw beyond the physical chains and recognized the mental and spiritual bondage forced upon his people. He knew that talking wasn't enough. He took it upon himself to lead the Southampton Rebellion, not just for his own freedom but for the generations that would come after. His responsibility wasn't about survival; it was about breaking a system that kept his people weak.

Turner's rebellion wasn't reckless; it was calculated, built on a vision of what true freedom meant. Many enslaved men feared retaliation, but Turner knew that fear was the very thing keeping them in chains. He understood that any movement toward liberation would come at a cost, and he was willing to pay it. His ability to move in silence, organize, and strike when the time was right demonstrated leadership and accountability. He didn't gossip about his plans, didn't seek approval, and didn't hesitate when the time came. Turner knew his mission was bigger than himself, and he carried it out without compromise.

Leading a rebellion meant facing death, but Turner embraced that reality because he valued responsibility over self-preservation.. Enslaved men were stripped of everything that made them men, and Turner chose to reclaim it through force. He understood that a man's word meant nothing if he wasn't willing to back it up. The rebellion shook the South to its core, showing the power of a Black man who refused to accept subjugation. Even in death, Turner's name carried weight because he stood on principle.

His execution didn't mark the end of his impact; it cemented his legacy as a man who refused to live on his knees. The rebellion led to harsher laws against enslaved people, but it also ignited fear in the hearts of those who thought Black men would remain passive. Turner's sacrifice was a blueprint for what it means to take responsibility, showing future generations that power isn't given; it's taken. His actions exposed the system's fear of a strong, principled Black man. Turner's life wasn't just about the rebellion; it was about redefining what it meant to be a man under oppression. His responsibility didn't end with his death; it lived on through every Black man who chose to stand instead of submit. Nat Turner was born into slavery, but from a young age, he knew he was meant for something greater. He was deeply religious and believed he was chosen by God to lead his people to freedom. Unlike other enslaved men who accepted their fate, Nat refused to live under oppression without resistance. He spent years observing the plantation system, understanding its weaknesses, and waiting for the right moment to strike. His visions and spiritual beliefs only strengthened his resolve, convincing him that rebellion was not just necessary but inevitable. When the time came, he didn't hesitate; he took responsibility for the lives of those around him and moved with purpose.

The 1831 rebellion he led in Southampton County, Virginia, was a direct challenge to the system that dehumanized his people. He and his followers killed slave owners, overseers, and anyone who stood in their way. This wasn't senseless violence; it was war, a declaration that Black men would no longer be passive victims. Nat understood that the cost of freedom was often blood, and he was willing to pay it. He moved strategically, gathering support and spreading fear among white enslavers who never thought their captives would rise up. His actions sent shockwaves through the South, proving that enslaved Black men were not broken; they were waiting for a leader. That's the responsibility of a true Black man: to act when the moment calls for it.

He knew death was the likely outcome, but that didn't stop him. After weeks of hiding, he was captured, tried, and executed, yet he never wavered in his beliefs. His sacrifice wasn't just his life; it was his willingness to challenge an entire system, knowing he wouldn't live to see the change he fought for. Nat Turner understood that his people's liberation was more important than his individual survival. His execution was meant to serve as a warning, but instead, it cemented his legacy. True men don't just live for themselves; they live for something bigger.

Nat Turner's rebellion led to harsher laws against enslaved people, but it also sparked fear in the hearts of enslavers. The very idea that Black men would rather die fighting than live in chains forced America to confront the reality of its own brutality. White Southerners increased restrictions on literacy and gatherings, proving how dangerous a knowledgeable and united Black men could be. Even in death, Nat Turner was a threat to the system. His actions didn't just inspire future revolts; they sent a message that the fight for freedom would never end. Black men today must understand that power doesn't come without sacrifice, and responsibility means taking action even when the odds are against you. Code #8 isn't about recklessness; it's about standing firm in your purpose, no matter the cost. Nat Turner didn't rebel out of emotion; he did it out of duty. He saw what needed to be done and accepted the consequences that came with it. Too many men today hesitate when it's time to take responsibility because they fear loss. They avoid difficult decisions, thinking self-preservation is the highest priority. But a real Black man understands that some things are bigger than himself. Nat's story reminds us that comfort is temporary, but legacy is forever.

His rebellion laid the groundwork for future resistance, from the Underground Railroad to the Civil Rights Movement. He was part of a long tradition of Black men who refused to submit, no matter the cost. The same spirit that drove Nat Turner lived in Madison Washington, Denmark Vesey, and Gabriel Prosser. It's the same spirit that made Fred Hampton willing to die for his people. Every generation has men who must make hard choices for the greater good. The question is, will you be one of them? The system still tries to make Black men fearful—fearful of speaking out, of standing up, of challenging oppression. They want you docile, content, and disconnected from your responsibilities. Nat Turner rejected that mindset completely. He didn't wait for permission to act, and he didn't seek validation for his decisions. He saw the problem and took action, which is what every Black man must do. Whether it's protecting your family, building your community, or standing on your principles, responsibility requires courage.

Nat Turner's legacy is not just about rebellion; it's about what it means to be a man His name still carries weight because he didn't fold under pressure. He reminds us that if you're not willing to stand for something, you'll fall for anything. A Black man's duty is to lead, protect, and fight for what is right, no matter the cost. That's what separates males from men.

FRED HAMPTON: The People's Revolutionary

Fred Hampton was a revolutionary leader who embodied what it meant to take responsibility for his people. As chairman of the Illinois chapter of the Black Panther Party, he understood that true power came from unity, discipline, and direct action. Unlike many so-called leaders today, he wasn't focused on being popular; he was focused on building something real. He didn't just talk about revolution; he organized free breakfast programs, political education classes, and self-defense training for the community. His belief in true liberation extended beyond race; he knew the system thrived by keeping poor people divided. That's why he formed the original Rainbow Coalition, bringing together Black, Brown, and White revolution-aries under one cause: taking power away from the oppressors.

The system saw what he was doing and immediately marked him as a threat. The FBI, under J. Edgar Hoover's COINTELPRO, feared his ability to unite people more than any gun in the Panthers' arsenal. Hampton's charisma, intelligence, and discipline made him dangerous because he wasn't just fighting; he was winning. While most so-called *"activists"* today chase clout and corporate sponsorships, Hampton was in the trenches, feeding kids and teaching self-defense. He wasn't asking for change; he was taking it. The government knew they couldn't beat him in open debate or break his movement through propaganda alone. So, they did what they always do when a Black man starts building something real: they infiltrated, sabotaged, and assassinated him.

William O'Neal, the so-called *"Security Chief"* of the of the Chicago chapter of the Black Panther Party, who was the government's inside man. He smiled in Hampton's face while feeding intelligence to the FBI, proving that betrayal always comes from the ones closest to you. O'Neal gave the FBI the layout of Hampton's apartment, ensuring that the raid on December 4, 1969, would be a guaranteed execution. The police stormed in, firing over 90 shots while the Panthers barely got a single one off. Hampton, drugged unconscious by O'Neal the night before, never even had a chance to defend himself. He was shot multiple times, including two point-blank shots to the head while he was already down. His pregnant fiancée, Deborah Johnson, lay next to him as his life was stolen by the same government that now pretends to celebrate civil rights.

His assassination showed exactly why Black men who take real responsibility for our people don't get statues, national holidays, or Netflix specials that tell the truth. They get bullets, betrayals, and historical erasure. The same system that murdered Hampton later repackaged his ideas and handed them to people who wouldn't use them against the state. The Rainbow Coalition, a movement about uniting oppressed people against a corrupt system, was hijacked by Jesse Jackson, who turned it into a Democratic Party puppet show. Now, the LGBT movement has taken the name completely, stripping it of its original revolutionary meaning. Hampton was about discipline, masculinity, and organized resistance; he would have never co-signed the watered-down, co-opted version of his vision. This is what the system does. It doesn't just kill our leaders, it steals from them, waters down their messages, and feeds us a corrupted version to keep us weak.

Fred Hampton lived Code #8 to the fullest because he was willing to sacrifice everything for his responsibilities. He didn't just fight for himself; he fought for his people, his community, and the next generation. He knew the risk and still did the work because that's what a real Black man does. O'Neal violated the Code in the worst way possible; not only did he abandon his responsibility, but he actively destroyed another man's. The betrayal of Hampton is the same story we've seen throughout history: the government picks a weak, desperate Black man and uses him to take down a strong one. Just like how Judas sold out Jesus, O'Neal sold out Hampton. And just like Judas, he couldn't live with himself, eventually taking his own life years later. The lesson? A Black man who betrays his responsibility will never find peace. The assassination of Fred

Hampton wasn't just about killing one man; it was about stopping a movement before it became too powerful to control. The government doesn't fear Black people who just march, complain, or make hashtags. It fears Black men who organize, strategize, and take responsibility for our people. That's why Hampton had to go. He was a young, disciplined, and fearless leader who didn't just talk about revolution; he lived it. And unlike the weak men today who sell out for clout, Hampton would never have compromised his mission for a seat at the table. He knew the system would never give real power to Black men; it had to be taken.

Fred Hampton's sacrifice is a reminder that a Black man's responsibility is bigger than himself. He died at 21, but he left a blueprint that still stands today. His story proves that leadership isn't about popularity; it's about responsibility, discipline, and sacrifice. The Panthers weren't perfect, but they understood something most Black men today have forgotten: a real man doesn't just survive; he builds, he protects, and, if necessary, he fights. Hampton didn't live long enough to see his vision come true, but his sacrifice should be a lesson to every Black man: if you don't take responsibility for your people, someone else will, and they won't have your best interests in mind.

Let's Talk About the Judases

William O'Neal was a man who had responsibility but chose betrayal. As Security Chief of the Illinois Black Panther Party, his job was to protect Fred Hampton and the organization from threats, both external and internal. Instead, he became the biggest threat of them all. He wasn't just a weak man; he was a man who sold out his brother for personal gain, proving that not every Black man can be trusted with leadership. The very man who was supposed to stand on the front lines chose to work for the enemy, violating one of the most sacred codes of manhood. When you have a duty to protect, there is no excuse for selling out. A Black man's word is his bond, and his responsibilities are not to be taken lightly. William O'Neal didn't just betray Hampton; he betrayed the entire movement. When a man is given the task of securing the safety of his people, it's no longer about personal survival; it's about the mission. O'Neal, however, put himself above the cause, proving that he was not fit to be called a man. Real men don't crumble under pressure; they stand firm, even when the enemy is offering them an easy way out. Responsibility is a weight that must be carried, not something that can be dropped when it gets too heavy.

Fred Hampton was a man who understood the risk of his position, but he expected loyalty from those around him. He knew that leadership came with a target on his back, but what he couldn't expect was that the man standing next to him would be the one to put the bullet in him. That's the cold reality of betrayal; it doesn't come from the outside; it comes from the people closest to you. O'Neal played his role well, pretending to be loyal while feeding the FBI everything they needed to execute their plan. A Black man who violates the trust of his brothers is worse than the enemy because he moves undetected.

Every Black man must ask himself where he stands in times of crisis. Are you the man who holds the line, or are you the man who folds when the pressure is on? O'Neal folded, and for what? Some money? A sense of power given to him by the very people who wanted to see him dead too? He thought he was playing the game, but he was only a pawn. Real men don't compromise their integrity for a paycheck, especially when that check is signed by the same system designed to destroy them. O'Neal was proof that a man without a code is a man without a soul. History remembers Fred Hampton as a revolutionary, a warrior, and a man who stood for something greater than himself. History remembers William O'Neal as a traitor, a coward, and a man who chose self-preservation over honor. His actions didn't just take down Hampton; they set back an entire movement. That's what makes betrayal so dangerous. When a man refuses to uphold his responsibilities, the damage doesn't stop with him; it spreads. O'Neal's choices didn't just cost a life; they cost progress. One man's cowardice can undo the work of a hundred warriors.

The FBI didn't need to send an army to take down the Black Panthers; they just needed a weak Black man with no sense of duty. That's the strategy that has been used against Black men for centuries: find the one who is willing to betray, offer him just enough to turn, and let him do the dirty work. O'Neal was that man. Instead of protecting his brotha, he made it easier for the enemy to strike. Instead of standing on principle, he let fear and greed guide him. A man who trades his integrity for security is already dead inside. There's a reason why the system works so hard to turn Black men against each other. They understand that unity is power, and a divided people are easier to control. O'Neal played right into their hands, believing that he was in control when, in reality, he was just a puppet. A man without integrity is a tool for destruction. The Panthers knew that the fight wasn't just against racism but also against the weakness within their own ranks. That's why Code #8 is so critical: a Black man must be willing to die for his responsibilities because anything less puts everything at risk.

O'Neal wasn't the first and won't be the last. There will always be men like him, Black men who trade their people for temporary gain. The question is, will there be more Hamptons or more O'Neals? More men willing to fight and sacrifice, or more men willing to fold and betray? Every generation has a choice, and every Black man must decide what side of history he wants to be on. O'Neal thought he could escape his choices, but guilt is a heavy burden. His suicide wasn't just an admission of regret; it was proof that even he knew he had broken something that could never be fixed. The greatest enemy to Black men is not always the white man in uniform, but the Black man who chooses to serve him. O'Neal's story is a reminder that the biggest threats often come from within. When a Black man is given a responsibility, he is given a purpose, and that purpose is greater than he is. O'Neal failed because he thought about himself first. A real man understands that his responsibilities come before his comfort. A man who values his own safety over the safety of his people is no man at all.

Bobby Rush, the Black Panther Defense Minister, was conveniently absent on the night of Hampton's assassination. That raised questions. How does the man in charge of security miss the night his leader is executed? Whether he was an informant or just negligent, his absence proved one thing: responsibility is not a title; it's an action. Being in a position of power means nothing if you aren't willing to fulfill the duties that come with it. That's why leadership is not for every man. It requires a level of sacrifice that many are unwilling to give. Some men are willing to die for the cause, while others just want to be close enough to benefit from it. O'Neal and Rush show the two types of men that exist in every movement: the ones who stand firm and the ones who step back when it's time to go all in; the ones who speak about revolution and the ones who live it. Hampton died because he lived what he preached. O'Neal survived because he chose comfort over courage. But in the end, even survival couldn't save him from himself. Betrayal doesn't just affect the man who commits it; it affects generations. O'Neal's actions didn't just take Hampton's life; they set a precedent for how easily a movement can be dismantled from within. When a Black man betrays his responsibilities, he doesn't just hurt himself; he weakens the foundation that other strong men have built. The effects of betrayal ripple through history, showing up in broken communities, weakened institutions, and movements that never reach their full potential. Every Black man must ask himself, *"Am I living by a code, or am I just existing?"* O'Neal existed, but he had no code. He thought his actions would buy him freedom, but they only trapped him in a different kind of prison. A man without principles is a man who will fall for anything. When the moment of decision comes, the only thing that separates men is whether they are willing to stand on what they believe in. Hampton stood. O'Neal folded.

A Black man without responsibility is dangerous, not just to himself but to everyone around him. O'Neal's story is a warning: when you abandon your duties, the consequences are greater than you can imagine. Responsibility isn't just about protecting yourself; it's about protecting the future. A man who lives by this code understands that his life is not just his own. He carries the weight of his people with every decision he makes. There is no excuse for betrayal. A Black man either stands on his responsibilities or falls under the weight of his cowardice. O'Neal proved that choosing comfort over commitment comes with consequences. Hampton proved that living for something greater than yourself makes you immortal. In the end, one man is remembered as a revolutionary, and the other as a traitor. Every Black man must decide which legacy he wants to leave behind.

MADISON WASHINGTON — A Man Who Would Not Be Shackled

Fred Hampton's sacrifice in the pursuit of freedom, a young life snatched too early by forces within his own ranks, serves as a painful reminder of the treachery that can fester close to home. But Hampton's life and death are also symbolic of the relentless fight for Black liberation, a fight that stretches back to the very foundations of this country. For many, resistance was not just a political stance but a matter of life and death, something that would be passed down through generations of Black men who would continue to challenge their chains in ways that would reshape history. And one such man, Madison Washington, embodies that relentless resistance in a way that speaks directly to the heart of *"The 14 Codes."* Madison Washington's journey, much like Fred Hampton's, was not about waiting for change to come; it was about making that change happen, no matter the cost. Born into slavery, Washington carried with him the weight of an inhumane system, yet his spirit refused to bend. In 1841, he led the revolt aboard the Creole, a ship transporting enslaved people to the South, where he made the ultimate decision to take his fate into his own hands. Like Hampton, Washington had a deep sense of responsibility, not just to himself, but to his fellow enslaved people who had no power, no voice, and no hope until he stepped in.

His sacrifice was profound, not just in terms of his personal risk, but in his commitment to a cause much larger than his own life. When the mutiny took place, it wasn't just for his own freedom. Washington secured the freedom of 128 men, women, and children, showing that his responsibility extended far beyond his personal plight. The rebellion on the Creole was one of the most successful slave revolts in American history, not because it resulted in massive bloodshed or destruction, but because it showed that the chains of slavery could be broken through sheer will, courage, and action. Washington's refusal to be shackled speaks directly to the core of *"The 14 Codes."* A Black man who will die for his responsibilities doesn't just seek personal liberation; he seeks to liberate all those who suffer alongside him. But Washington's story doesn't end with the mutiny. After securing his own freedom, he didn't simply fade into safety; he went back. His commitment to his responsibility didn't allow him to walk away from the pain and suffering of his loved ones. His wife, Susan, remained in bondage, and despite having the chance to disappear into freedom, Washington chose to return to the United States in an attempt to bring her out of slavery. This wasn't just a personal mission; it was a demonstration of what it means to live by The 14 Codes, sacrificing everything, even safety, for the ones you love and for the greater good of your people.

To be a Black man who lives by this code is to recognize the weight of responsibility in every decision, no matter how dire. His mutiny aboard the Creole wasn't just a fight for freedom; it was an act of defiance against a system that dehumanized him, his people, and his culture. It wasn't about heroism or glory; it was about doing what needed to be done to ensure the survival and freedom of others. Just like Hampton, who died for his cause, Washington was willing to risk everything for a greater responsibility that stretched far beyond his own life. What's crucial to understand is that it's not about dying for a cause; it's about living for it every day, knowing that sacrifice is inherent to any real change. Washington's story isn't about the death he could have faced but about the way he lived in the face of that death, choosing to act when others might have chosen safety. It's easy to talk about revolution from the comfort of a home or a secure position; it's another thing entirely to put everything on the line with no guarantee of success. But that's the reality for men like Washington, and it's that kind of action that builds the foundation for future genera-tions to follow.

Madison Washington didn't let fear of death or reprisal stop him. His actions were rooted in a deep understanding of his responsibility, not just to himself but to everyone who was held in chains. His story teaches us that to truly live by the *"14 Codes"* requires a willingness to sacrifice not just for the cause, but for the people who need us. Washington's fight is still felt today, as his story becomes part of the larger tapestry of resistance that shows Black men how to stand tall, make their own way, and fight for the freedoms they and their families deserve. This is how history remem-bers men like him: through their actions, their sacri-fices, and their undying commitment to the principles they hold dear. As we transition from Hampton to Washington, we see two men who faced different battles but shared a common mission: to free their people, protect them, and live by a set of unshakable principles. Both men put their lives on the line, but it wasn't the act of dying that defined them; it was the living that followed their principles until the end. They understood the responsibility they had to their people and their communities, and that understanding drove them to act, no matter the cost. The story of Madison Washington, like the story of Fred Hampton, is a call to action, a reminder that true Black men don't run from their responsibilities, no matter the sacrifice.

This lesson of sacrifice is as relevant today as it was

in Washington's time. In a world where Black men are often reduced to stereotypes or ignored altogether, the true challenge is in recognizing the depth of our responsibility, not just to our families but to the community and the larger struggle for liberation. Washington's legacy is one of courage, resilience, and undying love for his people. He didn't just fight for his own freedom; he fought for everyone who was still shackled by the chains of oppression. His life teaches us that we must do the same, live by the *"14 Codes,"* make our sacrifices, and lead by example for those who come after us. Washington's sacrifice didn't just secure the freedom of those on the Creole; it set a precedent for future generations of Black men who would follow his example. The fight for freedom is long and filled with challenges, but those who are willing to die for their responsibilities are the ones who make history. In the fight for justice, we are all responsible for each other. Washington's life wasn't just a flash in the pan of history; it was a legacy that continues to fuel the flames of resistance to this day. We must all remember that responsibility to the people, to the cause, and to the future is what truly defines us as Black men living by the *"14 Codes."*

Sacrifice vs. Death: The Real Meaning of This Code

Dying for a cause is often seen as the ultimate act of sacrifice, but the real test lies in the willingness to live for that cause. Death isn't the goal—sacrifice is about giving up something of yourself for something greater. The true measure of a Black man is not in his willingness to lay down his life, but in his ability to live with purpose, responsibility, and conviction. It's about staying committed even when the odds are stacked against him, even when the fight seems endless. The ultimate sacrifice is being willing to suffer, struggle, and endure, whether for your people, your family, or your community. It's about giving everything for the greater good without needing a heroic ending. Nat Turner and Fred Hampton understood the risks of leading the struggle for Black liberation. They knew their lives were on the line daily, yet they moved forward with unwavering dedication. They didn't let the fear of death deter them; instead, they embraced the responsibility to lead, knowing it could cost them everything. Malcolm X, with his fiery rhetoric and clear call for Black pride and self-determination, understood the risk of martyrdom, but his sacrifice was in how he lived. Dr. King, a man of peace, chose nonviolence but knew his message would eventually lead to his death. Both men sacrificed their safety and comfort to ignite change and build a future for Black Americans.

Black men today carry on this tradition of sacrifice, though the battlefield has changed. It's no longer about marching on the front lines or standing against an armed enemy; it's about the daily sacrifice of choosing responsibility. Protecting your family, raising your children with values, and refusing to bow to societal pressures all require strength and sacrifice. Building a thriving community takes more than hard work; it demands discipline, time, and commitment to something bigger than personal gain. Every day, Black men are challenged to hold our heads high, take responsibility for our actions, and not shy away from the hard work it takes to uplift our people. These are the sacrifices that matter today, not as visible as dying for a cause, but just as significant. A Black man's true responsibility lies in how he influences those around him, how he shapes the lives of his children, and how he builds the legacy that will outlast him. Sacrifice is often quiet, uncelebrated, and invisible to the outside world. It's in the hours spent at work to provide for the family, in the choices made to protect one's own, and in the moments when a man holds his tongue for the greater good. These acts of sacrifice don't require a headline or a commemorative statue; they live in the everyday actions that lay solid foundations for future generations. A Black man who understands this is more powerful than any warrior who dies on a battlefield. His life and his sacrifice become a testament to the ongoing struggle for Black liberation and empowerment.

It's easy to romanticize death for a cause, especially when looking at revolutionaries like Nat Turner or Fred Hampton. But what makes a Black man truly powerful is his ability to live for his cause even when it's inconvenient or uncomfortable. The real test is how much you're willing to sacrifice for what you believe in, not how much you're willing to give up in death. In the long run, the leaders who leave a lasting impact aren't always the ones who died young or violently; they are the ones who laid down their lives in service to others, even when it meant living through hardship. The true purpose of this code is not to glorify death but to elevate the power of responsible living. Many Black men in history understood that their duty was not just to themselves but to the larger community. Whether it was the soldiers who fought in the Civil War, the men who marched with King in the Civil Rights Movement, or the Black Panthers who risked their lives daily to protect their neighborhoods, they knew that real sacrifice wasn't about dying in the spotlight. It was about making sure the next generation could live better. Today, Black men still face the challenge of choosing sacrifice over immediate gratification, and the impact of those choices is felt by every generation. The battle has shifted from the streets and battlefields to boardrooms, schools, and homes. *"Sacrifice"* is about ensuring that the work done today builds a foundation for tomorrow.

In many ways, the life of a Black man is shaped by the need to protect, provide, and preserve. Sacrificing for the greater good means understanding that personal comfort may sometimes take a backseat to the needs of the collective. Black men are called to be protectors, not just of their families but of the legacy their ancestors fought for. This responsibility doesn't disappear after a few struggles; it's a continuous commitment to the betterment of all. The power of this Code is in recognizing that a true Black man never stops sacrificing for the community, even if it goes unnoticed. His actions build the world that others will inherit, and that legacy is his greatest offering. Sacrifice isn't just about enduring hardships; it's about giving up your own desires and comforts for something greater than yourself. A Black man who embodies this Code understands that his life is intertwined with the lives of others. Every choice he makes impacts his community, his family, and his culture. This understanding drives him to make sacrifices that may seem small in the moment but have far-reaching effects on the generations that follow. He knows that his responsibility is not just to his own survival but to the collective advancement of Black people everywhere. His sacrifices create a ripple effect that influences not just his children but his community at large.

One of the hardest truths for many Black men to face is that the weight of their responsibility often goes unseen. Their sacrifices, whether in time, effort, or emotional labor, are often overlooked. But these sacrifices are the quiet engines that power communities forward. A man who sacrifices his time for his family, his resources for his neighborhood, and his energy for the advancement of his people understands the true meaning of responsibility. It's not about recognition; it's about ensuring that when the next generation looks back, they see that progress was made, not because someone died for the cause, but because someone lived for it. Ultimately, the idea of sacrifice extends far beyond the concept of death. A Black man who lives by this *"Code"* isn't simply waiting for a moment of martyrdom; he is actively shaping the world around him. His sacrifices may go unnoticed, but they are felt in the strength of his children, the health of his community, and the advancement of his people. The true meaning of this Code is that responsibility doesn't end with death; it begins with the courage to live for something greater than yourself. And that, in the end, is the most powerful act of sacrifice a Black man can offer.

"Sacrifice," not death, is what Code #8 is all about. It's about what you're willing to give up for a cause that's bigger than you, not whether or not you live through it. Men like Fred Hampton and Madison Washington understood the stakes; death was a very real possibility, but they didn't back down. They knew their fight for justice could cost them their lives, but their true sacrifice wasn't in dying; it was in dedicating every moment to the liberation of their people. They lived with purpose, and that purpose was much greater than themselves. Sacrifice isn't just about the past; it's something we see in the daily decisions Black men make today. Sacrifice is about standing firm in your

beliefs, no matter how crazy the world gets. It's about protecting your family when the odds are stacked against you and making sure your community survives the storm. It's about taking on responsibility, even when that responsibility feels like too much to bear. Black men who honor this Code do so not for recognition, but for the future, because they understand the weight of their choices. Sacrifice is in the grind, the daily grind. It's about taking responsibility for your actions and for others. Malcolm X's transformation from hustler to revolutionary was all about sacrifice. He gave up his past life, his comforts, and eventually his life because the cause of Black liberation demanded more than his words; it demanded his whole being. Martin Luther King Jr. did the same. He put his own safety on the line for the dream of a better world, knowing that the violence hanging over him was real. These men understood that sacrifice is constant. It's not about waiting for some heroic moment to define your legacy; it's about every small, selfless act adding up. Manhood demands action every day. A true Black man walks with purpose, knowing he's living for more than just himself. He makes the hard choices, even when others won't, regardless of what it costs him.

For a Black man to truly live this Code, he must see beyond his own desires. Too many men today get lost in temporary pleasures, fame, comfort, and distractions, but sacrifice is about ignoring the immediate for the long term. It's about focusing on what will last and what will build, protect, and uplift. Sacrifice means laying a foundation for the next generation, even if you don't get to enjoy the fruits of your labor. Real sacrifice often goes unnoticed. It's the man who wakes up every day to provide for his family, despite the struggles. It's the father who puts aside his dreams so his children can chase theirs. Sacrifice isn't always flashy, but it's always necessary. A Black man who honors this Code knows the true power is not in what he gets for himself, but in what he gives for others. Code #8 reminds us that a man's ultimate responsibility is to his people. A Black man's sacrifice strengthens his community and builds his legacy. This isn't about martyrdom; it's about living with the awareness that your actions have weight. A man who follows this Code sacrifices for those who can't protect themselves: his family, his brothers, his people. He doesn't seek recognition, but his work speaks for itself. The world may measure a man by what he owns or achieves, but that's a shallow way of looking at things. A Black man's real worth is in what he's willing to sacrifice for his community. The 14 Codes don't glorify death; they call for living in service to something greater. A true man steps up when others step back, knowing the price could be high, but still pushing forward because the cause is worth more than his life.

The real sacrifice is in staying true to your responsibilities, even when it's hard. For Black men, it's a daily struggle, resisting the forces that try to pull them off course. Whether it's oppression, personal hardships, or societal pressures, the temptation to give up is real. But Code #8 calls for resilience. It's the strength to say, *"I'll endure because this is bigger than me."* It's understanding that the sacrifices you make today will pay off tomorrow, even if you don't see it right now. Sacrifice isn't about waiting for the perfect moment to act; it's about stepping up when it counts. The 14 Codes urge Black men to own their actions, to be the ones who take on the weight, and to keep pushing forward, even when the road is long and the end isn't in sight. That's what it means to live for something bigger than yourself and carry the torch for those who will follow. Code #8 tells us a man's worth is in his ability to sacrifice for his responsibilities, no matter the cost. It's about the legacy you leave, not just for your kids, but for your people. Sometimes the hardest path is the one that's worth walking. Men like Nat Turner, Fred Hampton, and Madison Washington understood that the fight was bigger than them, and they were ready to pay the price. The real power in Code #8 comes from understanding that sacrifice is the path to growth. It's not about losing everything for no reason; it's about giving up something for something greater. Sacrifice is the means to a better future. It's the blood, sweat, and tears that create change. A Black man who lives by this Code is part of that change, constantly working to improve not just himself but the world around him.

CODE NO. 9

A BLACK MAN UNDERSTANDS THAT IF HIS WORD MEAN NOTHING, HE IS WORTHLESS

"*My balls and my word.*"

A MAN'S word is the foundation of his identity. If people can't trust what you say, you might as well stay silent. A Black man with no credibility is a man with no power, influence, or respect. History shows us that Black men who stood firm on their word became leaders, while those who talked just to talk were ignored or exposed. Your word is more than noise; it's a contract, a reflection of your character. If you say something, people should know you mean it. From the elders who led communities to the warriors who fought for freedom, their word defined their legacy. In the past, a man's word was tied to his actions. If he spoke, he backed it up. Today, that standard has slipped. Too many say one thing and do another. The respect a man once earned for standing on his word is fading, replaced by empty promises and fast talk. But a real Black man knows that his word is a weapon, and he uses it wisely. Too many Black men today are trapped in reckless *"jaw-jacking."* Social media has turned too many into talkers, men who run their mouths without taking real action. Everyone wants to sound deep, but too few actually live what they preach. It's not just about lying; it's about speaking with no purpose, no conviction, and no results. The more a man speaks without delivering, the less seriously people take him. Eventually, he becomes just another loud voice in the background. A man's word should have weight. When he speaks, people should stop and listen. Think about leaders like Malcolm X and Khalid Muhammad. When they spoke, it wasn't for attention or clout; it was because they had something real to say. Their words carried the weight of action behind them. That's the difference between a man whose words change the world and one who just entertains. A Black man who wants respect must make his word something people can trust.

The system fears men who stand by their word. A Black man who speaks with conviction and refuses to fold is a threat to the status quo. That's why real leaders get targeted, while sellouts are promoted. The ones who mean what they say and won't back down inspire change; they make enemies. But a man who talks just for a check is never a threat because everyone knows his word is worthless. The difference between power and irrelevance is whether people believe what you say. For a Black man, your word is your currency. When people hear your word, they should know they can cash it in. The moment your word becomes worthless, so do you. That's why it's better to speak less and let your actions do the talking. A man who talks too much without following through loses credibility fast. But a man who speaks with intention, backs it up, and stands on his word? That man commands respect wherever he goes. A man is only as strong as his word. If your actions don't match your words, nobody's going to take you seriously. People respect consistency. When they know a man stands by what he says, they trust him. But if you're just talking to be heard, running your mouth with no follow-through, you're just noise. Black men can't afford to be seen as unreliable; the world is already waiting for us to slip. Your word should be a signature. When you speak, it should hold weight.

Too many men today talk just to get a reaction. But words without action are worthless. If people hear you making promises, setting expectations, or talking tough, they're going to watch what you do next. And if you don't follow through, you've just shown them everything they need to know: you're not to be taken seriously. Once a man is labeled as all talk, it's almost impossible to shake that reputation. You lose respect, opportunities, and your chance at real leadership. A

Black man's word must be solid, because without it, he's just another empty voice. When a Black man speaks, people should listen because they know he means business. This doesn't mean talking loudly or trying to intimidate; it means speaking with purpose. The most powerful men in history didn't beg for attention; their reputation commanded it. They said what they meant, backed it up with action, and that's why they had influence. Every time you open your mouth, you're setting the tone for how people will perceive you. If your words don't mean anything, neither do you.

Trust is everything. Once you lose it, it's almost impossible to get back. People will forgive a lot of things, but they don't forget a liar or a fraud. If you make a commitment, follow through, whether it's to your family, friends, or yourself. A man's integrity is built brick by brick, and each time he keeps his word, he strengthens that foundation. But every lie, excuse, or broken promise chips away at it. Black men can't afford to be shaky with their word because, in a world that already doubts us, our credibility is everything. That's why a Black man must take pride in every word he speaks. If you say you'll do something, do it. If you stand for something, don't waver. If you give advice, make sure you're living by it. A man who talks just to hear himself speak is useless. But a man whose words have meaning will always be respected. Your word is your reputation. Once that's damaged, so is your ability to lead. Black men don't get the luxury of being careless with their credibility. The men who built legacies weren't just great speakers; they were great doers. Every man who ever led a movement, built a business, or changed the world started with his word. The difference between those who succeed and those who fade into the background is whether people believe in what they say. If your words don't carry weight, you have no power. *"If your words don't inspire trust, you have no influence. And if your words don't mean anything, neither do you."*

The Power of a Man's Word

Khalid Muhammad wasn't just a speaker; he was a force of nature. He didn't sugarcoat, he didn't backtrack, and he damn sure didn't apologize. When he spoke, you felt it in your chest because every word came from a place of conviction. He wasn't just talking for the sake of talking; he was giving Black people the fire they needed to wake up and move with purpose. That's what made him dangerous. That's why the system had to shut him down. But even after they tried, his words still live on because they weren't just words; they were a blueprint for action. Born in Houston, Texas, in 1948, Khalid Muhammad was raised in an era when Black people were still fighting for basic human rights. He joined the Nation of Islam in the 1970s, drawn to the teachings of Elijah Muhammad and the power of discipline, self-reliance, and Black unity. Rising through the ranks, he became the National Spokesman for the NOI under Minister Louis Farrakhan. His speeches were fiery, direct, and uncompromising, making him one of the most electrifying voices in the movement. But unlike many so-called *"leaders,"* Khalid wasn't just interested in talking; he wanted real action. And that's where the problem started.

Khalid Muhammad's words weren't just about making people feel good; they were designed to make people do something. He didn't believe in begging the government or looking for a seat at the table; he was about Black self-determination by any means necessary. His speeches reflected that, calling out *"white supremacy,"* *"corrupt Black leadership,"* and anyone standing in the way of true Black liberation. He spoke with a level of fearlessness that made a lot of people uncomfortable, and that's how you know he was saying something real. The system doesn't go after men who are just talking; they go after men who inspire action. That's exactly why the FBI had him on their radar. The U.S. government has always targeted Black men who use their words to challenge the status quo. Huey P. Newton, Malcolm X, Martin Luther King Jr.—every one of them was watched, infiltrated, and neutralized when they became too powerful. Khalid was no different. His 1993 speech at Kean College, where he went all the way in on white supremacy, Jewish influence, and Black self-defense, sent shockwaves through the country. The media labeled him a dangerous radical, and under pressure, Louis Farrakhan expelled him from the Nation of Islam. But here's the difference between Khalid Muhammad and the frauds: he didn't change his stance. Most men, when stripped of their title and their platform, fold. They apologize, water down their message, or disappear altogether. Khalid Muhammad didn't do any of that. He stood ten toes down on everything he said. Instead of backing off, he doubled down, taking his fight for Black liberation to the streets by leading the New Black Panther Party. He understood that his mission was bigger than any organization. He didn't need the NOI's backing to keep speaking the truth. And because he never wavered, his influence grew instead of disappearing.

That's what real integrity looks like. That's what it means for a Black man's word to mean something. Too many so-called leaders shift their message depending on the crowd, the paycheck, or the political climate. Not Khalid. His message stayed consistent, and people trusted him for that. He wasn't looking to be liked; he was looking to wake people up. And because he never strayed from his principles, his words carried more power than those coming from politicians, preachers, and activists who played both sides. Khalid Muhammad understood that words have consequences, and he was willing to face them. He took the heat, the media slander, and even assassination attempts; yet he never backed down. He spoke in a way that commanded respect, not because he demanded it, but because his words carried weight. He wasn't just talking to entertain or to go viral; his words were meant to shift the mindset of Black people. And that's why the system feared him. They knew that a Black man who stands by his word is a Black man they can't control.

Even in death, Khalid Muhammad's words still shake the room. His speeches, which can still be found online, sound just as relevant today as they did in the 1990s. And that's because truth doesn't expire. A real man's words aren't based on trends, popularity, or money; they're based on principles. That's the difference between a man who talks for a check and a man who speaks for liberation. Khalid Muhammad's words weren't meant to gain him favor in politics or media circles; they were meant to inspire Black power, Black self-sufficiency, and Black unity. When a Black man speaks, people should feel it. They should know he means exactly what he says and is willing to stand on it no matter what. That's the lesson Khalid Muhammad left behind. His words weren't cheap, and neither should ours be. Too many Black men today talk just to be heard, gossip for entertainment, or lie to keep people comfortable. That's weak. If your word means nothing, you are nothing. A man is only as strong as his ability to stand by what he says.

This is where many so-called Black leaders fail. Instead of standing firm, they adjust their message to keep getting invited to the table. They say whatever needs to be said to avoid backlash, to keep their pockets fat, or to stay in good graces with white-owned media. That's why nobody trusts them. That's why they have followers but not believers. A Black man's word should be unshakable. If he says something, it should mean something. And if he can't live by what he says, he shouldn't be speaking at all. Khalid Muhammad represents the standard. He showed us what it looks like when a Black man speaks with authority, integrity, and fearlessness. His words carried weight because he lived by them. That's what makes a man different from a talking head. His words didn't just sound good; they meant something. And when a Black man's words mean something, he becomes a force that no system can break.

AL SHARPTON: The Price of a Bought Tongue

Khalid Muhammad was a man whose words carried weight. When he spoke, people listened, not because he entertained them, but because they knew he meant every syllable. His words had force behind them, and he stood by them, no matter the cost. That's why the system feared him. He wasn't just talking; he was moving minds, igniting action, and putting power back in the hands of Black men. But where Khalid was a threat, there were always those willing to play the system's game. Enter Al Sharpton, a man who talks a lot but stands on nothing. A man whose words are nothing more than tools for his own advancement. Al Sharpton built his name as a so-called activist, preacher, and community leader, but his track record tells a different story. He started in the church, then moved into civil rights, attaching himself to high-profile cases and controversies whenever the cameras were rolling. At first glance, he appeared to be fighting for Black people, but a closer look reveals a man who mastered the art of self-promotion. Every movement he aligned with somehow ended up benefiting him more than the people he claimed to represent. Unlike Khalid Muhammad, whose words inspired real action, Sharpton's words were always about the next hustle.

The biggest problem with Al Sharpton is that he has no core values. He has spent decades shifting positions whenever it benefits him. One minute, he's radical; the next, he's shaking hands with politicians who do nothing for Black people. He speaks with passion, but that passion is only for whatever lines his pockets. Unlike true leaders, who remain consistent in their mission, Sharpton bends to whatever narrative is popular. This isn't leadership; it's performance. And for those paying attention, it's clear that his loyalty has always been for sale. One of the most damning truths about Sharpton is his history as an FBI informant. Documents confirm that he worked with the feds, feeding them information. While Khalid Muhammad was targeted by the government for being a threat, Sharpton was working with the very people destroying

Black movements. That alone tells you everything you need to know. He wasn't fighting for Black liberation; he was securing his own position by selling out others. His words might sound militant at times, but in reality, he has always been an agent of the system.

For a man who claims to fight against white supremacy, Sharpton has spent a lot of time cozying up to white politicians and corporate interests. His National Action Network, supposedly an organization for justice, has been exposed for taking money from major corporations with questionable ethics. He talks about holding America accountable, but he has never held himself accountable for the ways he has profited off Black pain. His brand of activism isn't about change; it's about keeping himself relevant. And as long as he remains useful to the establishment, he will always have a platform. When comparing Khalid Muhammad to Al Sharpton, the difference is clear. One was a man of conviction, and the other is a man of convenience. Khalid spoke and lived his truth, refusing to back down even when it cost him everything. Sharpton, on the other hand, speaks whatever is necessary to stay in the room. He wants proximity to power, not revolution. That's why the system never silenced him: because he was never a real threat to begin with. He is a controlled voice, one that gives the illusion of resistance while maintaining the status quo.

Black men need to recognize the game being played. Sharpton's career is a blueprint for how to exploit the struggle rather than fight for it. He has spent decades making speeches, marching for cameras, and collecting checks while the conditions of Black America remain the same. His presence gives people the illusion that something is being done when, in reality, he ensures that nothing ever changes. Leaders like Khalid Muhammad were silenced because they were dangerous. Sharpton has been allowed to operate for decades because he is not. There is a reason why the mainstream media gives Sharpton a platform while silencing true revolutionaries. He is safe. He provides just enough fiery rhetoric to keep people entertained but never enough to truly challenge the system. The establishment knows it can trust him to play his role. Meanwhile, the real threats, the ones who tell Black men to stand on their own two feet, organize, and take power, are either discredited or removed. This is not by accident. The system needs Sharpton more than he needs it.

For Black men, the lesson is clear: your word must mean something. If people can't trust what you say, you are worthless. Sharpton has made a career of saying one thing and doing another, proving that his word holds no real value. A real man's words should carry weight, should be backed by action, and should stand firm regardless of money, fame, or pressure. This is why Khalid Muhammad will be remembered as a warrior, while Sharpton will be remembered as a hustler. Sharpton's legacy is not one of strength but of survival at any cost. He survived by making himself useful to those in power, even if it meant compromising the very people he claimed to fight for. And the worst part? Many Black people still fall for it. They hear his words but ignore his actions. They mistake volume for substance and longevity for credibility. But a long career of talking means nothing if it has not produced results.

Black men must stop being fooled by fancy speeches and well-rehearsed talking points. A man's power isn't in how loud he talks but in how well his actions back his words. That's why the system feared Khalid Muhammad but embraced Al Sharpton. One was a leader; the other a puppet. One stood on principle; the other chased profit. A Black MAN understands that his word is everything. If you say it, stand on it. If you don't mean it, don't say it. The world has no respect for men who talk big but fail to deliver. Sharpton has spent a lifetime proving that words without integrity are just noise. A real Black MAN knows that his speech must be backed by action, or else he's no better than a fraud selling dreams. A Black man's word should be like a contract: firm, unshakable, and non-negotiable. Too many men today talk just to hear themselves speak, throwing words around without weight. That kind of reckless talking weakens your presence and makes you look like a clown. If your word carries no weight, neither do you. Speak with clarity, directness, and purpose. People respect men who mean what they say and don't back down under pressure. The moment you start backpedaling, doubting yourself, or letting outsiders shake you, your credibility drops. Your words should be rooted in truth, not in feelings or emotions. Speaking with conviction isn't about being loud; it's about being certain. If you believe what you say, people will feel it.

There's a difference between talking to be heard and talking to be understood. Too many men run their mouths to sound important. That's a waste of breath. If you speak, make sure it has substance. People should walk away from your words with clarity, not confusion. When a Black man speaks, his words should hit like a hammer, not a feather. It's not about attention; it's about respect. Say it, mean it, and be ready to back it up. Empty words and broken promises will ruin a man faster than any outside enemy. Once people see that your words mean nothing, they will tune you out forever. A Black man must control his mouth. Loose lips don't just sink ships; they sink reputations, relationships, and opportunities. Gossiping, lying, or running your mouth about things you don't understand makes you look weak and unreliable. No one respects a man who talks too much but says too little of value. Silence is often more powerful than meaningless chatter. Gossip is weak because it's feminine behavior; real men focus on their own business, not someone else's. A strong Black man moves with integrity and never wastes words for cheap entertainment.

A wise man knows his words can build or destroy. What you say can start wars, mend relationships, or change lives. Every great leader, warrior, and strategist knew the power of controlling his tongue. Even in heated moments, a disciplined man speaks with purpose, not impulse. Black men must stop throwing words around like they have no consequences. Your reputation is tied to how well you control your mouth. If people associate your name with lies, exaggerations, or nonsense, it won't matter how smart, skilled, or talented you are. A man with a weak word is a man without respect. Your presence should command attention, but when you do speak, it should be worth listening to. Every time you open your mouth, you're either strengthening or weakening your reputation. In the past, a Black man's word was his bond. If he said something, he followed through. That was a matter of survival. That sense of honor has been lost in an era where men say anything for clout, clicks, or validation. It's time to bring back the power of a man's word. Being intentional with your words doesn't mean being silent; it means speaking with purpose. Some men stay quiet out of fear, but that's not strength either. Speak when necessary, listen when needed, and never waste words. A man who talks too much is ignored, but a man who speaks only when needed is respected. Choose your words like a warrior chooses his weapons.

The world is full of men who talk big but can't back it up. They lie, exaggerate, and flip-flop depending on who's listening. That's cowardice, not leadership. Black men should aim to be men whose words are trusted, whether in business, relationships, or the community. When a man's word means something, he means something. And when he means something, his presence carries power. A Black man's word is his signature; it should be strong, clear, and undeniable. If you don't mean it, don't say it. If you say it, stand on it. Let your words reflect your principles, strength, and integrity. Speak with conviction, cut out the nonsense, and make sure people take you seriously. If you want to be respected as a man, your word must mean something. In a world full of deception, a Black man's word should be a symbol of honor. If people can't trust what you say, you have no foundation, no standing, no power. A man's credibility is built on consistency, saying what he means and meaning what he says. If his words don't match his actions, he's just another empty voice. A real Black man doesn't just talk; his words move people, shift minds, and command respect. Anything less makes him weak, forgettable, and useless.

Khalid Muhammad is the perfect example of a man who stood by his word. When he spoke, people listened, not because he was loud, but because he was real. He didn't sugarcoat or pander; his words came from conviction and truth. The system feared him because he wasn't just running his mouth; he was shaping minds and inspiring action. He put himself on the line for what he believed, knowing the risks. That's why his words still carry weight long after his passing. Contrast that with Al Sharpton, a man who says whatever benefits him at the moment. He built a career off loud talking, empty promises, and playing both sides. He's been caught lying, fabricating stories, and working against the same people he claims to defend. He doesn't speak to empower; he speaks to stay relevant. His words have made him rich, but they've never made him a leader. A Black man's word should never be for sale. A man who will say anything for a check is a liability to his people. Real leaders like Khalid Muhammad were feared because they couldn't be bought. Meanwhile, men like Sharpton get TV deals and government access because their words serve the agenda. One man's words built warriors; the other's created confusion. A Black man must decide whether his words will be a weapon or a weakness.

When a Black man speaks, his actions should match his words. His life should be proof of his message. Khalid Muhammad's speeches weren't just words; they were a call to arms, backed by a man who lived what he preached. On the other hand, Sharpton talks *"revolution"* while shaking hands with the same people he claims to fight. The truth is in the results. A Black man's word is his power. If people trust your word, they will follow you, respect you, and stand with you. If your word is worthless, so are you. And once a man loses credibility, he becomes a joke, a liability, and a puppet for those who benefit from his weakness. The choice is simple: be a man whose words carry weight, or be another empty voice in the wind. Say what you mean. Mean what you say. Stand on it. Anything less, and you're just another talker, and the world already has enough of those.

BROTHERHOOD

No man is an island, and no king rules alone. Brotherhood is about aligning yourself with strong, disciplined men who share your values, vision, and drive. The company you keep reflects the kind of man you are; iron sharpens iron, and real men build together. A solid brotherhood holds each other accountable, protects one another, and ensures that no man in the circle moves without strategy and purpose. If your circle isn't making you sharper, you need a new one.

CODE NO. 10

A BLACK MAN GIVES REASONS, NOT EXCUSES

A reason and an excuse might sound similar, but they're not the same. A reason is based on reality and comes with a plan of action, while an excuse is just empty words meant to dodge responsibility. A real man doesn't waste time explaining why something didn't happen; he figures out how to make it happen. Excuses are what weak men use when they want sympathy instead of results. The difference between a man and a male is that a man takes control of his situation, while a male sits around complaining about it. The world doesn't care about your excuses, and nobody respects a grown man who begs for understanding instead of commanding respect. A man explains his circumstances, but he doesn't stop there; he follows up with a solution. If you're broke, don't just talk about how the system is unfair; go learn a skill, start a business, or work harder. If you're out of shape, don't cry about genetics; hit the gym, fix your diet, and be disciplined. Men don't get the luxury of whining because nobody is coming to save us. The moment you start making excuses, you strip yourself of power. A Black MAN doesn't accept being a victim because a victim has no control. Either you find a way, or you accept failure; there's no in-between. An excuse is nothing more than a plea for sympathy, and no one respects a man who begs for pity. The moment you start explaining why you couldn't do something, you sound like a child. *"I couldn't because of this... I would have, but that happened..."* Nobody cares. The only thing that matters is what you did! Life will always throw obstacles at you, but a real man adjusts and moves forward. Excuses don't change reality; they just make you look weak. The more you make them, the more you train yourself to accept failure instead of overcoming it. A Black MAN holds himself accountable at all times. If you fail, you take the hit and figure out what's next. You don't cry about why it happened; you fix it and make sure it doesn't happen again. There's honor in trying and failing; there's no honor in making excuses. This is why men who make excuses are never taken seriously, because their word means nothing. If your actions don't back up your words, then you might as well not speak at all. A man's reputation is built on what he does, not on what he says he meant to do.

Excuses have been used to justify weakness for too long. Too many Black men have been conditioned to think that complaining about their struggles is the same as overcoming them. Talking about oppression isn't the same as building power. Complaining about the system doesn't put money in your pocket or food on your table. Making excuses doesn't change the reality that life rewards results, not explanations. The most respected Black men in history didn't have fewer struggles; they just refused to let those struggles define them. They found a way. The moment you stop making excuses, you take back control of your life. Nobody respects a man who asks for sympathy because men are meant to lead, not beg. When you eliminate excuses, you force yourself to focus on action, and action is what separates men from boys. If you're not where you want to be in life, don't explain it; change it. A Black MAN doesn't ask for permission to be great. He takes what's his, puts in the work, and makes sure his results speak for themselves. That's what separates a MAN from a male. When a man stops making excuses, he steps into his true power. A Black man's word must be backed by action. If you say you want to be successful but never take the necessary steps, your words mean nothing. If you promise to take care of your family but always have an excuse for why you can't, you have failed as a man. Integrity means standing on your commitments, and a man filled with excuses will always be unreliable.

Women and children don't follow men who whine; they follow men who provide solutions. This is why many Black men struggle with leadership in relationships and the community. Too many have become comfortable explaining why they can't do something instead of finding a way to get it done. Women naturally respect men who handle business without complaint. The moment a man starts seeking sympathy instead of commanding respect, he loses his masculine presence. A Black MAN understands that life does not care about excuses. If you don't work, you don't eat. If you don't build, you will remain powerless. If you don't strategize, you will remain a pawn in someone else's game. The world rewards those who produce, not those who explain why they couldn't. Black men who make excuses spend years in the same position, watching other men pass them by simply because those men refused to let obstacles stop them. The solution is simple: kill the excuses. The only thing that matters is the results. If a problem exists, find a way around it. If one door is locked, build your own door. If you fail, adjust and try again. A man who refuses to make excuses is a man who will always find a way to succeed. The discipline of rejecting excuses forces a man to evolve, sharpen his skills, and create opportunities where none existed before. That is how power is built. A Black MAN does not waste time explaining why he couldn't; he focuses on what he will do next. Excuses are the language of men who have accepted their own defeat. Reasons, backed by action, are the foundation of true power. If you want to be respected, stop explaining why and start proving how.

We, as Black men, have become too comfortable with making excuses instead of finding solutions. Every time failure happens, there's always something or someone to blame: racism, the system, women, or lack of opportunities. While those things might be real obstacles, sitting around complaining about them doesn't change anything. The world doesn't care about a man's excuses; it only respects results. Too many Black men spend time justifying their shortcomings instead of figuring out how to push through. A Black MAN doesn't cry about the problem; he finds a way to beat it. The biggest issue is that whining has become normal. Social media is filled with Black men talking about how unfair life is, looking for sympathy instead of strategy. Every day, there's a new conversation about how Black men are the most disrespected, overlooked, and underappreciated. That may be true, but repeating it like a broken record does nothing. Instead of talking, men need to start moving, planning, and executing. *"Whining"* is feminine energy; solutions are masculine energy. The world doesn't move for weak men; it moves for men who take action. Black men have been conditioned to see themselves as victims, and too many have accepted that role. The government, media, and even some community leaders have pushed the idea that Black men are helpless without outside help. This has created a generation of men waiting for someone to save them instead of becoming their own saviors. No real man sits around hoping the world changes in his favor. He forces it to respect him through his work, discipline, and execution. Black men will never be taken seriously if they keep begging for recognition instead of earning it. No one respects a man who expects sympathy. In every other culture, men are measured by what they build, not by how much they struggle. No woman, child, or community wants to follow a man who constantly complains about his circumstances. Leadership isn't about who suffered the most; it's about who overcame the most. Every successful Black man in history faced obstacles, but they didn't let that stop them. A Black MAN either finds a way or makes one. Anything else is just weakness in disguise.

Blaming racism, the system, or Black women doesn't change the situation. Every generation before us faced some form of oppression, but they still built, fought, and demanded respect. The difference today is that too many Black men think talking about the problem is the same as solving it. It's not. Complaints without action are just noise. If a Black man wants to change his life, he needs a plan, not a pity party. The world only values the man who produces, not the one who complains about why he can't. Black men must let go of excuses and embrace accountability. The truth is, nobody cares about our struggles the way we think they do. The only thing that matters is whether we win or lose. If we want respect, power, and success, we have to take it; nobody is going to give it to us. That starts with dropping the victim's mindset and adopting a warrior's mentality. No more complaining, no more waiting, no more excuses. A Black MAN doesn't beg for respect; he commands it through his actions. Black men have become too comfortable using excuses as a shield against accountability. Instead of strategizing and pushing forward, too many justify their failures with reasons that hold no weight. Yes, racism exists, and the system is designed to make things harder, but history proves that excuses don't build legacies; action does. Our ancestors faced worse and still found ways to carve out success, whether through business, leadership, or community building. They understood that obstacles were part of the journey, not the reason to stop walking. A Black MAN doesn't sit in his struggle; he finds a way out. Blaming racism without a plan to counter it is just a dressed-up excuse. The system is real, but so is the power of adaptation, strategy, and discipline. If the rules are rigged, then the only logical response is to learn the game and play it to win. Too many Black men spend more time pointing out the problem than executing solutions. Nobody is coming to save us, and complaining won't change the outcome. The only thing that commands respect is results, and results don't come from excuses; they come from work.

Society has created a narrative that Black men are perpetual victims, and too many have embraced that identity. The moment you see yourself as powerless, you have already lost. The media, politicians, and even some within our own community push the idea that Black men can't win without outside help. That lie has stripped men of their natural instinct to lead, fight, and conquer. A man who waits for sympathy instead of demanding respect will always be at the mercy of someone else's handouts. That's not power; that's dependency. A grown man whining about his struggles is no different from a child throwing a tantrum. Life is unfair to everyone, but men are judged by how they respond, not by what they endure. Struggle is not unique to Black men; what's unique is how we've been conditioned to glorify suffering instead of overcoming it. When other groups face hardship, they mobilize, strategize, and push through. Too many Black men, instead of adapting, look for comfort in the idea that failure was inevitable. That mindset is poison to progress and a death sentence to ambition. The hard truth is that no one respects a man who constantly looks for pity. Women don't respect it, other men don't respect it, and society doesn't respect it. The world only moves for those who move with purpose. You can either be a man who finds a way or one who finds an excuse; there is no in-between. The Black men who command respect are the ones who refuse to accept defeat, no matter the circumstances. The ones who wait for sympathy will be left behind, talking about what could have been while real men are out there making things happen. A Black MAN either gets it done or he doesn't; there is no space for excuses. Respect is earned through action, not words. The ones who embrace struggle as fuel will always outshine those who see it as a reason to quit. Black men must reject the comfort of excuses and embrace the challenge of proving themselves through results. Every moment spent complaining is a moment that could have been spent building. A Black MAN does not justify failure; he finds a way to win.

Black men of the past didn't have the luxury of making excuses. They faced laws designed to keep them at the bottom, but they still built businesses, educated themselves, and protected their communities. Whether it was Black Wall Street, the Pullman Porters, or men like Frederick Douglass, they understood that excuses wouldn't change their condition; only action would. These men didn't cry about the system; they maneuvered within it, found ways to win, and forced the world to acknowledge them. Even under the harshest conditions, they commanded respect through their resilience. They knew that a man who whines is a man who gets ignored. Today, too many Black men use oppression as a crutch instead of a challenge to overcome. The system is still real, but complaining about it doesn't fix anything. Instead of building their own, too many wait for opportunities to be handed to them. Instead of taking control of their families and communities, they blame women for their problems. The world doesn't respect men who sit around crying about what they don't have. A Black MAN either makes a way or finds a way, but he never sits still waiting for a hand-out. The moment a man starts making excuses, he gives the world permission to dismiss him. Nobody respects a grown man who expects sympathy instead of solutions. The same society that claims to care about Black men will mock them the moment they start begging. Black men are expected to be strong, yet many have embraced weakness and victimhood as an identity. The more excuses a man makes, the less he's taken seriously. A Black MAN stands on his ability to handle business no matter the odds. Nobody wants to hear about what held you back, only what you did to move forward. History honors the men who built despite the barriers, not the ones who complained about them. You either figure it out, or you get left behind. A man's value is measured by what he overcomes, not by what he blames. The world isn't looking for Black men to succeed; it's waiting for them to fail. Excuses give them the justification they need to write you off. The only way to fight back is through results. Black men must kill the excuse-making and get back to producing, building, and leading. If you're not doing that, you're just another lost voice in the crowd.

Excuses are the language of the weak. A Black MAN does not waste time explaining why he couldn't get something done; he gets it done! Life will always give you obstacles, but a MAN finds a way through them.

When you rely on excuses, you're telling the world you're powerless, and a powerless man commands no respect. The moment a Black MAN allows excuses to become his norm, he begins his descent into irrelevance. Society does not respect a man who begs for understanding instead of demanding results. Every day, Black men are faced with challenges that test their resolve. The world will not slow down for our struggles, nor will it wait for us to get ourselves together. While others may complain about unfair conditions, a MAN adapts and strategizes. A Black MAN understands that excuses are just dressed-up justifications for failure. The only thing that moves a man forward is action, not explanation. When you stand on results, nobody questions your circumstances because they see your work. This modern era has made it easy for men to seek sympathy instead of solutions. Social media is filled with men crying about what they didn't have growing up, how society is unfair, and why they can't get ahead. But talking about problems without presenting solutions is just whining. A Black MAN does not engage in public displays of self-pity. The world does not owe him understanding; it owes him nothing. A man earns his respect through what he builds, not through what he complains about. History has shown that Black men who took action left their mark, while those who made excuses were forgotten. The men who fought for freedom, built businesses, and led movements did not have it easy, but they made it happen. They didn't have social media to complain about racism or make viral posts about struggle; they focused on solutions. The difference between a leader and a follower is the ability to turn struggle into strategy. A MAN is judged by what he overcomes, not by what he suffers through.

A Black man's word must mean something, or he is just another talker. If he says he's going to do something, he must follow through. This is why men of action are always respected. Their reputation precedes them because their word is backed by proof. Too many Black men have fallen into the trap of making promises they don't keep, then blaming circumstances when they fail. A MAN does not look for pity; he looks for ways to ensure he never has to explain why he didn't deliver. Excuses are addictive because they provide temporary comfort. They allow a man to feel justified in his shortcomings without requiring him to change. But comfort is the enemy of progress. A Black MAN understands that every excuse he makes weakens his position in the world. If you keep finding reasons why you can't do something, you are programming yourself to fail. A MAN holds himself accountable first, even before the world does. That's what separates him from the rest. Black men must reject the culture of explaining away failure and embrace a culture of execution. We cannot afford to be seen as men who are full of words but empty in results. Every time a man tries to justify his lack of progress, he lowers his own value. A MAN is not defined by how well he can explain his failures but by how effectively he corrects them. A warrior does not tell you why he lost the battle; he prepares for the next one and ensures victory. We live in an age where too many men seek validation through their struggles instead of their triumphs. The more you talk about how hard life is, the more people see you as incapable. Black men are not designed to be seen as victims. The moment you start looking for sympathy, you start losing the respect of both men and women. A Black MAN ensures that when he speaks, people listen, not out of pity, but out of recognition for what he has accomplished.

A Black man's presence should command respect without the need for explanations. His results should speak for themselves. If a Black MAN is respected, it is because he has built something tangible: his career, his family, his legacy. He does not sit around waiting for someone to acknowledge his hardships. The only thing that matters in this world is what a man produces. Everything else is just noise. A Black MAN does not ask for fairness; he creates his own opportunities. He does not expect life to be easy, nor does he spend time complaining when it isn't. He understands that every moment spent making excuses is a moment wasted. Strength is built through hardship, and the strongest men are those who refuse to be defined by struggle. A MAN takes the hand he's dealt and plays it to win, no matter what. If Black men want respect, they must stop seeking excuses and start seeking results. Nobody cares why you couldn't do something; they only care about what you did. If you want to be a leader, start by eliminating every excuse from your vocabulary. Focus on solutions, and let your actions do the talking. Words without action are meaningless. A Black man's legacy is built on what he did, not what he could have done if circumstances were different. A MAN either gets it done, or he doesn't. There is no in-between. The world only remembers those who built something worth remembering. If you want your name to carry weight, make sure it is associated with results, not excuses. Black men must reclaim their image by becoming men of execution. When a Black MAN speaks, his words must carry weight because they are always backed by action.

CODE NO. 11

A BLACK MAN IS "PROACTIVE," NOT REACTIVE

Black men have been conditioned to move only when we're forced, never when it's time. We've been trained to wait until we're under attack before we respond; preparation is a luxury instead of a necessity. But power doesn't work like that. White supremacy doesn't wait; it moves first, plans ahead, and stays ten steps in front. The system strategizes, executes, and leaves Black men scrambling to react. By the time we recognize the setup, we're already in the trap. That's why every step forward has been met with an even harder pushback, because we weren't ready for the counterpunch. Every Black movement that gained traction was met with a calculated response designed to wipe out progress before it could solidify. The Harlem Renaissance built culture and economic power; then the Great Depression and financial sabotage crushed it. The Civil Rights Movement won legal victories, but mass incarceration and redlining made sure those wins didn't lead to real independence. Even today, Black athletes and entertainers reach the top, but real ownership and power remain out of reach. The system stays ahead because it doesn't move off emotions; it moves off long-term strategy. A Black MAN can't afford to live life on defense. If you're always reacting, you're never leading. Power belongs to those who make the first move, not the ones who waste their lives responding. That's why Code #11 exists, because playing defense won't win the game. The difference between a survivor and a conqueror is simple: one reacts to the storm, the other builds before it comes. A Black MAN doesn't wait for the flood; he strengthens his foundation before the first drop of rain.

Look at history. Every major fight we've had was a response to oppression, not a proactive move for power. We didn't fight slavery before the shackles were on—we reacted after generations of brutality. The Civil Rights Movement didn't start until segregation was already suffocating us. Even now, Black communities don't mobilize until we're already in crisis. By the time we stand up, the system already has its next move lined up. That's why every win is temporary, because we're not thinking ahead. Every time there's a police killing, we march, we protest, we demand justice, then go back to business as usual. Meanwhile, the system is already passing new laws and adjusting its tactics to keep the oppression going. It doesn't react to us; it plans ahead so that whatever we do is already accounted for. That's why nothing ever truly changes. Real power isn't in reaction; it's in setting the tone. A Black MAN doesn't wait for the enemy to strike first. He studies, prepares, and ensures he's never caught slipping. The moment you're forced to react, you've already lost control. That's the difference between being a pawn and being the one moving the pieces. Power is about anticipation, not reaction. And until Black men master that, the cycle will keep repeating. The biggest advantage white supremacy has isn't just money or resources; it's long-term thinking. The system plans decades ahead while too many Black men can't see past the next crisis. Every attack against us was plotted long before we saw it coming. The *"War on Drugs"* wasn't an accident; it was a strategy to dismantle Black families. Gentrification wasn't random; it was planned years in advance. By the time we realize what's happening, the damage is already done. Meanwhile, too many of us move off emotion instead of strategy. We get mad, we react, we protest, but we don't plan. White supremacy isn't emotional; it's cold, calculated, and precise. That's why it wins. The system has mastered control while we're still playing catch-up. If we don't shift from reaction to preparation, we'll keep getting played.

Code #11 is about breaking that pattern. A Black MAN doesn't let emotions dictate his actions; he moves with purpose. He doesn't wait for an attack; he anticipates and counters before it happens. He stays ahead, so when the game shifts, he's already in position. The system is planning for the next 50 years, so should we. Suga Free said it best: *"Stay ready, and you ain't gotta get ready."* That's the mindset every Black MAN needs. If you're always prepared, nothing can catch you off guard. But for too long, we've been conditioned to be reactive. White supremacy has made sure we stay distracted, emotional, and unprepared, so we're never in control. And every time we think we've gained ground, the system reminds us who's really running the show. From Reconstruction to the Civil Rights era, from Black Wall Street to the War on Drugs, the pattern has been the same: reaction instead of action. It's time to study those lessons and change the approach.

From the moment Black people were kidnapped and enslaved, we were forced into a reactionary position. Every move was dictated by the oppressor, and every breath was controlled by violence. Our names, our culture, and our sense of self were stripped away, leaving us with nothing but survival mode. The plantation was a battlefield where we had no weapons, no time to plan, and no way to organize without risking death. Any attempt to fight back was met with whippings, mutilation, lynching, and family members being sold away. White supremacy didn't just enslave Black bodies; it conditioned generations to focus on survival instead of strategy. Revolts happened, but they were crushed before they could gain momentum. The Haitian Revolution showed that enslaved people could overthrow their oppressors, but in the U.S., every rebellion, from Nat Turner to the Stono Rebellion, was met with overwhelming force. White fear of Black resistance led to laws banning us from gathering, reading, or even defending ourselves. The system ensured that Black reaction was always outmatched by white retaliation. The ones who truly broke free did so by moving strategically, like Harriet Tubman and the Underground Railroad, acting before desperation set in. But for most, reacting to suffering was all they knew.

This cycle isn't an accident; it's by design. White supremacy keeps Black people in reaction mode, so we're always responding to oppression instead of preventing it. But history has also shown that when Black men recognize this pattern and take proactive steps, they become the biggest threat to the system. Huey Newton and Bobby Seale understood this when they created the Black Panther Party. Instead of waiting for police brutality to continue unchecked, they armed themselves with knowledge, weapons, and strategy. They made it clear that Black people would no longer be passive victims. The Panthers didn't just fight back against violence; they built programs that addressed food insecurity, education, and healthcare, creating an independent system that strengthened the Black community. Their movement was proof that real power comes from preparation, organization, and discipline. Every time Black people built something valuable, white supremacy destroyed it before they could protect it. Tulsa's Black Wall Street wasn't just about jealousy; it was a preemptive strike to make sure Black people never reached the point of controlling their own destiny. The massacre in Rosewood and the destruction of thriving Black communities in East St. Louis and Wilmington were all part of the same strategy. The system never lets Black success stand unchallenged.

The most dangerous part of reactionary thinking is assuming that the system will play fair. Black communities believed that hard work and following the rules would protect them, but white supremacy moves the goalposts whenever we get too close to real power. Civil rights victories didn't end the fight; they triggered mass incarceration, economic exclusion, and political manipulation. Assassinations of Black leaders weren't random; they were calculated moves to disrupt momentum. When Malcolm X and MLK were murdered, there was no clear succession plan. The Black Panther Party, one of the strongest proactive movements, was dismantled through COINTELPRO because the government knew that an organized Black force was the greatest threat to white supremacy. Code #11 is the difference between being controlled and being in control. A Black MAN doesn't wait for permission; he moves with intention, making sure he's never caught off guard. The time for reaction is over, it's time to play offense.

Proactive Resistance: Huey P. Newton, Bobby Seale, and the Black Panther Party's Fight Against Systemic Injustice

Huey P. Newton and Bobby Seale understood this when they founded the Black Panther Party. Instead of waiting for police brutality to continue unchecked, they armed themselves with knowledge, weapons, and strategy, making it clear that Black people would no longer be passive victims. The Panthers didn't just fight back against violence; they built programs that addressed food insecurity, education, and healthcare, essentially creating an independent system that strengthened the Black community from within. Their movement was a direct response to the failures of reactionary activism, proving that true power comes from preparation, organization, and unwavering discipline. Huey P. Newton was born on February 17, 1942, in Monroe, Louisiana, a place deeply entrenched in the oppressive structures of Jim Crow segregation. His parents, Walter and Armelia Newton, were hardworking and deeply religious, instilling in him a strong sense of discipline and self-respect. The Newton family was part of the Great Migration, moving to Oakland, California, in search of better opportunities and an escape from the violent racism of the South. Though they left the South physically, the systemic racism they faced in Oakland proved that oppression had no borders. Huey's upbringing in a household that emphasized education, self-reliance, and Black pride laid the foundation for the revolutionary path he would take. Huey P. Newton understood that power doesn't come from begging; it comes from force, strategy, and preparation. Unlike previous Black movements that focused on peaceful resistance, Newton saw the necessity of armed self-defense. He realized that white supremacy was violent by nature and that waiting for justice meant accepting oppression. Instead of reacting to police brutality after the fact, he studied California gun laws, learned how to legally arm Black men, and trained them in disciplined, strategic defense. The mere sight of organized, armed Black men patrolling their own neighborhoods sent shockwaves through the system. For the first time, the oppressor had to think twice before making a move.

Newton wasn't just about guns; he was about structure. He knew that for Black people to break free from white dependency, they needed to create systems for themselves. The Panthers weren't just patrolling the streets; they were feeding the hungry, educating the youth, and providing medical assistance to the neglected. Newton studied power at its core and understood that true independence required infrastructure. While the government treated Black communities like war zones, he built programs that gave Black people what they were being denied. He forced the system to recognize Black strength, and that's why they feared him. His leadership style was both intellectual and militant. Newton was heavily influenced by revolutionary theory, drawing from the works of Frantz Fanon, Karl Marx, and Mao Zedong. He saw the Black struggle as part of a global fight against imperialism and capitalism, understanding that racism wasn't just about skin color but about maintaining a system of economic and political control. He used this knowledge to build the Panthers into more than just an armed self-defense group; they became a political force challenging the very foundation of white supremacy. Newton also recognized the power of media and propaganda. He understood that the narrative of the Black Panther Party had to be controlled by Black people, not distorted by the white press. He made sure the Panthers had their own newspaper, *"The Black Panther,"* which spread revolutionary education and exposed police brutality. This strategic use of media made it harder for the government to demonize the movement without opposition. Newton knew that perception was just as powerful as physical force, and he made sure the Panthers used every tool available to shift the balance of power. Despite his brilliance, Newton was heavily targeted by the FBI's COINTELPRO, which saw him as a direct threat to American stability. He faced constant surveillance, legal battles, and internal betrayals, all orchestrated to dismantle the movement. The government understood that if Newton's ideas spread unchecked, Black people would no longer rely on the system for survival. His downfall wasn't just personal; it was a calculated effort to neutralize Black resistance.

Even in his later years, when internal struggles and external pressures weighed heavily on him, Newton remained a symbol of fearless Black power. His legacy is a reminder that real change doesn't come from compliance; it comes from preparation, discipline, and the willingness to confront oppression head-on.

The FBI labeled Newton a threat because he wasn't playing checkers; he was playing chess. He didn't wait for white America to give him a seat at the table; he built his own. He used the media to expose police brutality, flipping the narrative before they could paint Black men as criminals. He educated his people on their legal rights, making sure they could defend themselves in court as well as on the streets. Newton's proactive mindset forced the system to change its tactics because, for once, Black men weren't just reacting; they were leading the charge. White supremacy thrives on division, but Newton's proactive thinking created a united front that shook the foundation of American power structures. The government saw Newton's vision as a direct threat, and they came at him with COINTELPRO, an FBI operation designed to destroy Black resistance from the inside out. But Newton wasn't naïve; he saw the attack coming. He trained Panthers to spot informants, secure their communications, and switch up their tactics to stay ahead of the system. The government couldn't take him down in a fair fight, so they had to resort to illegal sabotage. But Newton wasn't the type to sit back and wait to be crushed; he struck first.

Even behind bars, he remained dangerous. He kept writing, teaching, and strategizing, making sure the movement didn't die with him. The Black Panther Party was never just about one man; it was about an ideology that couldn't be killed. Newton's proactive approach to Black liberation left a battle plan that still holds weight today. If more Black men moved like him —thinking ahead, staying ready, and building for themselves—the system wouldn't stand a chance at keeping them boxed in.

Bobby Seale was the one who kept the Black Panther Party moving like a well-oiled machine. Newton was the mastermind, but Seale was the builder, the one who made sure the vision actually became a reality. He wasn't about empty talk; he structured the movement from the ground up. From recruitment to training to organizing Panther chapters across the country, Seale ensured the movement had direction and discipline. Without him, the Panthers wouldn't have expanded as quickly or as effectively as they did. He wasn't just proactive; he was relentless. Seale knew that an army without discipline was just a mob, and he refused to let the Panthers fall into chaos. He drilled them in organization, making sure every member carried themselves with professionalism and precision. Every Panther had to know their rights, their responsibilities, and their purpose in the struggle. There was no room for loose cannons. This wasn't street violence; this was controlled power. When the Panthers marched with rifles, they weren't gangsters; they were soldiers. Seale made sure of that.

Bobby Seale was born on October 22, 1936, in Liberty, Texas, another stronghold of the Southern racial caste system. His parents, George and Thelma Seale, moved the family to California when he was still young, hoping for a better life, just like thousands of other Black families escaping the South. But moving west didn't mean escaping racism; it just meant experiencing it in a different form. Seale grew up in Oakland's toughest neighborhoods, where Black families were locked out of opportunity and boxed into poverty. His father was a carpenter, his mother a homemaker, both doing their best to provide stability in a world designed to keep them struggling. Seale saw the same discrimination his parents had tried to leave behind, but instead of running from it, he decided to fight. His lineage was one of survival and resistance, and it shaped his revolutionary mindset. That same fire led him to co-found the Black Panther Party alongside Huey Newton, turning frustration into action and oppression into organized rebellion. Community programs didn't just happen; they were built through planning and execution. Seale spearheaded initiatives like the *"Free Breakfast Program,"* which fed thousands of Black children every morning. He made sure Panthers were on the ground, meeting the needs of the people whom the government had abandoned. He knew that true revolution wasn't just about fighting the police; it was about replacing the system with something better. That's why the Panthers' survival programs were seen as a bigger threat than their weapons. The government could handle armed resistance, but they couldn't handle Black self-sufficiency. Seale also understood the importance of political influence. While many viewed the Panthers as an underground movement, he pushed for direct engagement with the political system. He ran for mayor of Oakland, not just to win but to force the city to acknowledge Black power. His campaign put pressure on politicians, proving that the Panthers weren't just about protest; they were about governance.

Seale saw the bigger picture: if Black men wanted control, they had to take it on every level. When Seale was arrested and put on trial, he refused to be a victim. He famously demanded his right to defend himself, exposing the racist court system in the process. When they tried to silence him by literally gagging him in court, it only made him a bigger symbol of resistance. Seale's defiance showed that the Panthers weren't just fighting in the streets; they were fighting in every arena, refusing to bow to white supremacy in any form. Seale's proactive mindset ensured that the Panthers left a lasting impact. He built something that couldn't be erased, even when the government tried. His dedication to organization, discipline, and community upliftment made him one of the strongest examples of what Black leadership should look like. His legacy proves that without structure, movements fall apart. If more Black men followed his model—building with precision, staying disciplined, and keeping their eyes on the long game—Black power wouldn't just be an idea; it would be a reality. The Black Panther Party wasn't just a movement; it was a declaration of war against systemic oppression. Unlike past generations that relied on nonviolent protest, the Panthers refused to wait for white approval. They saw the problem, analyzed the system, and built a solution that forced the enemy to adjust. Their approach was direct: arm the people, educate the people, and feed the people. They didn't ask for justice; they ensured it. Patrolling Black neighborhoods wasn't just about carrying guns; it was about enforcing accountability. The Panthers made sure that police brutality had consequences. When officers stopped a Black man, Panthers were there, legally armed and watching. The law was on their side, and they knew it. This forced the police to rethink their actions, proving that power respects power. The Panthers understood that without enforcement, rights meant nothing.

Their Free Breakfast Program exposed the government's neglect. The Panthers proved that feeding Black children wasn't impossible; the system just didn't care to do it. By stepping in and solving the problem, they showed that Black self-sufficiency was a real threat. The government eventually launched its own breakfast programs, but only because the Panthers had already done it first. That's what proactive leadership looks like: making the system react to you, not the other way around. Education was another weapon. The Panthers didn't rely on white schools to teach Black children their history. They created their own curriculum, ensuring that young Black minds weren't poisoned with lies about their inferiority. They taught self-defense, politics, and economic empowerment. They didn't just prepare Black children to survive; they prepared them to lead. The Black Panther Party forced America to confront its hypocrisy. The system called them criminals, but all they did was hold America to its own laws. They didn't start the violence; they responded to it with intelligence and strategy. That's why the government attacked them so viciously. The Panthers proved that when Black men think ahead, organize, and move with purpose, they become unstoppable. The blueprint is still there. The question is whether Black men today are willing to follow it.

The Black Panther Party showed the power of armed resistance, community organization, and direct confrontation with the system. But there was another approach to Black empowerment that was just as proactive—one that focused on economic independence, self-discipline, and spiritual fortification. Before the Panthers, Elijah Muhammad and the Nation of Islam had already built a blueprint for Black self-sufficiency, proving that true power isn't just about defending yourself in the streets but also about controlling your own institutions, wealth, and destiny. Where the Panthers focused on immediate resistance, the Nation of Islam played the long game, creating a system that could sustain itself beyond any one leader or political moment. Their approach wasn't just about fighting white supremacy, it was about making it irrelevant.

Proactive Vision: Elijah Muhammad and the Nation of Islam's Blueprint for Black Empowerment

The Black Panther Party showed the power of armed resistance, community organization, and direct confrontation with the system. But there was another approach to Black empowerment that was just as proactive—one that focused on economic independence, self-discipline, and spiritual fortification. Before the Panthers, Elijah Muhammad and the Nation of Islam had already built a blueprint for Black self-sufficiency, proving that true power isn't just about defending yourself in the streets but also about controlling your own institutions, wealth, and destiny. While the Panthers focused on immediate resistance, the Nation of Islam played the long game, creating a system that could sustain itself beyond any one leader or political moment. Their approach wasn't just about fighting white supremacy; it was about making it irrelevant. Elijah Muhammad understood that true freedom required Black people to control their own resources, businesses, and infrastructure without needing validation or support from a system designed to keep them in a permanent state of dependence.

Elijah Muhammad was born Elijah Robert Poole on October 7, 1897, in Sandersville, Georgia. He came from a lineage of formerly enslaved Black people who had survived the brutal conditions of the American South. His parents, William and Mariah Poole, were sharecroppers, and his father was also a Baptist preacher. Their roots traced back to the Deep South, where Black people were systematically oppressed through racial terror, economic exploitation, and segregation. Growing up in the harsh environment of post-Reconstruction Georgia, Elijah Muhammad witnessed firsthand the horrors of Jim Crow, lynchings, and the daily struggles of Black families trying to survive under white supremacy. These early experiences shaped his views on Black self-sufficiency, independence, and the need for a spiritual and economic revolution among his people. Elijah Muhammad's path to Islam began when he was introduced to Wallace D. Fard, also known as Master Fard Muhammad, arrived in Detroit in 1931. At the time, Elijah was searching for answers beyond Christianity, which he felt had failed Black people by keeping them spiritually and economically dependent on white society. Fard's teachings emphasized that Black people were the original people of the Earth and that Islam was their true religion, not the faith forced upon them through slavery. This message resonated deeply with Elijah Muhammad, who saw it as a way to uplift and reprogram the minds of Black men and women suffering under white supremacy. Fard also preached separation from white society, self-sufficiency, and the need for Black people to create their own businesses, institutions, and communities. These ideas aligned with Elijah's own frustrations about Black dependency and inspired him to dedicate his life to the mission of Black empowerment through Islam.

After studying under Fard, Elijah Muhammad quickly rose through the ranks of what would become the Nation of Islam, proving himself to be a devoted and disciplined follower. Fard entrusted him with leadership responsibilities, and when Fard mysteriously disappeared in 1934, Elijah Muhammad stepped up to continue his teacher's work. He expanded upon Fard's teachings, refining the doctrine that would shape the Nation of Islam into a powerful movement. Unlike mainstream Islam, Elijah incorporated elements of Black nationalism, economic empowerment, and strict moral discipline into his teachings. He also emphasized self-mastery, requiring his followers to reject destructive habits like drinking, smoking, and unhealthy eating. His leadership transformed the Nation of Islam from a small Detroit-based movement into a national organization, proving that the right teacher can awaken a leader who changes history. Elijah Muhammad understood that Black people would never have real power if they depended on white society for survival.

He didn't just preach separation; he built an infrastructure to support it. Under his leadership, the Nation of Islam (NOI) created a self-sustaining economic system, owning businesses, farms, grocery stores, bakeries, and restaurants. He knew that if Black men didn't control their own resources, they would always be at the mercy of a system that wanted them weak and dependent. He didn't wait for handouts or government programs; he made Black people build for themselves. His philosophy was simple: *"Ownership equals power."*

Most Black organizations at the time were focused on integration, fighting for a seat at a table that wasn't meant for them. Elijah Muhammad rejected that approach. He taught that Black men needed to build their own table, set their own rules, and create a system where they controlled their own destiny. He saw how other ethnic groups pooled their money, kept wealth circulating within their communities, and built institutions that ensured their long-term success. The NOI followed that model, developing an economic blueprint that emphasized self-reliance. While other leaders begged for access, Elijah Muhammad created his own economy that could sustain Black people without outside interference. His vision was not just about fighting racism; it was about ensuring that Black people no longer needed to depend on their oppressors for anything. He also implemented strict financial discipline within the NOI, requiring members to contribute regularly to the movement. This wasn't just about collecting donations; it was about training Black people to think long-term about money and wealth accumulation. Every dollar had a purpose. The NOI reinvested these funds into buying land, businesses, and properties, ensuring economic security for future generations. Elijah Muhammad understood that money wasn't just about luxury; it was about control, influence, and power. Without economic independence, Black men would always be under someone else's rule. One of the most significant aspects of the NOI's economic movement was its focus on job creation. Instead of waiting for white employers to offer opportunities, the Nation provided jobs for its members, giving Black men a way to provide for their families without compromising their dignity. This was a radical shift from the typical Black experience in America, where employment was often tied to racism, discrimination, and exploitation. By owning businesses and hiring within the community, Elijah Muhammad gave Black men a way to earn a living without selling their soul to a system that never valued them.

Farming was another key element of the NOI's economic strategy. Elijah Muhammad knew that food was power. He acquired thousands of acres of farmland to ensure that Black people had control over what they ate. The Nation didn't just talk about independence; they grew it from the ground up. Owning land meant that they weren't reliant on white-owned grocery chains or government assistance. It also meant that they had an economic base that couldn't easily be taken away. In a world where Black communities were constantly stripped of their wealth, owning land and producing food was an act of war against economic oppression. Elijah Muhammad's economic model wasn't just about money; it was about freedom. He showed Black people that the key to liberation wasn't in marching or protesting but in owning, controlling, and producing. He wasn't interested in temporary solutions or symbolic victories; he wanted real, tangible power that could be passed down through generations. His vision was clear: if Black men didn't take control of their economy, they would always be under the control of someone else. Elijah Muhammad understood that economic power meant nothing if Black men didn't have the discipline, knowledge, and self-respect to maintain it. He saw that slavery and white supremacy had done more than just destroy Black wealth; it had destroyed Black minds. That's why he focused just as much on spiritual and mental reprogramming as he did on economics. He didn't just want Black men to make money; he wanted them to think, act, and move like men of power. Without a strong foundation of self-worth, any economic progress would eventually crumble. One of his most revolutionary teachings was the idea that Black people were the original people of the Earth, not the cursed, inferior race that white supremacy had painted them to be. This was a radical shift from the Christian doctrine that had been weaponized against Black people for centuries. Instead of teaching submission and forgiveness for oppression, Elijah Muhammad taught strength, discipline, and divine purpose. He gave Black men a spiritual identity that empowered them, not one that kept them begging for acceptance. Self-discipline was a cornerstone of his teachings. He knew that if Black men wanted to be leaders, they had to control their desires, vices, and weaknesses. The NOI's strict lifestyle—no alcohol, no drugs, no pork, no reckless behavior—wasn't just about religious rules; it was about creating a disciplined, focused, and productive Black man. He understood that white supremacy used addiction, temptation, and distractions to keep Black men weak. By eliminating these self-destructive habits, the NOI produced men who were sharp, reliable, and ready for leadership. Elijah Muhammad also emphasized the importance of education, but not in the traditional sense of relying on white institutions. He believed that Black people needed an education that served their interests, not one that prepared them to be servants in someone else's system. The NOI established its own schools, ensuring that Black children were raised with a sense of pride, purpose, and responsibility. He knew that if the next generation wasn't trained properly, the cycle of dependence and submission would continue. Real power wasn't just about making money; it was about controlling the knowledge that shaped the future. A major part of his spiritual teachings was the rejection of victimhood. He didn't allow Black men to make excuses for their condition. Instead of blaming white people for everything, he focused on what Black men could do to change their situation. This was a radical departure from the mainstream civil rights movement, which focused on demanding justice from white America. Elijah Muhammad wasn't interested in waiting for justice; he was interested in building power. He instilled in Black men the mentality that no one was coming to save them, so they had to save themselves.

Proactive Leadership: Adam Clayton Powell Jr. and His Fight for Black Political Power

The combination of economic power and spiritual discipline made the Nation of Islam one of the strongest organizations in Black history. Elijah Muhammad didn't just create a movement; he built an institution that transformed how Black men saw themselves and their place in the world. His teachings forced Black men to take control of their lives, to think for themselves, and to build for themselves. He proved that when Black men are proactive, disciplined, and economically independent, they become unstoppable. Elijah Muhammad and the Nation of Islam showed Black people the power of proactive leadership, how economic independence and spiritual discipline could create a foundation for true self-sufficiency. But while the NOI focused on building an internal system separate from white America, another Black leader took the fight directly into the political arena. Adam Clayton Powell Jr. was a different kind of warrior, one who understood that if Black people were going to navigate the system of white supremacy, they had to play the game of power at the highest levels. Where Elijah Muhammad built an independent economy, Powell used legislation, boycotts, and political maneuvering to force America to recognize Black people's rights. He didn't ask for change; he demanded it. Powell was the blueprint for how Black politicians should operate: unapologetic, strategic, and always moving with a purpose.

Adam Clayton Powell Jr. was born on November 29, 1908, in New Haven, Connecticut, but his roots were deeply tied to the South and the struggle for Black advancement. His father, Adam Clayton Powell Sr., was born to formerly enslaved parents in Franklin County, Virginia, and rose to become one of the most influential Black pastors of his time. His mother, Mattie Buster Shaffer, was of mixed Indigenous and European ancestry, with her family tracing lineage back to the Creek and Cherokee nations. Powell Jr.'s lineage was one of resilience, intellect, and leadership; his father led the Abyssinian Baptist Church in Harlem, transforming it into one of the most powerful Black institutions in America. Raised in privilege compared to most Black children of his era, Powell still understood the racial barriers that limited Black success and used his position to challenge them. His family's legacy of education, faith, and activism shaped him into the fearless leader he became, proving that strong roots produce powerful men.

Adam Clayton Powell Jr. wasn't just a politician; he was a disruptor, a strategist, and the godfather of modern Black political power. Before the Civil Rights Movement had national momentum, Powell was already forcing America to recognize Black people as a political force. He didn't wait for integration to be handed to him; he demanded it, using his position to make tangible moves instead of symbolic gestures. While other leaders were pleading for change, he was commanding it through legislation, activism, and economic pressure. His approach wasn't about asking permission; it was about using the system's rules against it to get what Black people deserved. Powell's legacy is the blueprint for what it means to be proactive in politics, forcing the government to act instead of waiting for it to offer scraps.

Before Powell ever stepped into Congress, he was already making power plays in Harlem. As a pastor at Abyssinian Baptist Church, he understood that the church wasn't just a place of worship; it was a stronghold for organizing Black economic and political power. He used his influence to mobilize Harlem's Black community, launching boycotts against businesses that refused to hire Black workers. His motto was simple: *"Don't buy where you can't work."* This wasn't just a protest; it was an economic strategy that forced white-owned businesses to either hire Black employees or lose Black dollars. Powell didn't wait for legislative action; he created economic consequences that left these businesses with no choice but to comply. This level of strategic action laid the foundation for future boycotts, including the Montgomery Bus Boycott led by Martin Luther King Jr.

When Powell entered Congress in 1945, he wasted no time making noise. He understood that being the first Black congressman from New York wasn't enough; his presence had to mean something. While many Black politicians were satisfied just to have a seat at the table, Powell made sure he controlled the conversation. He introduced legislation that directly benefited Black Americans, focusing on fair employment, education, and anti-discrimination policies. He didn't just talk about civil rights; he embedded them into the laws of the nation, forcing America to deal with Black issues on a legal level. His aggressive, no-nonsense approach made him a threat to white lawmakers who were used to Black politicians being passive or compromising. Powell wasn't just pushing for laws; he was making sure they had *"teeth."* When he became chairman of the House Education and Labor Committee in 1961, he controlled billions in federal funding for education, jobs, and social programs. He used this power to ensure Black communities got their fair share, redirecting funds to historically Black colleges and implementing policies that benefited Black workers. Every piece of legislation that crossed his desk had to answer one question: *"How does this help Black people?"* He wasn't interested in empty symbolism or bipartisan appeasement. Powell knew that real power came from controlling the purse, and he used federal dollars to strengthen Black institutions in a way that couldn't be easily reversed. One of Powell's greatest contributions was the Powell Amendment, which changed the way federal money was distributed. He introduced a simple but powerful rule: if an institution or program received federal funding, it had to be desegregated. This forced white institutions to choose between their racism and their money, and most of them chose the money. The Powell Amendment became the foundation for future civil rights legislation, including the Civil Rights Act of 1964. This was a proactive move; Powell wasn't waiting for the courts to rule on segregation; he was using financial leverage to break it down. He understood that racism wasn't just about hate; it was about power and economics. And the best way to dismantle it was to hit where it hurt the most: the pockets.

Powell also mastered the art of political strategy, making sure Black power wasn't just concentrated in activism but in legislation. He built relationships when necessary but was never afraid to burn bridges if it meant getting results. Unlike many politicians who feared white backlash, Powell welcomed it, knowing that his enemies' opposition only meant he was doing something right. He challenged presidents, called out racist congressmen on the House floor, and made it clear that Black people were not to be ignored. While other leaders were focused on morality, Powell focused on leverage, understanding that politics isn't about fairness; it's about making sure your side has the strongest position. His ability to think ahead and anticipate counterattacks kept him ahead of the game, making him one of the most effective Black leaders in American history. Despite his accomplishments, Powell's enemies eventually found a way to undermine him. Accusations of corruption and misuse of funds were used to remove him from Congress in 1967, even though white politicians were guilty of far worse and faced no consequences. This was the system's way of neutralizing a Black man who refused to play by its rules. But even in his downfall, Powell had already laid the foundation for Black political power, showing future generations how to navigate the system and use it for their benefit. His political career proved that Black people couldn't afford to wait for justice; it had to be demanded, enforced, and protected at every level. The moment you stop being proactive, the system finds a way to strip you of everything you've built.

Powell's blueprint is still relevant today because the same tactics he used are still effective. Black politicians who focus on symbolism over substance accomplish nothing, while those who understand power and strategy can force real change. Powell didn't just react to racism; he attacked it before it had the chance to tighten its grip. His success shows that if you control the money, write the laws, and dictate the terms, the opposition has no choice but to play by your rules. The lesson is simple: a Black MAN cannot afford to wait for justice. He must anticipate the moves of his enemies, position himself accordingly, and make power respect him. Adam Clayton Powell Jr. was more than a politician; he was the embodiment of Code #11. He understood that the only way to win in a system built against you is to outthink, outmaneuver, and outwork it at every turn. He didn't react; he planned, executed, and forced the system to adjust to him. His legacy is a reminder that being proactive isn't just a strategy; it's a necessity for survival and success. If Black men want real power, they have to stop playing catch-up and start controlling the game. Powell did it, and his blueprint is right there for the taking if you're ready to use it.

Proactivity is about action.

Newton, Seale, Muhammad, and Powell all understood one thing: waiting for change is the same as accepting oppression. They didn't ask for power; they took it. They knew the system wasn't designed for them, so they built their own. White supremacy thrives when Black men stay passive, so they chose to be proactive, not reactive. The system respects force, discipline, and organization, and these men embodied all three. That's why they weren't just opposed; they were targeted. Their blueprint still applies today; ignore it, and Black men will keep making the same mistakes. The system fears a Black man who refuses to be a victim. That's why COINTELPRO, sabotage, and media smear campaigns were used to dismantle their movements. Newton and Seale mastered the law and used it against their oppressors. Muhammad built an economic empire to take power out of white hands. Powell leveraged politics to push an unapologetically Black agenda. None of them sat back waiting for change; they moved first. Their approach forced the system to adjust to them, not the other way around. The message was clear: *"Stay ready so you ain't got to get ready."* Black men today can't afford to react when oppression strikes; it's already too late by then. That's why Newton focused on self-defense, Muhammad preached economic self-sufficiency, and Seale enforced strict organization. They knew that if you're not structured before the attack comes, you've already lost. Preparation is power, and power commands respect.

The biggest mistake a Black man can make is thinking the system will ever play fair. Newton knew better, so he studied the law and legally armed the Panthers. Muhammad knew better, so he built businesses that didn't rely on white approval. Powell knew better, so he played politics with strategy, not emotion. The system values dominance, not fairness. Any Black man who wants to survive must do the same. Playing by an oppressor's rules will never lead to liberation. Being proactive means controlling your environment before it controls you. Newton knew the police couldn't be trusted to protect Black neighborhoods, so he created armed patrols. Muhammad knew Black people couldn't rely on white businesses for survival, so he built a supply chain. Powell knew waiting for white politicians to deliver justice was a waste of time, so he took office himself. Their actions were direct, calculated, and effective. They didn't ask permission; they made moves and forced the system to respond. One of the core principles of The 14 Codes is that a Black man must be proactive, not reactive. That means solving problems before they become crises. It means securing your finances before you go broke, developing discipline before adversity hits, and building a foundation before you're forced to fight for survival. Black men can't afford to drift through life aimlessly. Strategy separates those who survive from those swallowed by the system.

Organization is key to power. The Panthers weren't just armed men; they were a structured movement with leadership, training, and a clear agenda. The Nation of Islam wasn't just a religious group; it was an economic powerhouse controlling businesses, schools, and food distribution. Powell wasn't just a politician; he used his seat to challenge white lawmakers and funnel resources into Black communities. Their success wasn't luck; it was the result of planning, discipline, and execution. The easiest way to weaken a people is to keep them disorganized. The system doesn't fear loud protests; it fears well-structured resistance. That's why the Panthers were infiltrated, the Nation of Islam was monitored, and Powell was targeted for removal from Congress. White supremacy thrives when Black people move without purpose. Without structure, movements crumble, and power fades. Black men must take control of our own education. The system will never teach us how to free ourselves. That's why Newton studied political theory, Muhammad emphasized knowledge of self, and Powell mastered the political game. They knew that ignorance is a weapon used against Black people. Schools won't teach real Black history, the media won't highlight Black success, and the government won't create policies that benefit us. That means we must educate ourselves.

Economic independence is a pillar of power. Muhammad built a financial system within the Nation of Islam, proving that Black dollars should circulate in the community first. Depending on white businesses leaves Black people vulnerable. Newton understood this too, which is why the Panthers created free breakfast programs and healthcare initiatives instead of waiting for government handouts. Power comes from ownership, and ownership requires discipline and vision. Discipline separates men from males. These men were dangerous to the system because they were disciplined. They didn't move off emotion; they moved strategically. They weren't chasing clout; they were chasing results. The Panthers didn't carry guns for show; they studied the law, trained with precision, and stayed ten steps ahead. The Nation of Islam didn't just talk about self-sufficiency; they built institutions to back it up. Powell didn't just talk about power; he exercised it. Without discipline, all efforts collapse. If you wait until war comes to prepare, you've already lost. The system doesn't give second chances to unprepared Black men. That's why *"The 14 Codes"* exist: to ensure Black men move with purpose, intelligence, and strength. Newton, Seale, Muhammad, and Powell set the standard: stay ready so you never have to scramble for survival. If more Black men embraced that mindset, the system wouldn't stand a chance at keeping them in check. The future of Black power depends on whether or not Black men follow these principles. Strategy, organization, economic independence, education, and discipline—these aren't just ideas; they're necessities. The system will always find new ways to attack, but the solution remains the same: be prepared before the attack comes. A Black man who follows *"The 14 Codes"* will never be caught off guard. He won't beg for change; he will create it. He won't wait for power; he will take it. That is true leadership. That is the legacy that must continue.

CODE NO. 12

A BLACK MAN UNDERSTANDS: IF HE CAN'T PRODUCE, HE IS A DEAD MAN

Production isn't just about working; it's about proving your worth in the real world. A Black MAN isn't here to just exist, consume, or sit back complaining. He's here to build, create, and leave a legacy that speaks long after he's gone. True production isn't just about survival; it's about creating wealth, influence, and history. It's about owning, innovating, and making sure what you put down lasts longer than you do. A man who doesn't produce is a man at the mercy of those who do, always depending on someone else's system, handouts, or control. For the Black man, production has always been a necessity and a weapon. The system has never made it easy, denied opportunities, stripped resources, and placed roadblocks at every turn. But the real ones found a way. Paul Cuffe built Black enterprise on the water. A.G. Gaston carved out a business empire. The ones who understood the power of production left their mark, no matter the obstacles. The ones who didn't? Forgotten, erased, left behind as wasted potential. A Black MAN who waits on opportunities that aren't coming is already a dead man walking.

To produce is to force your will onto the world instead of letting it shape you. It isn't just about getting money; it's about building institutions, ideas, and movements that stand the test of time. Reginald F. Lewis didn't just chase dollars; he broke down doors in high finance. William Still didn't just document history; he preserved the blueprint of Black resistance. Every great Black MAN in history is remembered for what he built, not what he consumed. A Black MAN who doesn't produce has no voice, no respect, and no power. The world doesn't care about men who just take up space. Women don't admire men who can't build. Children don't look up to fathers who leave them with nothing but excuses. A man who produces controls his name, his legacy, and his destiny. He doesn't beg for chances; he makes them. Production isn't a luxury; it's the only path to freedom, respect, and power. A man survives by what he creates, commands, and controls. History proves this: Paul Cuffe, A.G. Gaston, the men of Black Wall Street—they built their own and secured their independence. The ones who didn't? Trapped in cycles of struggle, waiting on a system designed to leave them behind. A Black MAN who doesn't produce is disposable. The one who does? He controls his future.

"*Legacy*" isn't just a word; it's what a man leaves

behind. Reginald F. Lewis shattered financial barriers. William Still made sure Black stories were never erased. What a man builds outlives him. A Black MAN who doesn't produce dies twice: once when his body drops, and again when his name fades from history. Respect isn't given; it's taken through proof of value. The world doesn't respect men who contribute nothing. That's why the system works to keep Black men dependent instead of dominant. The Panthers built, and the system dismantled them. The Nation of Islam created economic power, and they were infiltrated. Every time Black men organize, structure, and build, the system moves to stop them. Why? Because a Black MAN with production can't be ignored, dismissed, or controlled. Production is the root of power. Oppression has always attacked Black men's ability to build through redlining, economic sabotage, and mass incarceration. But the ones who follow the Code never stop creating. They know survival, legacy, and respect all come from what they produce. The choice is simple: build and be remembered or do nothing and be erased. Every powerful Black MAN in history was known for what he created. Every weak man was forgotten for what he failed to build. Production isn't an option; it's manhood itself.

A Black MAN who doesn't produce doesn't survive. Power runs the world, and production is the only way to claim it. A man who can't provide is left begging, weak, and irrelevant. White supremacy knows this;

that's why its biggest weapon has always been stopping Black men from building, whether through mass incarceration, engineered dependency, or economic sabotage. A Black MAN who can't produce can't protect, can't lead, can't sustain. That's not just failure; that's defeat. Legacy is the only way to ensure a Black man's name doesn't die with him. Every empire, every dynasty, every bloodline that lasted was built by men who produced. White supremacy keeps Black men stuck in survival mode, so they never build wealth, institutions, or long-term power. A Black MAN who stays a laborer instead of an owner remains replaceable, forgotten when his usefulness runs out. But the one who follows the Code understands that what he builds today isn't just for him, it's for generations to come.

Respect isn't requested; it's seized through undeniable results. The world only respects men who create, sustain, and own. That's why the system fuels joblessness, economic instability, and distractions, because a Black MAN who builds can't be controlled. He doesn't ask for respect; he commands it through what he produces. Freedom isn't given; it's taken. And the biggest threat to white supremacy is a Black MAN who doesn't depend on anybody. That's why Black production has always been attacked. Because once a Black MAN embraces the Code, he stops waiting for a seat at the table; he builds his own. A man's worth isn't in his words or dreams; it's in what he produces. A Black MAN who doesn't produce has already lost, whether he realizes it or not. History proves this: the men who built, owned, and created dictated their existence. The ones who didn't? Used, discarded, forgotten. White supremacy thrives on Black economic and social dependence because a dependent man is a controlled man. A Black MAN who follows the Code and produces becomes a force; he sets his own terms, creates his own options, and commands his own destiny. But those who don't? They stay pawns on the board, waiting to be moved or removed.

White supremacy doesn't need chains to control Black men; it uses economics to keep them locked in place. A Black MAN who produces breaks free. He owns his time, his resources, his future. The system doesn't fear the Black MAN who complains; it fears the one who builds. That's why every tool—economic barriers, legal restrictions, psychological warfare—has been used to shut Black production down. But the Black MAN who builds anyway? He becomes the system's worst nightmare. The Code is clear: production is the key to power, and power is the only path to true freedom. Every Black MAN must choose: will he be a producer or a pawn? A builder or a beggar? A master of his fate or a servant to another? White supremacy has already made its move, keeping Black men distracted, divided, and dependent. But the Code doesn't allow passivity. It demands action, ownership, and production. The ones who refuse will always be at the mercy of the ones who don't. History makes it plain: the Black MAN who produces is a king; the one who doesn't is a pawn. Only one controls the board.

A.G. Gaston: Building Black Wealth in the Face of Oppression

Men like A.G. Gaston embodied this code. Born into a system designed to keep Black men in submission, he refused to be a mere laborer. He built businesses, created wealth, and shaped his environment on his own terms. In doing so, he commanded respect, not by asking for it, but by producing undeniable results. White supremacy thrives on keeping Black men waiting and hoping; Gaston took control instead. His success was not just financial, it was an act of defiance, proving that a Black MAN who produces cannot be ignored.

For every Gaston, there is a man who chose dependence, surrendering control and becoming disposable. White supremacy fears the Black MAN who produces because he cannot be manipulated. The system cannot erase a man who builds; it can only hope to stop him before he starts. That's why economic sabotage has always been a primary weapon against Black production, from redlining to legal restrictions. The Code makes it clear: true power is not in what a man consumes but in what he creates. A Black MAN who produces does not ask for permission, he moves with authority.

White supremacy thrives when Black men are dependent, unable to build and sustain our own. Gaston rejected that system entirely. He didn't just create wealth; he created a blueprint for Black men to secure our futures without waiting for validation. The attack on Black economic success has always been about control. A Black MAN who produces determines his own survival, and that's why Gaston faced resistance, not just for making money but for making other Black men self-sufficient. White supremacy can tolerate an exceptional Black man, but it cannot withstand a system of Black men who know their power.

A Black MAN who does not produce remains a pawn in someone else's game. Gaston refused that role. He lived by results, not excuses, proving that opportunity isn't given; it's created. White supremacy distracts Black men from building tangible assets, but Gaston stayed focused, demonstrating that economic production is the true measure of power. His wealth wasn't just personal; it secured a future for Black people in a system built to erase them. The Code teaches that a Black MAN must produce, and Gaston showed the world exactly why. The battle against Black production has never been about money; it has always been about control. A Black MAN who owns cannot be dictated to, and white supremacy knew that. This is why access to loans, fair wages, and business licenses was restricted for Black men, not out of fairness but to ensure dependency. But Gaston built anyway, refusing to wait for the rules to change. The greatest act of defiance a Black MAN can commit is to produce in a system designed to keep him consuming. Gaston didn't just make money; he made a statement: a Black MAN who builds is a Black MAN who cannot be broken.

Production extends beyond finance; it is psychological, cultural, and generational. When a Black MAN produces, he sets a precedent, proving that survival is not enough; ownership is the goal. Gaston knew that a Black man's value lies in what he creates, and white supremacy fears this mindset more than anything. A Black MAN who produces liberates not just himself but those around him. Gaston proved that the Code isn't just an idea; it's a necessity. His success wasn't luck or accident; it was the result of following the Code, rejecting dependency, and producing at all costs.

Gaston's life is the perfect example of why production is the difference between freedom and servitude. White supremacy pushes the narrative that Black men must assimilate, beg for inclusion, or wait for change. Gaston rejected that entirely. He proved that a Black MAN who follows the Code doesn't wait for opportunities; he creates them. His businesses, schools, and financial institutions weren't just for him; they were for the Black men who would come after him. This is why white supremacy works to erase Black production, because once a Black MAN understands his power, he can never be controlled again.

The Code demands that a Black MAN produces,

and Gaston answered that call with undeniable success. His wealth, influence, and impact were the direct results of refusing to accept limitations. White supremacy will always try to stop Black men from following the Code because once production begins, control ends. Gaston's story is not just history; it's a lesson, a warning, and a challenge to every Black MAN reclaiming his power. The greatest battle a Black MAN will ever fight is the battle to produce in a world that wants him dependent. Gaston won that battle, and his victory stands as proof that a Black MAN who builds cannot be erased.

A.G. Gaston built wealth in a world determined to keep Black men impoverished. His success in insurance, banking, funeral services, and real estate wasn't just financial; it was a direct challenge to white supremacy's foundation. The system was designed so that Black men could work but never own, survive but never build, exist but never thrive. Gaston shattered that expectation, proving that ownership is the only path to true power. White supremacy relies on Black men waiting for approval and accepting limitations. Gaston understood the Code: a Black MAN must produce, and through that production, he forces the system to acknowledge him. Production is resistance because it makes a Black MAN self-sufficient in a world that wants him powerless. Gaston knew that ownership meant controlling his own destiny. His businesses didn't just generate income; they built infrastructure for Black power. White supremacy fears Black ownership because ownership eliminates the need for permission. By creating institutions that served Black people, Gaston weakened white power's grip on Black economic survival. Building something from nothing was his act of defiance. A Black MAN who produces forces the world to respect him, whether they want to or not.

Self-reliance was at the core of Gaston's mission, and white supremacy works to prevent it. A Black MAN dependent on another for survival is easily controlled and broken. This is why Black men were denied capital, land, and ownership: dependency keeps a man weak. Gaston rejected that model, creating a financial network so Black people didn't have to beg for inclusion. His success was not luck but discipline, vision, and an unshakable commitment to economic power. White supremacy survives by keeping Black men distracted, but Gaston remained focused, on production, ownership, and control.

Building multiple businesses wasn't just about wealth; it was about creating a foundation that could not be erased. Gaston knew that wealth is temporary without infrastructure that sustains itself across generations. White supremacy has always worked to keep Black men economically unstable because when each generation starts over, power remains in white hands. By establishing banks, insurance companies, and real estate holdings, Gaston ensured that Black money remained in Black hands. White supremacy thrives on extracting wealth from Black labor, but Gaston disrupted that cycle by keeping Black dollars circulating within the Black community. Job creation was another critical weapon in Gaston's arsenal. White supremacy depends on Black unemployment and economic instability to maintain control. Gaston countered this by hiring, training, and empowering Black men, giving them the tools to be self-sufficient. He understood that power isn't in complaining about oppression; it's in building something undeniable. White supremacy erects barriers to Black economic control, from discriminatory laws to outright sabotage. Yet, Gaston proved that a Black MAN committed to production will always find a way to rise.

Gaston's influence extended beyond economics; it reshaped the social and political dynamics of Birmingham. White supremacy thrives when Black men lack leverage and a voice. But Gaston's financial empire made him too powerful to ignore, giving him access to political influence and the ability to shape policies affecting Black people. A Black MAN with resources cannot be silenced. White supremacy fights Black economic strength because financial independence breeds political and cultural independence. Gaston's wealth made him more than rich, it made him a force white power had to reckon with.

Gaston's commitment to the Code uplifted the Black community, proving that a Black MAN who produces secures not only his own future but that of his people. White supremacy teaches Black men to seek individual success while avoiding collective power because collective power leads to true liberation. Gaston rejected that mindset, building businesses that benefited entire communities. His impact ensured Black families, workers, and entrepreneurs had the tools to succeed. White supremacy survives by ensuring Black wealth is temporary, but Gaston's model proved that lasting institutions are the key to true independence.

The biggest lesson from Gaston's life is that no matter how oppressive the system, a Black MAN who produces will always find a way to create power. White supremacy is not invincible; it assumes Black men will remain dependent, waiting instead of taking control. Gaston shattered that illusion, proving that economic power is always within reach for those willing to work for it. His story is a testament to the Code: excuses don't matter when a Black MAN is committed to ownership and self-reliance. White supremacy will always try to block Black progress, but Gaston proved that a Black MAN who refuses limits will build regardless. His life is the blueprint for how a Black MAN defies oppression through production.

Paul Cuffe: Charting a Course for Black Economic Independence

Paul Cuffe was a Black MAN who understood that ownership is the foundation of power. In the late 1700s, when free Black men were expected to remain laborers, he refused to be confined by white supremacy's limitations. Instead of seeking approval, he built, owned, and expanded, creating wealth on his own terms. The system was designed to keep Black men out of global commerce, ensuring our dependence on white-controlled economies. But Cuffe followed the Code: a Black MAN who produces dictates his own future. His success wasn't just financial; it was an act of defiance against a world determined to keep Black men powerless.

Survival was never enough for Cuffe; true power came from controlling resources, trade, and wealth. White supremacy thrived on keeping Black men in cycles of dependency, working but never accumulating, producing but never owning. Cuffe disrupted that system by mastering the industry that dictated global power: shipping and trade. His ability to move goods, control commerce, and establish networks made him a threat, allowing him to operate outside of white economic dominance. A Black MAN who owns the means of production isn't just surviving, he's setting the terms of engagement with the world.

Cuffe knew that a Black man's worth is measured by what he leaves behind. White supremacy ensured that Black men lived and died without passing down anything of significance, forcing each generation to start from nothing. He rejected that cycle, creating an economic framework that would outlive him and give future Black men something to build upon. He followed the Code: a Black MAN produces not just for himself, but for those who come after him. His trade networks, wealth, and business practices weren't just about personal gain, they were a blueprint for Black economic independence.

Respect wasn't something Cuffe asked for; it was something he commanded through production. White supremacy operates on the idea that Black men must constantly prove themselves worthy of a seat at the table. But Cuffe knew results spoke louder than valida-tion. His ability to move goods across continents, generate wealth, and sustain enterprise made him impossible to ignore. The system sought to keep Black men in subjugation, but Cuffe's success proved that a Black MAN who follows the Code isn't waiting for inclusion, he builds his own.

White supremacy's greatest fear has always been the independent Black MAN who doesn't need approval or assistance to thrive. Cuffe embodied that fear, proving that a Black MAN who produces is a Black MAN who is free. The system was designed to keep Black men as consumers, not creators, because creation leads to ownership, and ownership leads to power. Cuffe shat-tered that design by mastering maritime trade, control-ling the very industry that sustained white economies. His life was proof that white supremacy can only function as long as Black men remain inactive and dependent.

A Black MAN who produces is a Black MAN who disrupts, and Cuffe's entire existence was a disruption. White supremacy relied on the belief that Black men couldn't build, organize, or sustain wealth across generations. Cuffe destroyed that notion by doing exactly what they claimed was impossible, proving that economic power is the only true equalizer. The code is clear: a Black MAN is measured by his ability to produce, and Cuffe's mastery of this principle made him a direct challenge to the system.

For Cuffe, production wasn't just about money; it was about control, influence, and the ability to dictate the terms of his own existence. As long as Black men remained reliant on white-controlled economies, they would always be subject to the whims of the system. White supremacy keeps Black men in a reactive position, always responding, never initiating. Cuffe refused to accept that fate. He didn't see barriers, only opportunities, and that mindset made him a threat. His life was a testament to the Code: a Black MAN who builds cannot be broken. Power isn't granted; it's built. White supremacy operates on the belief that Black men can only go as far as the system allows, but Cuffe ignored those boundaries and forged his own path. A Black MAN who understands his value doesn't ask for permission to succeed; he takes what he is owed through production and ownership. Cuffe's success wasn't an exception; it was proof that any Black MAN who follows the Code can do the same.

Ownership has always been the dividing line between freedom and dependence, and Cuffe's mission was to ensure that Black men had the ability to own. He knew that wealth without structure was meaningless, so he used his success to advocate for Black self-sufficiency. White supremacy fears Black men who produce because production eliminates the need for validation or handouts. A system built on Black male dependency will always move to destroy those who break the cycle, which is why Cuffe faced resistance at every turn. But the Code is clear: a Black MAN must produce at all costs, because survival without ownership is just another form of enslavement.

Cuffe's fight for Black property ownership and voting rights wasn't just about politics; it was about controlling one's own survival. White supremacy has always tied political power to economic dependence, ensuring that Black men who cannot own also cannot govern. Cuffe knew that a Black MAN who produces must also protect what he builds, which means securing a say in the laws that govern him. A Black man's true measure isn't in what he says, but in what he creates. White supremacy promotes the lie that Black men are powerless, but Cuffe proved that power isn't given; it's built. His trade empire stood as evidence that nothing could stop a Black MAN who follows the Code. The greatest threat to the system isn't rebellion; it's self-sufficiency. A Black MAN who doesn't seek validation is a Black MAN who cannot be controlled. Cuffe's legacy isn't just about wealth; it's about breaking the psychological chains of dependency. His life is proof that a Black MAN's strength lies in his ability to produce, no matter the obstacles placed before him.

Cuffe's legacy is the embodiment of what it means to be a builder, a producer, and a MAN who commands his own destiny. White supremacy has always tried to erase Black success, ensuring that each generation starts from nothing. But Cuffe made sure his knowledge, strategies, and wealth would serve as a guide for future Black men. The Code demands that a Black MAN leaves something behind, that his work outlasts him, and Cuffe fulfilled that duty with precision. His success wasn't a miracle; it was the result of discipline, foresight, and an unshakable commitment to production. He wasn't just a businessman; he was the very definition of a Black MAN who refuses to be conquered. The fight has always been about control, and Cuffe's success showed that we, as Black men, reclaim our power when we take command of our own economic future. He built, he produced, and he left a legacy that could not be erased. The Code demands that a Black MAN create, not just for himself, but for future generations. White supremacy thrives on keeping Black men focused on temporary gains, but Cuffe's legacy shows that lasting success requires infrastructure, discipline, and self-sufficiency. His story is more than history; it's a blueprint for securing economic independence. Cuffe didn't just make money; he made history by refusing to be controlled. Production eliminates the need for permission, validation, or external control. That's why white supremacy resists it; it depends on Black dependence, ensuring each generation starts from scratch. Cuffe's legacy poses a challenge to every Black MAN today: will you build, or will you remain a worker in another man's system? The answer determines whether Black men remain in survival mode or step into true power. The code is clear: a Black MAN must produce, because without production, there is no respect, no legacy, and no freedom. Paul Cuffe understood this truth, and so did Reginald F. Lewis.

REGINALD F. Lewis: The Titan Who Took What Was His

Where Cuffe laid the foundation for Black economic independence, Reginald F. Lewis elevated it to a global scale. He wasn't just a businessman; he was a strategist who understood the power of ownership in a system designed to exclude Black men. White supremacy evolved from physical barriers to financial ones, ensuring Black men remained locked out of major economic opportunities. But, like Cuffe, Lewis refused to accept limitations. He proved that a Black MAN who follows the Code can play and win at the highest levels. Born in 1942 in Baltimore, Maryland,

Lewis grew up in a working-class family that instilled discipline, education, and perseverance. His grandfather emphasized self-sufficiency and ownership, shaping Lewis's mindset early on. Excelling in both academics and athletics, he embodied the 14 Codes long before he ever defined them. Lewis understood that true success comes from ownership, not just participation. The system is designed to keep Black men working but never owning, consuming but never controlling. Lewis recognized early that to win, he had to master the rules and then rewrite them. His transition from law to business wasn't just about wealth; it was about dominance in an arena never meant for him. A Black MAN who follows the Code knows that without production, he's just a pawn in another man's empire.

The acquisition of TLC Beatrice International wasn't just a financial move; it was a direct challenge to a system that historically denied Black men the right to build. White supremacy ensures Black men remain employees rather than owners, allowing wealth to pass through them but never to them. Lewis shattered that structure, proving that a Black MAN who commands his own destiny cannot be controlled. Ownership is power, and Lewis showed that a Black MAN does not ask for opportunities; he takes them. His billion-dollar deal proved that strategy, discipline, and execution make any structure vulnerable. A Black man's success isn't based on talent alone; strategy dictates the level of success. The system distracts Black men with meaningless battles while real power is quietly transferred. Lewis never fell for it. He stayed focused on his mission, knowing that a Black MAN who controls his emotions controls his destiny. White supremacy thrives when Black men are unorganized, emotional, and undisciplined, Lewis embodied the opposite.

A Black man's word is his bond, and without it, he is useless. Lewis understood that credibility is currency, and without execution, the system would use failure as justification to deny future Black men the same opportunities. White supremacy feeds off Black men breaking our word, overpromising, and falling short. But Lewis moved with purpose and precision proving that when a Black man backs his word with action, it can't be denied. In our Code, excuses don't exist and Lewis never made room for any. The system hands us every excuse to settle for less, but a Black MAN who lives by the Code knows that only results count. White supremacy trains us to see ourselves as victims of our situation, but Lewis refused to live like that. A Black MAN who follows the Code gives reason, not excuse; he finds a way to win or creates one. The system fears this mindset because once Black men collectively reject excuses, they become unstoppable.

Lewis operated with the understanding that without production, he was as good as dead. A Black man's value is measured by what he builds, and without production, he has no leverage. White supremacy encourages Black men to consume rather than create, to work rather than own, keeping them dependent. Lewis proved that the only escape is to build something so powerful that it cannot be ignored. A Black MAN must do more than survive; he must thrive, create, and dominate in his field. Respect is not requested; it is commanded. Lewis did not beg for a seat at the table; he bought the table and dictated the rules. White supremacy conditions Black men to ask for acceptance, to wait for permission to lead. Lewis rejected this entirely, understanding that power is taken, not given. A Black MAN who follows the Code never lowers himself to begging; he builds, owns, and commands respect through action. The system fights this because a Black MAN who knows his worth cannot be controlled. A Black MAN who fails to produce is powerless, at the mercy of a system designed to use and discard him. White supremacy thrives on Black men who waste time, seek validation, or react instead of build. When Black men fail to produce, they contribute to their own oppression, reinforcing the false narrative that they are incapable of leadership. The system doesn't have to actively oppress a Black MAN who does not produce; his own inaction ensures his downfall. The choice is clear: follow the Code and build, or ignore it and be controlled. Reginald F. Lewis exemplified what happens when a Black MAN follows the Code. His success wasn't accidental; it was the result of strategy, discipline, and execution. White supremacy does everything possible to prevent Black men from thinking like Lewis, from realizing that true power comes from ownership. A Black MAN who follows the Code understands he doesn't need permission to succeed; he creates his own opportunities. The system can only control those who lack discipline, fail to produce, or seek validation instead of respect.

"A Broke Nigga Might as Well Be a Dead Nigga" Nipsey Hussle

We, as Black men, must make a choice: will we control our future, or will we let the system dictate our path? Reginald F. Lewis made his choice, and his billion-dollar deal was proof that a Black MAN who follows the Code cannot be stopped. The system will always set traps and create distractions to prevent Black men from following the blueprint that Lewis laid out. But the truth is clear: a Black MAN who builds, produces, and controls his own resources is the system's biggest threat. The real question is, will Black men embrace the Code and claim what's rightfully theirs? A Black MAN who does not produce has already accepted his downfall. The world doesn't reward potential; it rewards action, creation, and value. Many Black men have had the talent and opportunities to carve out their destinies, but they let distractions weaken them. White supremacy knows that a Black MAN without production is one it can control. The Code is simple: either you build, or you remain at the mercy of those who do.

History proves that Black men who do not produce are forgotten, disrespected, and powerless. Potential is nothing without action. White supremacy doesn't fear talent; it fears a Black MAN who turns that talent into power. A man who chooses laziness, distractions, or dependency over discipline and focus is playing into the system that's designed to break him. Without production, he has no leverage, and without leverage, he's at the mercy of those who control the world. Production separates leaders from liabilities, builders from beggars, and legends from cautionary tales. Too many Black men have chosen comfort over creation, entertainment over enterprise, and excuses over action. The system doesn't need to destroy a Black MAN who refuses to build; he destroys himself through inaction. White supremacy doesn't block every opportunity; it convinces Black men not to take them. A Black MAN without production has no power. He lives under the rules of those who create, stripped of authority over his own life. True dominance isn't achieved through violence or law, but through economic control, because he who owns, rules. Dependency is the system's greatest weapon, thriving when Black men surrender their ability to provide for themselves. Production is not just about money; it's about sovereignty. A Black MAN who builds ensures he is never under another man's thumb. White supremacy wants Black men reliant, but a Black MAN who owns cannot be owned. He doesn't ask for a seat at the table; he builds his own.

The Code is clear: if you don't produce, you don't matter. The world respects creators, not consumers. Every moment spent on distractions steals from the future. A Black MAN who refuses to build will always be at the mercy of those who do. The question is simple: will you master your fate, or be a pawn in someone else's game? Paul Cuffe understood this. Reginald F. Lewis mastered it. Their legacies challenge Black men today: build or be forgotten. The Code demands that a Black MAN produces because, without production, there is no respect, no legacy, and no freedom. A Black MAN must reject the illusion that success is solely individual. Wealth means nothing if the collective remains powerless. White supremacy thrives on Black consumption and dependency, ensuring Black men don't build for themselves. Efforts have been made to keep them divided, competing for scraps instead of pooling resources to create sustainable industries. The Code calls for more than personal success; it requires creating opportunities for others, ensuring future generations don't start from nothing. True power lies in collective economic strength, not fleeting individual wins. Every Black MAN faces a choice: to produce or serve. There's no middle ground. A man who does not produce is forever at the mercy of someone else's system, forced to follow rules he didn't create. White supremacy's greatest weapon is convincing Black men that they can be respected without ownership and free without power. But respect is never given; it's taken. A

Black MAN who lives by the Code understands the only path to independence is through production.

The system is designed to keep Black men at the bottom, making them believe their only options are to work for someone else or beg for inclusion. But a Black MAN who produces is dangerous because he exposes the lie of dependency. He can't be contained because he creates his own opportunities, controls his own wealth, and shapes his own destiny. This is why production is non-negotiable; it's the difference between power and submission. When Black men reject dependency, they become unstoppable. Production isn't just about survival; it's about domination. The war against Black men has always been economic. Slavery wasn't just about labor; it was about making sure Black men remained workers, not owners. Even after the chains came off, financial bondage remained, disguised as policies, social conditioning, and economic barriers. A Black MAN who follows the Code doesn't fall for these traps. He knows that power is never given; it's taken. White supremacy's greatest fear is a Black MAN who refuses to be controlled, who doesn't wait for opportunities but creates them. The system only wins if Black men refuse to play the game on their own terms. Black production has always been under attack, and it always will be. This isn't about fairness or morality; it's about power. The world doesn't care about Black men's complaints; it respects results. A Black MAN who follows the Code doesn't waste time blaming the system. He studies it, masters it, and outsmarts it. White supremacy can't stop a man who refuses to be stopped. The only thing standing between a Black MAN and his power is his willingness to produce. This fight isn't about equality; it's about sovereignty. There's no freedom without ownership, no respect without production, and no power without control. For centuries, the system has kept Black men at the bottom, but the Code offers the only solution: build, own, and control. A Black MAN who produces doesn't seek validation; his work speaks for itself. The world respects those who control resources. If we, as Black men, fail to take this truth seriously, we'll remain at the mercy of those who do. A Black MAN must decide: will he build, or be ruled? There's no third option. A Black MAN who cannot produce is already dead. The only question is whether he accepts it or changes his fate.

SOVEREIGNTY

Dependence is weakness; ownership is power. Sovereignty means taking full control of your life, your mind, your money, and your decisions. A man who owns his resources, time, and influence is a man who cannot be manipulated or controlled. This principle applies to economics, education, and self-sufficiency. You must build and protect what is yours, ensuring that you answer to no one but yourself and your Creator.

CODE NO. 13

A BLACK MAN HOLDS HIS PEERS
ACCOUNTABLE

Accountability is the backbone of real leadership and integrity. A Black man who refuses to check his people is a man who lets weakness, dysfunction, and failure run wild. Without accountability, there's no growth, no discipline, and no power—just chaos. Holding each other to a higher standard isn't about control; it's about ensuring that we, as Black men, uphold strength and excellence. A community without accountability is one that allows mediocrity to define it, and mediocrity is death to a people who are already fighting against a system that wants to see them fail. Black history has shown us that the strongest men, the real leaders, were those who weren't afraid to check their peers. Men like Malcolm X, Fred Hampton, and Dick Gregory understood that progress comes from discipline, responsibility, and an unshakable commitment to greatness. They called out the system for its injustices, but they also called out their own people when necessary. *"Accountability isn't hate; it's love."* A weak man avoids accountability because he fears conflict; a strong man embraces it because he knows it's the only path to power.

A Black man who is never held accountable is a man who will continue to make the same mistakes, stuck in a cycle of failure. Iron sharpens iron, and without that pressure, men stay dull, unpolished, and ineffective. When we hold each other accountable, we create a culture where strength, discipline, and success are expected. Without it, we fall into habits that destroy us: excuses, laziness, and self-destruction. A real man doesn't make excuses; he makes corrections. A real brotherhood doesn't let its men fall; they pull them up, whether they like it or not. But here's the deeper truth: white supremacy has never been held accountable for the damage it has done to Black people, especially Black men. This country was built on the exploitation, degradation, and destruction of Black men, and yet, no real responsibility has ever been taken. The system kills, incarcerates, and strips Black men of opportunity, then turns around and blames them for their condition. America has never admitted to its crimes, never repaid its debts, and never truly acknowledged the suffering it has caused. Instead, it shifts the blame onto Black men, expecting us to fix a problem we didn't create while it continues to profit from our struggle.

For centuries, this system has been built on Black

labor, Black bodies, and Black suffering. From slavery to Jim Crow to mass incarceration, America has found new ways to break the Black man while avoiding any real accountability. When the chains of slavery were broken, they created the prison-industrial complex. When segregation was outlawed, they flooded our communities with drugs and guns. When we demanded justice, they assassinated our leaders. Every time Black men have risen, the system has worked to knock us back down. And yet, despite all of this, they still refuse to acknowledge their hand in our oppression. They tell us to *"pull ourselves up by the bootstraps"* while making sure we don't even own the boots. The failure of white supremacy to take accountability is why Black men must hold themselves to an even higher standard. If the world refuses to be fair, then we must be so strong, so disciplined, and so unstoppable that the system can't ignore us. We can't wait for justice; we must demand it. But that demand starts from within. If Black men are to rise, they must first police themselves. We can't afford to let weakness slide, to let destructive behavior fester, or to allow excuses to rule our actions. The world already counts us out; we can't do the same to ourselves.

Historically, the Black men who held their people accountable were seen as threats, not just by their own, but by the system itself. Malcolm X, Fred Hampton, and even Jim Brown weren't just fighting racism; they were fighting complacency within the Black community. That's what made them dangerous. The system fears a Black man who refuses to be weak, a Black man who demands accountability from himself and his brothers, because that man cannot be controlled. Accountability is not public humiliation; it's real love. It's refusing to let your brother fail. It's speaking the truth, even when it's hard. It's understanding that without discipline, there is no progress. A strong brotherhood is one where men push each other to be their best because anything less is unacceptable. Without accountability, there is no power, no respect, no future. Either we hold ourselves to the highest standard, or we let the world define us. And history has shown, when we let others define us, they will always define us as less than what we are.

The time for excuses is over. Black men must take their power back, and that starts with holding each other accountable. It means checking your brother when he's slipping, correcting bad habits before they become permanent, and setting expectations so high that failure is not an option. It means refusing to entertain self-destructive behavior, whether it's in the home, in the streets, or in the workplace. It means making accountability a culture, a lifestyle, and a requirement for every Black man who wants to see his people rise. If we don't do this, we leave the door open for the same system that has been killing us for centuries to keep doing its work. But if we take accountability seriously, if we demand it from ourselves and our brothers, then there's nothing this world can do to stop us. A community built on accountability is a community built on power. And power is the only language this world respects. It's time to speak it fluently.

DICK GREGORY: The Unfiltered Truth-Teller Who Held Black America Accountable

Dick Gregory was more than just a comedian; he was a force of nature who used his platform to challenge both Black and white audiences. Born in 1932 in St. Louis, Missouri, Gregory grew up in poverty and faced firsthand the struggles of being Black in America. Comedy became his entryway into the entertainment world, but he never saw himself as just an entertainer. His humor was sharp, biting, and rooted in the painful realities of racism, injustice, and inequality. Unlike many Black comedians of his time, he refused to shy away from controversial topics or make himself the butt of jokes for white amusement. Instead, he flipped the script, using comedy to expose uncomfortable truths. Gregory's big break came when Hugh Hefner invited him to perform at the Playboy Club in 1961, where he impressed an all-white audience with his unfiltered honesty. This moment catapulted him into mainstream success, but he never lost sight of his greater purpose. While other Black comedians focused on making people laugh, Gregory used laughter as a weapon against oppression. He quickly became known as a fearless truth-teller, willing to call out injustice regardless of the consequences. His comedy laid the foundation for a new kind of Black entertainer, one who didn't just entertain but educated and agitated. Gregory never played it safe, and that refusal to conform defined his career.

Beyond comedy, he was deeply involved in activism, risking everything to fight for civil rights and social justice. He joined protests, went on hunger strikes, and faced arrest multiple times for standing up to racial oppression. Unlike celebrities who stayed neutral to protect their careers, Gregory put his on the line without hesitation. He believed that having a platform meant having a responsibility to use it for good. Many Black entertainers at the time feared losing white approval, but Gregory never cared about being palatable to the mainstream. His loyalty was to the truth, not to his audience's comfort.

Gregory saw himself as more than a performer; he was a soldier in the fight for justice. He walked alongside Martin Luther King Jr., marched in Selma, and participated in protests against segregation and police brutality. While his peers chased Hollywood fame, he turned his back on the industry to commit himself fully to activism. He understood that making white people laugh was not nearly as important as making them uncomfortable with the reality of Black suffering. This commitment cost him roles, endorsements, and financial security, but Gregory never wavered. He valued his integrity more than his income, a rare quality in an era when entertainers were expected to *"stay in their lane."*

Even in his later years, Gregory never softened his approach or became complacent. He remained an outspoken critic of racial injustice, government corruption, and systemic oppression. Unlike many activists who mellowed with age, he only became more radical and unfiltered. He spoke truth to power, whether addressing college students, news reporters, or fellow activists. Gregory never sought approval or validation; he was only interested in exposing lies and waking people up. His refusal to conform made him a polarizing figure, but history vindicated his words time and time again. To many, he was a prophet, one who saw through the illusions of society and called them out without hesitation. He dissected the ways racism operated not just through laws but through the media, the food industry, and government policies. Gregory was one of the first public figures to expose the role of diet in Black health, urging people to abandon the unhealthy habits that were killing them. His activism extended beyond race; he was also deeply involved in anti-war movements, environmental activism, and government transparency. He believed that oppression existed on multiple levels, and Black people had to wake up to all of them. His life was a blueprint for speaking truthfully and fearlessly, no matter the cost.

Dick Gregory was not the type to sugarcoat his words when it came to the Black community. He believed that Black people needed to take responsibility for their own progress, not just blame racism. While he acknowledged systemic oppression, he also challenged the complacency, self-destruction, and division within the community. He called out the obsession with materialism, celebrity worship, and lack of discipline among Black people. Many were uncomfortable with his words, but he didn't care; his goal was to spark change, not to win popularity. Gregory saw accountability as love, not as criticism.

He often questioned why Black people would spend billions on designer brands while neglecting their own economic empowerment. Gregory exposed the irony of protesting white racism while continuing to support white-owned businesses. He urged Black people to prioritize education, entrepreneurship, and self-reliance over entertainment and consumerism. Many resented his blunt approach, but he believed in *"tough love."* Unlike others who pandered to emotions, Gregory pushed Black people to examine their own role in their oppression. He believed that empowerment started with self-awareness and self-discipline.

Gregory also criticized Black celebrities who used their fame for selfish gain instead of uplifting the community. He saw how many entertainers remained silent on injustice to protect their careers, and he called them out without hesitation. To him, being Black and successful came with a duty to the people, not just to personal wealth. He was especially critical of those who engaged in destructive behavior while being role models for young Black children. Gregory didn't care how rich or famous someone was; if they weren't contributing to the upliftment of the race, he had no respect for them. He believed that true success wasn't about money but about making a lasting impact. Another area where Gregory held Black people accountable was health. He was ahead of his time in promoting plant-based diets, fasting, and holistic living. He pointed out how the food industry was poisoning Black people with processed junk, leading to high rates of diabetes, hypertension, and obesity. While others ignored the issue, Gregory made it his mission to educate the community about the link between diet and disease. He argued that poor health weakened Black resistance, making it easier for systemic oppression to continue. His message wasn't just about surviving racism; it was about thriving despite it.

Gregory didn't just talk about accountability; he lived it. He practiced everything he preached, from healthy eating to financial independence. He never waited for government handouts or white approval to make moves; he built his own lane. Gregory showed that Black people didn't need validation from the mainstream to succeed. His example proved that discipline, knowledge, and integrity were more valuable than wealth. He was a walking testament to what self-reliance looked like in action. While many viewed his critiques as harsh, Gregory saw them as necessary. He didn't believe in false optimism or feel-good rhetoric that ignored real issues. He knew that Black people couldn't afford to be comfortable in a world that worked against them. Gregory's message was clear: no one was coming to save Black people but themselves. He believed that true liberation required internal change as much as external resistance. His accountability forced people to reflect, even when they didn't want to hear it.

Dick Gregory didn't just talk about change; he put himself on the front lines of the Civil Rights Movement. Unlike many Black entertainers who distanced themselves from activism, he risked his career, wealth, and personal safety for the cause. He was present at pivotal moments in history, marching alongside Dr. Martin Luther King Jr. and other leaders. Gregory didn't just give speeches from a safe distance; he was in the trenches, getting arrested and enduring brutal conditions to make a difference. He understood that fighting for justice meant more than making bold statements; it required action. His activism set him apart from those who only talked about progress but refused to sacrifice for it.

Gregory used his platform to expose the hypocrisy of America, calling out the government for its treatment of Black people. During his speeches, he fearlessly condemned police brutality, segregation, and economic oppression. He didn't hold back, even when his words made powerful people uncomfortable. He publicly criticized the Vietnam War, exposing how Black soldiers were sent to fight overseas while being denied basic rights at home. This stance cost him opportunities in Hollywood, but he never cared about approval. Gregory's mission was bigger than entertainment; it was about awakening the minds of his people. One of his most powerful moments came when he ran for mayor of Chicago in 1967 and then for president in 1968. He knew he wouldn't win, but that wasn't the point; his goal was to challenge the system and expose its corruption. His presidential campaign, though unconventional, forced America to acknowledge the issues facing Black people. Gregory used his candidacy to push radical ideas, like reparations and economic self-sufficiency. While the mainstream media dismissed him as a joke, his campaign inspired countless young activists. He proved that real power wasn't in seeking validation but in challenging the status quo.

Gregory also played a critical role in voter registration drives, encouraging Black people to understand the power of their vote. He believed that political engagement was just as crucial as protest and economic empowerment. Unlike many entertainers who remained silent about politics, Gregory was vocal about how policies affected Black lives. He used his humor to break down complex political issues, making them accessible to everyday people. His speeches weren't just about pointing out problems; they were about mobilizing people to act. Gregory understood that knowledge without action was useless. His activism extended beyond race; he was deeply involved in social justice on multiple fronts. He spoke out against police violence, government corruption, and economic exploitation. His speeches were filled with historical knowledge, proving that injustice was not an isolated issue. He taught that fighting oppression required understanding its roots, not just reacting to its symptoms.

Gregory's commitment to truth made him a target for government surveillance. The FBI monitored him closely, labeling him a *"dangerous radical."* His phone was tapped, his events were watched, and he was constantly harassed for his outspoken nature. But instead of being intimidated, he exposed the government's hypocrisy even further. He knew that any Black person willing to challenge the system would be seen as a threat. Gregory saw it as proof that he was on the right path, if the enemy wasn't watching him, he wasn't doing enough.

Dick Gregory's fearless accountability forced Black people to confront uncomfortable truths about themselves. He didn't allow excuses, complacency, or victimhood to dominate the conversation. While he acknowledged systemic racism, he also emphasized personal responsibility, discipline, and unity. Many Black leaders avoided these discussions because they were unpopular, but Gregory wasn't concerned with popularity. His message was simple: if Black people wanted real change, they had to be willing to change themselves. His words were often harsh, but they were rooted in love and a deep desire for progress. Gregory was one of the first public figures to address the dangers of unhealthy eating habits in the Black community. He exposed how poor diets were being weaponized against Black people through processed foods, fast-food chains, and government neglect. While others focused solely on political oppression, Gregory understood that health was a form of power. He believed that a physically strong and mentally sharp Black population was harder to oppress. His message encouraged many people to adopt plant-based diets, fast regularly, and take control of their health. This legacy of wellness is still felt today.

His willingness to hold Black people accountable also extended to economic habits. He criticized the obsession with materialism and the lack of investment in Black-owned businesses. Gregory urged Black people to circulate their money within their own communities instead of enriching corporations that didn't care about them. He warned that economic dependence on white-owned industries would always keep Black people in a vulnerable position. While many were offended by his critiques, they were undeniable truths. Gregory believed that financial independence was the key to true freedom. He also exposed the failures of Black leadership, particularly those who sought personal gain over collective progress. He wasn't afraid to call out politicians, religious figures, and celebrities who exploited their own people. He saw how many *"so-called"* leaders made deals behind closed doors while pretending to fight for justice. Gregory refused to play that game; his loyalty was to the truth, not to titles or institutions. He believed that Black people had to stop blindly following leaders without questioning their motives. His words inspired a new generation to demand transparency and accountability from those in power.

Gregory's impact went beyond just speeches; his actions proved that accountability required sacrifice. He walked away from Hollywood fame to focus on activism full-time, losing millions in potential earnings. He endured hunger strikes, arrests, and financial hardship because he refused to compromise his principles. While many entertainers chased luxury, Gregory lived modestly and gave his money to the causes in which he believed in. His life was a testament to the fact that true leadership requires putting the mission above personal comfort. He set a standard that few were willing to follow. Perhaps Gregory's greatest legacy was his ability to make people think. Even those who disagreed with him couldn't ignore the logic behind his arguments. He challenged both Black and white people to look beyond propaganda and see the truth for themselves. His speeches, books, and interviews remain relevant today because they addressed root issues, not just temporary problems. Gregory knew that real change started with the mind; if people changed their way of thinking, they could change their circumstances. His accountability forced Black people to *"wake up"* and take charge of their destiny.

Dick Gregory never sought validation from the mainstream, and that's what made him so powerful. He was never afraid to tell Black and white people exactly what they needed to hear. He didn't pander, sugarcoat, or water down his message to be more acceptable. Gregory was a truth-teller in the purest sense, willing to risk everything for the greater good. His influence extended beyond his lifetime, continuing to inspire activists, comedians, and leaders. He proved that real power lies in honesty, courage, and unwavering integrity. His impact on the Civil Rights Movement, health activism, and economic empowerment cannot be overstated. Gregory didn't just talk about change; he embodied it. He left behind a blueprint for future generations on how to hold themselves accountable. His work serves as a reminder that progress requires both external resistance and internal discipline. Gregory's life was proof that speaking the truth is always worth it, no matter the cost. In a world full of cowards, he was a fearless warrior for justice.

Dick Gregory's fearless commitment to truth and accountability set a powerful precedent for Black leadership. He was never afraid to challenge both the system and his own people, urging them to take responsibility for their progress. But while Gregory used comedy and activism to call out hypocrisy, another Black man in history held a different kind of power, one that forced the U.S. military and government to reckon with their own contradictions.

DAVID FAGAN: A Rebel Who Demanded Accountability in the Face of Injustice

David Fagen was born in 1875 in Tampa, Florida, during the height of Reconstruction, a time when Black Americans faced severe racial discrimination despite their formal emancipation. His early life was shaped by the systemic racism that limited opportunities for Black men, making the military one of the few places where they could earn a steady income and gain a sense of purpose. At the age of 24, he enlisted in the U.S. Army and was assigned to the 24th Infantry Regiment, a unit composed entirely of Black soldiers, known as *"Buffalo Soldiers."* The Buffalo Soldiers had a long history of service, having fought in the Indian Wars and the Spanish-American War, often in support of U.S. expansionist policies. While their bravery was undeniable, they frequently faced racism from their white officers and the U.S. government. Despite this, Fagen joined in hopes of proving himself as a soldier and securing a better future.

In 1899, Fagen and his regiment were deployed to the Philippines as part of the U.S. effort to suppress the Filipino independence movement. The war had begun after the U.S. defeated Spain in 1898 and took control of the Philippines instead of granting them independence. Filipino rebels, led by Emilio Aguinaldo, resisted American occupation, launching a guerrilla war against U.S. forces. Fagen quickly saw the parallels between the Filipinos' struggle and the plight of Black Americans back home. The U.S. justified its war in the Philippines with claims of bringing *"civilization"* to a *"lesser"* people, a rhetoric eerily similar to the arguments used to justify slavery and segregation in America. Fagen, like many Black soldiers, began questioning his role in enforcing an imperialist agenda against another oppressed people. Throughout his service, Fagen experienced racism firsthand from white officers who viewed Black troops as inferior. Black soldiers were often given the most grueling tasks, subjected to harsher discipline, and denied promotions despite their competence. Meanwhile, they were expected to enforce American rule over Filipinos, who were also being demeaned as racially inferior. Many Black soldiers found themselves in an ethical dilemma: Should they continue fighting for a country that oppressed both them and the people they were sent to conquer? Some Black troops sympathized with the Filipinos, seeing their fight for freedom as no different from the struggle of Black Americans. This internal conflict led to growing tensions within the ranks, culminating in Fagen's bold decision to defect.

In November 1899, David Fagen deserted the U.S. Army and joined the Filipino resistance. His defection was not an impulsive act but a deliberate rejection of American imperialism and racial oppression. By choosing to fight alongside the Filipinos, he made a powerful statement: he would not be a pawn in America's colonial ambitions. His knowledge of U.S. military tactics and weaponry made him a valuable asset to the Filipino guerrilla forces. He quickly earned the respect of Filipino commanders, who recognized his skills and leadership. Within months, he was promoted to the rank of captain in the Filipino army, a remarkable achievement for a former U.S. soldier. Fagen's defection sent shockwaves through the U.S. military, which considered him a traitor. White officers saw his actions as an unforgivable betrayal, while Black soldiers silently admired his courage. For Fagen, this was not just a personal rebellion but an act of solidarity with the oppressed. His story spread quickly, becoming a symbol of Black resistance against racial and colonial subjugation. Some Black soldiers debated following in his footsteps, but most knew the consequences of desertion were severe. The U.S. military responded by intensifying its campaign against guerrillas and placing a bounty on Fagen's head.

The U.S. labeled Fagen an outlaw, using propaganda to paint him as a dangerous renegade. Posters and reports described him as a ruthless enemy of America, but to Filipinos, he was a hero. His presence inspired other defectors, including a few Black and white soldiers who saw through America's false promises.

Fagen's understanding of U.S. military strategy helped the Filipino resistance launch successful attacks against American forces. His knowledge of terrain, supply lines, and troop movements allowed the guerrillas to evade capture and strike at critical moments. The longer he remained free, the more he embarrassed the U.S. military.

As a leader in the Filipino resistance, Fagen commanded a group of fighters who specialized in hit-and-run tactics. The U.S. military, trained for conventional warfare, struggled against the elusive guerrilla forces. Fagen's ability to think like an American soldier gave the Filipinos an edge, allowing them to anticipate enemy movements and adapt accordingly. His troops ambushed U.S. patrols, sabotaged supply lines, and disrupted American control over key areas. Despite limited resources, Fagen's unit inflicted damage that far exceeded its numbers. The U.S. Army launched numerous missions to capture him, but he always managed to slip away.

Fagen's defiance of the U.S. military was not just about personal survival; it was about proving that Black men could fight for justice on their own terms. He refused to be an instrument of oppression and instead became a symbol of rebellion. His actions embarrassed American officials, who feared that his defection could inspire more Black soldiers to question their loyalty. Reports of Fagen's exploits were suppressed in the U.S., but within Black communities, his story spread through word of mouth. His leadership represented a challenge to both U.S. imperialism and the notion that Black men had to serve a nation that denied them basic rights. He was not just a soldier; he was a revolutionary.

David Fagen's defection and leadership in the Filipino resistance highlighted the contradictions of American democracy. The U.S. claimed to be a land of freedom while simultaneously subjugating both Black Americans and Filipinos. His actions forced uncomfortable questions about Black soldiers' roles in enforcing American imperialism. Should Black men fight for a country that treated them as second-class citizens? Could they justify oppressing others while demanding equality at home? These questions remain relevant in discussions about Black participation in U.S. military conflicts today. The U.S. military never captured Fagen, and his fate remains uncertain. Some reports claim he was killed by Filipino scouts seeking a reward, while others suggest he escaped and lived in hiding. Regardless of his final days, his story continues to inspire those who resist injustice. His defection proved that Black men could take a stand against oppression, even at great personal risk. In the decades that followed, his legacy lived on in Black resistance movements, influencing leaders who questioned America's moral authority. Though erased from mainstream history, David Fagen remains a symbol of defiance and courage.

JIM BROWN: A Relentless Leader Who Held Himself and His Community Accountable

Jim Brown's reputation in the realm of activism extended far beyond his athletic career. He became an advocate for social change and used his celebrity status to challenge systemic racism and support Black empowerment. What sets Brown apart is his willingness to hold his peers accountable, something he consistently demonstrated in his interactions with other Black men. Brown saw the potential for change within the Black community, but he recognized that this required a collective effort to embrace responsibility. This approach was especially evident in his work with gangs, where he believed that true liberation came from both individual accountability and community support. Brown's philosophy was grounded in the idea that Black men could take ownership of their destinies by adhering to a code of conduct that valued respect, integrity, and leadership. By holding others to these standards, Brown became a pivotal figure in transforming Black masculinity into a force for positive change.

While Jim Brown was an undeniable force on the football field, his legacy as a civil rights leader is just as significant. Brown didn't just use his platform to entertain; he used it to advance the cause of Black equality. He was unafraid to speak out against the injustices that plagued the Black community, holding both the government and his peers accountable for their role in perpetuating systemic oppression. This extended beyond rhetoric into action, as Brown worked closely with figures like Muhammad Ali, Kareem Abdul-Jabbar, and others to push for Black empowerment. He understood that holding his peers accountable meant challenging them to use their voices and influence for more than just personal gain. Brown's refusal to back down in the face of adversity showcased the core of Code #13: demanding responsibility from those in positions of power and influence. This commitment to accountability was not a fleeting moment; it was a life-long pursuit that would guide his work in the years to come.

Jim Brown's involvement in civil rights was revolutionary, especially given the context of his time. As a successful athlete in the 1960s, he was one of the few prominent Black men who boldly spoke out about the issues facing Black America. In an era when most Black athletes were expected to focus solely on their sport, Brown defied these expectations by taking an active role in shaping the civil rights movement. He consistently held his peers accountable for their lack of engagement, encouraging athletes to not only acknowledge the struggles of Black people but also to actively fight for change. Brown's refusal to be complacent and his call for his fellow athletes to use their platforms for justice showcased a commitment to social responsibility that mirrored "*Code #13*" in action. His leadership was a call for all Black men, whether in sports or outside of it, to recognize the power of their voices and to use them for the collective good. By holding his peers accountable in this way, Brown helped to shift the narrative on Black manhood in America.

One of Jim Brown's most impactful ventures was the creation of the Black Economic Union, an organization designed to empower Black communities through economic independence. His goal was to provide an alternative to the societal structures that oppressed Black people, offering avenues for financial and social growth. This initiative was deeply tied to his belief in the power of self-reliance and accountability. Brown knew that real change came from within the community and that holding one's peers accountable meant ensuring they took responsibility for their own economic futures. The Black Economic Union sought to shift the focus from dependence on outside forces to the building of a strong, self-sustaining Black economy. Brown didn't just talk about change; he actively worked to create opportunities for Black people to take charge of their lives. His push for economic empowerment was a direct challenge to the systemic issues that kept Black men in cycles of poverty and criminality, calling on them to break free by embracing responsibility.

Brown's most remarkable contributions to the community were his efforts in gang intervention, particularly in Los Angeles during the 1980s. At a time when gang violence was ravaging Black communities, Jim Brown stepped in to offer a path toward peace and redemption. Rather than viewing gang members as irredeemable, he saw them as individuals who could be held accountable for their actions but could also be given the tools to change. Brown reached out to gang leaders directly, not through grand speeches or lofty ideals, but through real conversations where he challenged them to rethink their impact on the community. His approach wasn't about force; it was about understanding, empathy, and ultimately holding people accountable for their choices. Brown's role in gang intervention illustrated the deep connection between personal responsibility and collective well-being. His work with the gangs demonstrated how Code #13 could be applied in even the most dangerous and seemingly hopeless environments.

Brown's willingness to engage directly with gang leaders was a testament to his belief in accountability. He didn't shy away from the difficult conversations or the potential risks involved in reaching out to those entrenched in violence. His approach was grounded in the understanding that many of these men had been shaped by systemic oppression, but that didn't excuse their actions. Brown used his status to gain access to gang leaders, offering them an alternative to the lifestyle they had chosen. He held these men accountable by challenging them to take responsibility for their actions and their impact on the community. Through these conversations, Brown emphasized that true leadership meant steering people away from self-destructive behaviors and toward constructive goals. His commitment to engaging with the most marginalized members of society reflected his broader philosophy of accountability, where everyone was responsible for the health and safety of the community.

For Brown, personal responsibility was not just an abstract concept; it was a way of life that he expected others to adopt. He believed that the gang members he worked with could break free from their violent lifestyles if they took ownership of their actions. This wasn't about excusing bad behavior but acknowledging the power of individual choice. Brown's efforts weren't about pretending the violence didn't exist; they were about holding people accountable for their role in perpetuating it. He pushed for gang members to recognize their influence on the community, not just in terms of violence but also in terms of their ability to inspire positive change. His philosophy was rooted in the idea that every Black man had the capacity to be a leader, but leadership required discipline, integrity, and accountability. By encouraging gang members to embrace responsibility, Brown gave them a chance at redemption and a pathway out of violence.

Brown's work with gang members wasn't solely about reducing violence; it also involved offering tangible alternatives for success. Education and employment became central pillars of his approach. He understood that without these opportunities, it would be nearly impossible for these men to break free from the cycle of gang life. Brown worked to create pathways for gang members to access job training, education, and employment opportunities that would provide a sustainable future. By providing these resources, he held them accountable not just for their past actions but for their future choices. His goal was to ensure that the men he worked with could see the possibility of a different life, one where their decisions could lead to success rather than destruction. Brown's intervention was about giving them the tools to build their own futures, thereby holding them accountable for their role in shaping their own destinies.

Jim Brown's commitment to accountability didn't stop with gang members; it extended to the broader Black community as well. He often spoke out about the need for Black men to take responsibility for our actions and our place in society. This was not a call for self-blame but for self-determination. Brown recognized that Black men were often subjected to systemic forces beyond their control, but that did not absolve them of their personal responsibility. He believed that accountability required acknowledging one's flaws while also striving to improve. This meant taking ownership of both successes and failures and ensuring that one's actions aligned with the greater good of the community. Brown's philosophy was clear: true freedom and empowerment came from holding oneself accountable for one's choices, no matter the circumstances. The influence of Jim Brown's work in gang intervention and his broader social activism has left an indelible mark on the Black community. His belief in holding others accountable, whether on the field or in the streets, created a blueprint for leadership that many have followed. While his approach was not always popular or easy, it was effective in fostering change. Today, Brown's legacy is a reminder that accountability is not a punitive measure but a necessary step toward empowerment and progress. He proved that even the most entrenched problems could be addressed through personal responsibility and collective effort. His work has inspired a new generation of Black leaders who understand that true progress comes from holding one's peers to high standards. Jim Brown's life was a testament to the power of accountability, and his contributions will continue to inspire for generations to come.

The Unbreakable Bond: A Key to Black Liberation and Strength

The essence of Code #13 lies in the understanding that Black men are strongest when they stand together, holding each other accountable. A Black man who refuses to hold himself and his peers accountable is a man who leaves his community vulnerable to destruction. Accountability is not just a personal principle; it is a weapon—one of the most powerful weapons against white supremacy. White supremacy has never taken responsibility for the centuries of oppression, systemic racism, and deliberate mistreatment of Black people, especially Black men. It has thrived by deflecting blame, rewriting history, and portraying Black men as the problem rather than acknowledging the structural injustices designed to keep them down. This is why Black men cannot afford to operate without a strict code of accountability, because the enemy will never hold itself accountable. A community that polices itself is a community that cannot be controlled by outside forces. That is why accountability is a threat to white supremacy. When Black men embrace accountability, they strip away the excuses, eliminate the distractions, and build a foundation so strong that no outside force can dismantle it. This is the essence of Code #13.

Code #13 requires Black men to look in the mirror and ask: *"Am I living up to the standard? Am I pushing myself and my brothers to be better? Am I setting the tone for the next generation?"* Men like Dick Gregory, David Fagan, and Jim Brown understood this principle. They didn't just demand accountability from others; they lived by it themselves. Gregory never let up on his people, challenging Black men to rise above self-imposed limitations. Fagan took accountability to another level by enforcing discipline in the ranks, ensuring that even in chaos, there was order. Jim Brown did the same in sports and activism, showing that discipline, work ethic, and responsibility were non-negotiable. These men knew that accountability is what separates the strong from the weak. Holding each other accountable is not an act of aggression or control; it is an act of love. It is a declaration that we refuse to let our brothers fall victim to mediocrity, self-destruction, or external manipulation.

Black men have been conditioned to fear accountability because it forces them to confront uncomfortable truths. Many have been taught to see correction as an attack rather than a tool for growth. But the reality is that accountability is the foundation of real power. A man who cannot be corrected cannot be trusted. A man who cannot hold others accountable is a liability. White supremacy grows stronger when we, as Black men, stop holding each other accountable when we let reckless behavior slide and drop our standards just to keep the peace. But true strength comes from embracing accountability, not as a burden but as a responsibility. One of the greatest lies ever told to Black men is that they do not need each other. That independence means isolation. That correction is criticism. That brotherhood is optional. But history has shown that when Black men hold each other accountable, they build movements that shake the world. Accountability was the driving force behind the Civil Rights Movement, the Black Panther Party, and every successful effort to uplift Black people. Without it, chaos reigns, weakness spreads, and white supremacy remains unchecked.

The refusal of white supremacy to take accountability is exactly why Black men must double down on it. We cannot expect justice from those who have never given it. We cannot expect fairness from a system built on exploitation. But what we can do is build our own system, one rooted in responsibility, discipline, and self-respect. The stronger we become through accountability, the less power white supremacy has over us. Accountability is a weapon, and it must be wielded without hesitation. It is what makes the difference between success and failure, between progress and stagnation, between power and submission. This code cannot be violated because it is the foundation upon which all true Black manhood is built. By holding ourselves and our peers accountable, we ensure that the fight for justice, empowerment, and freedom never falters. The responsibility is ours to carry, and it is through this accountability that we will continue to build a stronger, more unified community for generations to come.

CODE NO. 14

A BLACK MAN UNDERSTANDS THAT HIS DICK CAN MAKE OR BREAK HIM

A Black man's greatest downfall often lies between his legs. Weak men move on impulse, chasing pleasure without thought, while disciplined men control their dicks, understanding the consequences of where they place their seed. History proves that when a man's desire for women goes unchecked, it has cost him everything, kingdoms, wealth, reputation, even his life. Black men, in particular, have been targeted for our sexuality, feared and exploited in equal measure. Picking the right women to continue your legacy is vital; it is a choice that dictates legacy, survival, and power. A Black man who masters his urges masters himself. Powerful men been crashing out since the beginning of time because they couldn't keep their thirst in check. Tiger Woods was not defeated by an opponent on the golf course but by his own reckless choices off of it. At the height of his career, Woods was untouchable, a symbol of excellence and dominance in his sport. However, his downfall did not come from injury or competition—it came from his inability to control his dick. His secret life of infidelity was exposed in 2009, shattering his public image and costing him millions in endorsements. The scandal led to his divorce, a decline in his performance, and years of personal and professional struggle. Like so many great men before him, Woods's legacy was nearly destroyed not by an enemy, but by a weakness he failed to control. History continues to repeat itself. From politicians to athletes and entertainers, countless powerful men have seen their empires crumble due to reckless sexual choices. Their downfall is not at the hands of rivals or external forces but from within. A man's greatest enemy is often himself, and those who fail to discipline their desires risk losing everything they've built.

A man who cannot control his dick will always be controlled. White supremacy has long understood the power of Black male sexuality and sought to neutralize it. Laws against interracial relationships, propaganda painting Black men as threats, and the castration of lynching victims were all methods to suppress Black male dominance. White supremacy stays alive when we, as Black men, look the other way instead of checking each other, let damaging actions go unchallenged, and water down our standards just to avoid confrontation. A man who stays distracted stays weak and nothing throws him off more than chasing ass with no discipline. White women have historically been used as bait and weapons against Black men. From Emmett Till to countless others lynched over false accusations, their tears have been a death sentence. Even now, fetishization leads many Black men into dangerous situations where they are set up, manipulated, or destroyed. The courts will always favor their tears over a Black man's truth. Falling for this trap has led to the downfall of many who failed to see the game at play. Choosing the right woman is one of the most important decisions a man will make. Women either elevate a man or destroy him; there is no in-between. A reckless man impregnates a woman who brings chaos, tying himself to dysfunction for generations. A disciplined man chooses a woman who nurtures his legacy, supports his mission, and strengthens his foundation. Many Black men have suffered financially, emotionally, and even physically because they chose the wrong woman. A king cannot build an empire on quicksand. Prisons and graveyards are full of Black men who followed their dicks instead of their minds. Too many have been set up by women they trusted, lured into deadly situations by jealous exes, manipulative lovers, or vindictive partners. The wrong woman can lead a man to his grave without ever pulling the trigger. A Black man who values his life must value where he places his trust and his seed.

Sex is more than physical; it is an exchange of

energy. The wrong exchange drains a man of everything. Lack of discipline leads to wasted time, money, and potential. This is why so many talented men end up broke, lost, or distracted. True power comes from knowing when to act and when to abstain, when to pursue and when to walk away. A Black man who controls his urges controls his future. Society pushes Black men to stay chasing women nonstop because they know it keeps us soft and unfocused. The glorification of sex, reckless relationships, and instant gratification strips men of discipline. A focused Black man is dangerous; he cannot be controlled by temptation or led astray by short-term pleasure. Black men must reject the idea that our worth is tied to sexual conquest and instead build our worth through legacy, power, and self-mastery. A man who values himself does not let his "*dick*" dictate his decisions.

A Black MAN understands that his dick can make or break him. He don't let chasing women cloud his judgment or let a quick fix mess up his long-term grind. He is strategic in choosing the right woman because he knows his seed carries power. He values discipline, knowing that true control comes from mastering himself. A weak man chases, but a strong man chooses. A Black MAN always chooses wisely. History shows any man who can't control his urge for women is on a crash course to ruin. Samson lost his strength to Delilah. Many Black men have met the same fate, trusting the wrong women and paying the price. The system doesn't need to destroy you if you're willing to destroy yourself. White supremacy understands this, which is why Black men are constantly baited with sex, indulgence, and vanity. A man without discipline has no defense. Dr. Martin Luther King Jr.'s legacy was attacked through sexual scandal because his enemies knew they couldn't stop him by force. *"The world does not need to defeat you if it can make you defeat yourself."* Malcolm X, before his transformation, was a reckless man, lost in lust and crime. Only when he mastered himself did he step into his true power. Had he remained undisciplined, he would have been just another statistic. The world respects a man who governs himself but laughs at a man governed by his dick. A Black MAN chooses mastery over destruction.

The entertainment industry is littered with Black men who had it all and lost everything because they lacked discipline. Athletes, musicians, and actors have been ruined by scandals, child support battles, and betrayals by the women they entertained. Some lost their careers, fortunes, and even their lives. The same system that profits from their success profits from their downfall, exploiting their weaknesses. A man who thinks with his *"dick"* instead of his mind is a man who will be played. Every Black man must recognize that his dick can be his strength or his downfall. The difference between a great man and a forgotten one is his ability to control what controls him. The world is full of distractions designed to weaken and destroy him.

Chasing women ain't just a personal flaw—it's a trap, a weapon used to break down any man who ain't got it under control. A man who loses control over himself has already lost the battle. A Black MAN knows the blueprint—history already laid out what happens when you don't keep your dick in check. He does not ignore the lessons of fallen men or assume he is immune. His enemies do not need to fight him if they can seduce him into fighting himself. His power is not in his ability to attract women but in his ability to control his urges. A true Black MAN don't fold for temptation—he stands tall, knowing his legacy means more than a few minutes of feel-good. Since the first encounters with white society, Black male sexuality has been under attack. White supremacy has always feared Black men's power, not just physically but genetically. The ability of a Black man to erase whiteness through reproduction threatens the foundation of white supremacy. This is why anti-miscegenation laws existed, why propaganda portrayed Black men as hypersexual beasts, and why castration was a common practice in lynchings. Controlling Black male sexuality has always been about controlling Black male power. A man who does not see the war waged against him will fall into its traps. Lynching was more than just murder; it was psychological warfare designed to instill fear and submission in the Black community. Castration was often part of the ritual, a symbolic act to eliminate Black men's ability to reproduce. White mobs sought not just to kill but to erase the threat of Black male existence entirely. Even in death, white supremacy sought to control Black men's reproductive power. False accusations of sexual violence have long been used to destroy Black men. From Emmett Till to countless nameless victims, history proves the pattern. White women, positioned as the most *"valuable"* and *"vulnerable"* in white society, wield accusations as weapons. A mere accusation is enough to justify a Black man's destruction. Today, Black men remain disproportionately accused, convicted, and sentenced for crimes involving white women. The justice system was never meant to protect Black men; it was built to control them.

Media reinforces white supremacy's grip on Black male sexuality. Black men are portrayed as either weak and emasculated or dangerously hypersexual. One makes them non-threatening; the other reduces them to mindless predators. Both narratives serve to prevent Black men from being seen as balanced, disciplined, and powerful. Controlling how the world sees Black men controls how Black men see themselves. Even within the Black community, white supremacy fuels division through the promotion of reckless sexual behavior, dysfunctional relationships, and broken families. Putting short-term pleasure above long-term success only weakens Black men. A man consumed by desire is easily sidetracked, played, and controlled. White supremacy knows a man who cannot control his *"dick"* cannot control his destiny. The legal system is another weapon used against Black men. Prisons are filled with Black men who were falsely accused, unfairly sentenced, or entrapped by their sexual choices. Child support laws, alimony, and biased family court rulings ensure that even when Black men create families, they remain financially crippled. The system finds ways to make Black men pay for our natural role as men. Sports and entertainment exploit and punish Black male sexuality. Black athletes and entertainers are surrounded by white women who serve as both status symbols and traps. Many have lost fortunes, reputations, and even their freedom because they failed to see the setup. Whether through false accusations, paternity traps, or financial ruin via divorce, the system profits off our rise and ensures our fall. Too many Black men fail to see the game being played against them. A Black MAN must recognize that his sexuality is both a gift and a weapon, one that can be used to build or destroy. White supremacy has never stopped targeting Black male sexuality because it understands the power it holds. The question is: do Black men understand it? A Black man who moves without awareness will always be a casualty of the war being waged against him, but a Black man who moves with discipline, strategy, and purpose will always be in control. White supremacy fears the day Black men master our own desires because a man who controls himself can never be controlled by another.

Even in interracial relationships, Black men must

understand the historical and political implications. White supremacy fears not just the act of a Black man with a white woman but what it represents, the erasure of whiteness and disruption of racial hierarchy. For centuries, laws, social conditioning, and financial incentives discouraged these unions. The attack on Black male sexuality is about control, who he loves, who he sleeps with, and who he reproduces with. A Black man who fails to understand this plays a dangerous game without knowing the rules. White women have historically been one of the most effective weapons used against Black men. Whether through false accusations, manipulation, or seduction, they have played a central role in the oppression and destruction of Black men. From slavery to Jim Crow to the modern era, their perceived innocence has been used as a shield while Black men have suffered the consequences. The mere accusation of a Black man harming or disrespecting a white woman has led to death, imprisonment, and social exile. A Black man who does not understand this historical pattern is walking blindly into a trap set for generations.

False accusations from white women have cost Black men their lives and freedom since the days of slavery. The infamous case of Emmett Till is one of the most well-known examples, where a white woman's lie led to the brutal murder of a 14-year-old boy. But Emmett was not the first, nor the last. Countless Black men have been lynched, jailed, or executed over accusations that were later proven false or exaggerated. During slavery, a simple claim that a Black man looked at a white woman the wrong way could result in death. Jim Crow laws reinforced this, ensuring that white women's words carried more weight than any Black man's truth. The legal system has always favored white women over Black men, reinforcing the imbalance of power. Courts historically ruled in favor of white women in cases of assault, domestic disputes, and even consensual relationships. Black men have been sentenced to prison for crimes they didn't commit simply because a white woman's tears held more weight than facts. Even in modern times, the *"Karen"* phenomenon proves that white women still weaponize their privilege, using law enforcement as their personal attack dogs against Black men. A Black man who does not understand this dynamic is setting himself up for failure, believing he is playing a fair game when the rules were never meant to protect him. Interracial relationships, particularly between Black men and white women, have always been about more than just attraction; they are tied to power, control, and racial hierarchy. Too many Black men have believed they could transcend race by being with a white woman, only to find themselves abandoned, betrayed, or worse when society reminded them of their place. A Black man who does not choose wisely in relationships can quickly become another statistic in a long history of downfall. The weaponization of white women against Black men continues today, just in different forms. Whether through false allegations in the workplace, viral social media accusations, or legal battles over children, white women still wield their privilege as a sword against Black men. Ignoring these lessons only leads to repeated mistakes. A Black man who understands history knows to move strategically, never placing blind trust in a system or a woman who has historically been used as his downfall.

None of this means that every white woman is an enemy, but history proves that a Black man must always be aware of the power dynamics at play. A naïve man believes he is different, that he won't suffer the same fate as those before him. A wise man moves with caution, understanding that he is navigating a system that was never built for his benefit. He don't let lust, ego, or feelings mess with his clarity. He recognizes that while the world has changed, the game remains the same, and survival requires strategy, not wishful thinking. A Black MAN does not put himself in situations where he can be used as a pawn in a game he didn't create. He understands that white women have been a tool of white supremacy, used to justify the destruction of Black men for centuries. He moves wisely, understanding that every decision he makes can either strengthen or weaken his position in life. A Black MAN is not ruled by desire, he is ruled by discipline, strategy, and an unbreakable understanding of the world around him.

The woman a man chooses to plant his seed in will determine the quality of his legacy. Too many men think having a child is just about reproduction, but it's about continuation, continuing your values, your mindset, and your bloodline. A wise man understands that he is only half of the equation, and the mother of his child will have just as much influence on the outcome. Choosing the wrong woman can destroy not just a man's present but also his future and the future of his lineage. Too many Black men have been set up, sabotaged, or even killed because they trusted the wrong woman. A woman can be a man's greatest asset or his deadliest liability, and the difference is in how well he chooses. A man must understand that a woman is either a multiplier or a divider. A good woman takes what a man provides and turns it into something greater. She multiplies his success, his peace, and his stability. A bad woman, however, will drain him, destroy his focus, and drag him into dysfunction. The wrong woman will cost a man more than just money; she will cost him peace, time, and energy. Black men must reject the lie that they have no control over their lineage. Every choice matters, and who a man creates life with determines the strength or weakness of his bloodline. A disciplined man moves with purpose, never letting momentary pleasure dictate his future. He understands that his seed is valuable, not something to be wasted on women who don't deserve it. White supremacy has always feared the power of Black male genetics, which is why so many systems have been put in place to weaken the Black family. The easiest way to destroy a nation is to corrupt its women and control its men, and Black men must wake up to this reality. A strong Black man is intentional about where he plants his seed because he understands that fatherhood is more than just DNA; it's about legacy. A real man doesn't let lust steer his path.; he moves with strategy, ensuring that the mother of his children aligns with his mission. He does not choose based on temporary pleasure but on the long-term impact she will have on his bloodline. A weak man leaves his future up to chance, but a strong man takes control of it. A Black MAN ensures that his lineage is strong, disciplined, and built to last.

Sexual mastery is about more than just control; it's about breaking generational cycles. Too many Black men come from broken homes because their fathers lacked discipline, creating children they were not ready to raise. Every man must ask himself: Is he building a legacy or just leaving behind a trail of broken families? Choosing the right woman to create life with is one of the most powerful decisions a man can make. A Black man who understands the weight of his seed does not plant it carelessly. He knows that the woman he chooses will determine the future of his bloodline. Being a man is about control—control of your mind, your actions, and your future. I love Black women, and I love sex, but I love power, purpose, and legacy even more. A man who is a slave to his desires will always be at the mercy of the world around him. But a man who masters himself? He is unstoppable. A Black man understands that his sexuality can either make him or break him, and he chooses to elevate himself rather than fall victim to his impulses. If you're out here acting recklessly, letting your urges dictate your actions, you will pay the price—financially, emotionally, or even with your life. A real Black man understands that every choice has consequences, especially when it comes to his body and his sexuality. Enjoy yourself, but do so with a clear mind, knowing the bigger picture. Letting your dick lead you can throw you off course, making you vulnerable to traps, both from others and from yourself. Your sexuality should be an asset, not your downfall. History has shown us what happens when men lack control. Powerful kings, generals, and leaders have fallen because they couldn't master their dicks. Kingdoms crumbled, empires fell, and lives were lost, all over a fleeting moment of pleasure. Some of the greatest men in history lost everything because they chased what felt good in the moment rather than thinking about their legacy.

We, as Black men, are dealing with the Black American woman, the most powerful, seductive, and nurturing being on the planet. To understand how powerful she truly is, I remember the first time I heard Dr. Claude Anderson tell the story of Emily West. The story of Emily West, also known as Emily

Morgan, stands as a testament to the undeniable influence of Black women. A free Black woman from New York, she found herself caught in the chaos of the Texas Revolution in 1836. Captured by General Santa Anna's forces, she was allegedly in his tent at the moment Sam Houston's army launched their decisive attack at San Jacinto. Whether by chance or silent intent, she played a role in the battle that secured Texas's independence. Her story, though clouded by legend, represents the unexpected ways in which Black women have shaped history. Emily West, like many others, was not given a seat at the table of historical recognition, but her presence altered its course nonetheless.

This connects directly to Code #14: A Black man understands that his dick can make or break him. But let's be clear, General Santa Anna was not a Black man. He was the most powerful man in Mexico at the time, yet he violated this code because of a Black American woman. He found himself distracted in the arms of Emily West, which ultimately led to his capture and the collapse of his forces at San Jacinto. This serves as a lesson to Black men: indulgence without discipline can be a fatal weakness. The choices a man makes in moments of pleasure can shape the course of his future, for better or worse. A Black man must always be aware that his actions in the bedroom can have consequences beyond the moment. The power of the Black woman is such that even those outside of our lineage fall victim when they fail to recognize the discipline required in her presence.

"The Yellow Rose of Texas," a song inspired by Emily West, further illustrates how Black women's presence echoes through time. Though originally written as a folk tune, its connection to her story highlights how Black individuals have been woven into the fabric of American history, often without proper credit. The song romanticizes her image, but the truth is that she was a Black woman in a war-torn land, surviving and, in her own way, influencing the course of events. Her story should serve as a reminder that recognition may not always be immediate, but significance is undeniable. Black men must carry this same resolve, knowing that every action, every step, and every moment of composure sends a message. Black women have always been powerful, but their power demands that we, as men, rise to the challenge of discipline and control. Emily West's presence was not loud, nor was it planned, but it was undeniable. She did not need a sword to leave an imprint on history; her existence in the right place at the right time made the difference. Like her, Black men must understand that our desires, when unchecked, can be the very thing that leads to our ruin. This is why self-control is essential; whether in battle, in business, or in daily life, one must move with discipline and foresight. Influence is not always spoken; it is often simply felt. The lesson is clear: unchecked lust leads to destruction. If you are serious about your

future, you must be intentional with your choices, especially when in the presence of a Black woman whose power is undeniable.

Now, let's talk about why white supremacy has always been obsessed with controlling Black male sexuality. They know the power of the Black man's seed. They fear genetic annihilation. That fear has led to centuries of attempts to manipulate, control, and limit Black reproduction. From lynchings to laws, the system has always worked to suppress Black male power. Understand that the attack on Black male sexuality is not random; it is strategic. White women have been used as tools in this manipulation, whether knowingly or not. History is filled with examples of Black men losing their lives over false accusations, all because they could not keep their dicks in check. White women's tears have been weaponized against Black men for generations. When you chase the wrong woman, whether for validation or a quick thrill, you're playing a risky game one that history shows can cost you everything. Choosing the right woman to plant your seed in is one of the most important decisions you will ever make. Not every woman is fit to carry your legacy. There is power in your seed; it is about more than just having a child; it is about creating a future, a lineage. Choose a woman who respects you, your vision, and your purpose. The wrong woman can destroy you, plain and simple. The right woman will help you build, elevate, and secure your legacy. A Black man's sexual discipline is what separates the successful from the unsuccessful. If you are out here recklessly spreading your seed, you are wasting energy—energy that could be used to build something greater. You cannot move forward if your focus is always on the next woman. Channel your sexual energy into your goals, your business, and your dreams. The more you master your urges, the more you will elevate. Control your sexuality, and you control your destiny. The spiritual and psychological aspects of sex are deep; do not take them lightly. Every woman you sleep with leaves an imprint on you. Soul ties are real. If you are not careful, you will carry negative energy that is not even yours. Each time you give yourself to someone, you give away a piece of yourself. The more you give away carelessly, the less you have left to invest in your purpose. Protect your energy. Protect your seed. Protect your soul. Your sexuality is not just a physical act; it is a spiritual one. Your choices have ripple effects that extend beyond the moment.

So yes, enjoy life, experience pleasure, but always be intentional. Know who you are dealing with because your legacy depends on it.

LEGACY

Every decision you make should contribute to something greater than yourself. A man's true worth is measured by what he leaves behind, not just in wealth, but in wisdom, influence, and impact. Legacy is about setting up future generations to be stronger, wiser, and more powerful than you were. This means guiding your family, mentoring younger men, and making sure your name is remembered for what you built, not for what you wasted.

HONORARY CODES

1. A Black Man Knows When To Walk Away

A Black MAN understands that walking away isn't weakness; it's wisdom. Too many men stay in situations that drain them, whether it's a dead-end job, a toxic relationship, or a pointless argument fueled by ego. Knowing when to walk away means knowing your value. If a woman isn't respecting you, you leave. If a job isn't paying you what you're worth, you move on. If your ego is pushing you into a fight that doesn't serve you, you let it go. A MAN doesn't stay where he isn't valued, appreciated, or progressing. Walking away is about control, not cowardice. The weak man stays in dysfunction because he fears change. He holds onto people, places, and things that no longer serve him out of comfort or pride. But a Black MAN is always moving forward. He doesn't argue for the sake of arguing; he understands that silence and distance are often more powerful than words. A man who knows when to walk away commands respect because he isn't desperate. He chooses his battles wisely and never lets emotions or circumstances dictate his decisions. This applies to everything. If a woman is playing games, disrespecting you, or making you prove yourself constantly, you walk away. If your job treats you like you're replaceable, then replace them. If your own ego is leading you into pointless conflict, you check yourself and step away. A Black MAN values his time, energy, and peace above all else. He understands that every step away from nonsense is a step toward something better. Walking away isn't about quitting; it's about making room for what you truly deserve. —O.G. Reggie

2. A Black Man Understands The Law Of Cause & Effect

A Black MAN knows that every action has a consequence. Nothing in this world happens by accident; everything is a result of a previous choice, whether good or bad. If you put in the work, you reap the rewards. If you slack off, you suffer the consequences. Too many men want results without effort, respect without character, or success without sacrifice. But the Law of Cause & Effect doesn't care about feelings; it only responds to what you put in. A Black MAN moves with intention, knowing that his present actions shape his future reality. This applies to every aspect of life. If you entertain the wrong women, don't be surprised when your life is full of drama. If you waste money instead of investing, don't cry about being broke. If you let your emotions control you, expect to be manipulated by those who see your weakness. A wise man understands that the choices he makes today determine the life he will have tomorrow. There is no escaping the Law of Cause & Effect, either you master it, or you become a victim of it. A Black MAN doesn't make excuses; he makes adjustments. He doesn't blame others for where he is in life because he understands that his decisions, not outside forces, shape his destiny. Every choice is a seed, and every result is the harvest. That's why he moves strategically, thinks long-term, and never lets temporary emotions dictate permanent decisions. The weak react, but a MAN calculates. He understands that success, power, and respect aren't given; they are earned through disciplined action and the wisdom to control his own fate. —BoarderLine

3. **A Black Man Only Deals With *"Receipts,"* Not *"Beliefs"***

A Black MAN moves on facts, not feelings. Too many people get caught up in what they believe to be true instead of what they can prove. Beliefs don't build wealth, power, or legacy; results do. A MAN doesn't argue about what should be; he focuses on what is. If a woman says she respects you, the proof is in her actions, not her words. If a man calls himself a leader, his track record should show it. A Black MAN deals in receipts, cold, hard evidence, because anything else is just talk. The world doesn't care about what you believe; it only responds to what you can back up. Too many men get hustled, played, or misled because they take words at face value instead of demanding proof. If a business deal sounds too good to be true, where's the paperwork? If someone claims to be loyal, when have they proven it? A Black MAN moves with logic, not blind trust. He understands that believing without proof is how men get scammed, betrayed, and set back in life. This applies to everything. If a woman says she's different, her actions will show it. If a job promises you a raise, you don't count on it until you see it in writing. If a movement claims to have your best interests at heart, look at the results, not the rhetoric. A MAN doesn't waste time on fairy tales; he demands results. Receipts don't lie, but emotions do. That's why a Black MAN trusts evidence over opinions and proof over promises. —Brotha Mocco

4. A Black MAN Attracts Attention; He Doesn't Seek It

A Black MAN moves with purpose, not desperation. He doesn't beg for eyes to be on him; his presence alone commands respect. Weak men chase attention, flexing for validation, but a true MAN lets his actions speak for him. When you handle business, carry yourself with discipline, and stay solid, people will take notice. You don't have to announce your value; those who matter will recognize it. A MAN understands that attention is a byproduct of greatness, not the goal. Seeking attention is a sign of insecurity. Men who constantly show off, brag, or chase clout are trying to fill a void within themselves. But a Black MAN doesn't need the world to see him to know his worth. He is confident in who he is, whether people are watching or not. Attention-seekers burn out fast because their value depends on others noticing them. But a MAN who stays on his grind, improves himself, and moves with integrity will always draw the right kind of attention, without ever asking for it. This applies everywhere. In business, the man who focuses on results will get the recognition, while the loudmouth gets ignored. In relationships, the man who knows his worth won't chase women; they will chase him. In life, a MAN doesn't compete for attention; he lets attention come to him. The world naturally follows those who lead with confidence and control. A Black MAN shines because of who he is, not because he demands to be seen.

5. A Black MAN Will Never Put His Hands On A Black Woman, Unless It's To Protect Himself

A Black MAN is disciplined, controlled, and strategic in his actions. He understands that violence against a Black woman is not only a betrayal of his own principles but also a losing battle in every way. A MAN moves with logic, not emotion, and never allows himself to be provoked into reckless decisions. If a woman disrespects him, he walks away. If she challenges his authority, he lets his actions speak louder than his words. But if his life is in danger, self-preservation comes first; no one has the right to harm him, and he will defend himself accordingly. Too many men let emotions get the best of them, reacting instead of thinking. But a Black MAN understands that raising his hands in anger only leads to regret, consequences, and a loss of control. A man who cannot control his temper is a man who can be easily destroyed. Society will never side with him, no matter the situation, so he must always move wisely. If a woman is violent, unstable, or trying to provoke him, he removes himself from the equation. He will not be manipulated into ruining his future over a temporary moment of frustration. At the same time, protection is non-negotiable. A Black MAN will always defend himself if his life or well-being is truly at risk. He understands that self-defense is not about ego; it's about survival. However, he also knows that the best way to win is to avoid situations that force him into that position in the first place. A MAN picks his battles, and any situation where he has to physically engage with a woman is already a loss. That's why he keeps his mind sharp, his emotions in check, and his actions aligned with his principles. —DJuanB & Mz.Dee

6. **A Black MAN Only Battles His Equal Or Better**

A Black MAN doesn't waste energy on lesser opponents. He understands that fighting someone beneath him, physically, mentally, or financially, is a sign of weakness, not strength. A real MAN chooses his battles wisely, knowing that true competition comes from those who can challenge and sharpen him. If a man is beneath him in status, mindset, or discipline, engaging with him is a waste of time. A lion doesn't concern himself with the opinions of sheep. A Black MAN focuses on elevating himself, not proving himself to people who don't matter. Battling the weak is an ego trip, not a power move. Too many men get caught up in petty conflicts with those who are no threat to them. Arguing with fools, fighting over nonsense, or trying to dominate someone who is already beneath them is pointless. A MAN understands that true battles, whether in business, competition, or personal growth, should push him forward, not drag him down. He steps into arenas where he is tested, where victory means something, and where his skills, discipline, and intelligence are put to the ultimate test. This applies to all aspects of life. A Black MAN doesn't fight over petty drama; he fights for legacy, respect, and power. He doesn't waste time debating people who can't teach him anything; he engages with those who sharpen his mind. He doesn't compete with men who have nothing to lose; he levels up and stands against those who will make him stronger. A MAN understands that steel sharpens steel, and battling the weak only dulls his edge. That's why he only competes with his equal or better, because real power comes from proving yourself against the best.

7. **A Black MAN Never Pocket Watches Another Man**

A Black MAN minds his own business and stays in his own lane. He understands that watching another man's pockets is a waste of time and energy. What another man earns, spends, or does with his money has nothing to do with him. Weak men gossip about what the next man has instead of focusing on their own grind. A real MAN knows that envy is a distraction; while you're watching him, he's building. Success doesn't come from hating; it comes from putting in the work. Pocket-watching is a sign of insecurity and laziness. A Black MAN doesn't waste time worrying about how another man got his money; he focuses on getting his own. If someone has more, that should be motivation, not jealousy. If you spend your time watching another man's plate, you'll never eat. A real MAN understands that success isn't about comparison; it's about progression. He measures himself by his own growth, not by someone else's achievements. This applies to everything in life. A Black MAN doesn't concern himself with another man's success, his women, or his lifestyle. He focuses on his own path, his own money, and his own legacy. Hating on another man's wins won't put money in your pocket or food on your table. That's why a real MAN stays locked in, grinding toward his own goals. He understands the truth: *"What another man eats doesn't make him shit,"* so why waste time watching? — Candice Eddings

The Honorary Codes serve as an essential extension of the 14 Codes, offering deeper layers of understanding and reinforcing the core principles that define a Black MAN's character. While the 14 Codes provide the foundation for what a MAN must be, the Honorary Codes elevate these standards, addressing nuances and circumstances that require a higher level of wisdom, self-awareness, and control. These Honorary Codes complement the 14 by giving practical insight into how a Black MAN should navigate the complexities of life, from relationships to personal growth. Together, the 14 Codes and the Honorary Codes form a comprehensive blueprint for Black manhood, showing that it's not just about strength, but also about discernment, discipline, and understanding the value of every action and decision. A Black MAN who abides by these principles doesn't just survive; he thrives. The Honorary Codes fine-tune the guidance laid out in the 14, adding the layers of knowledge and self-control necessary to succeed in a world that often works against him. They stand as the ultimate complement to the foundation already established; together, they represent the highest standard of Black manhood.

CONCLUSION

The 14 Codes: Black Manhood, Ancient Kemet, and the Osirian Path to Power.

My connection to Ancient Kemet runs deeper than just an interest in ancient history; it is a profound part of my identity. Ancient Kemet, as the cradle of Black civilization, has long been a symbol of strength, wisdom, and resilience. The Black men of Ancient Kemet embodied the very qualities that I believe define true masculinity: courage, leadership, wisdom, and a deep respect for tradition. In Ancient Kemet, manhood was not just about physical strength but the ability to lead, provide, protect, and serve as a reflection of divine order. The Ancient Kemites understood that their legacy was rooted in the cultivation of strong men who upheld values that transcended time. Ancient Kemetic society was structured around the idea that manhood was an essential force in maintaining balance in the world. The Pharaoh, as both a leader and spiritual figure, exemplified this ideal, where manhood was not separate from duty or responsibility. This sense of purpose is deeply embedded in the *"14 Codes,"* which reflect the strength, integrity, and wisdom required to lead a life of responsibility and respect. Just as the Pharaohs upheld the laws of Maat—truth, justice, and order—Black men today must strive to live in accordance with their own set of principles. Black men today must also recognize their role as the cornerstone of their communities.

Ancient Kemet's legacy is one of transformation, evolving through time while staying true to core values. The ancient Kemites were constantly innovating, creating new technologies, philosophies, and systems, yet they remained rooted in the traditions that defined them. *"The 14 Codes"* are designed with the same principle in mind: to help Black men evolve, adapt, and thrive in the modern world while staying grounded in the timeless values of strength, integrity, and wisdom. Just as Ancient Kemite's legacy has endured, so too must the legacy of Black manhood, passed down from generation to generation. The Codes are a blueprint for that legacy, ensuring that Black men not only survive but thrive, just as the ancient Kemites did.

Like the Laws of Maat, these codes need to be written in stone. They need to be put into practice so much that they become a fabric of your being. I chose number 14 based on the Osirian drama. The Osirian (also known as Asar) myth is one of the most significant and well-known myths in ancient Kemetic mythology. It revolves around Osiris, the god of the afterlife, death, resurrection, and fertility, and his relationship with his wife, Isis (also known as Aset), and his brother, Set (also known as Sutekh). The myth has been passed down through various texts, most notably the Pyramid Texts and *"Coffin Texts,"* and is central to ancient Kemetic religious beliefs. Osiris was initially a beloved ruler of ancient Kemet, known for bringing civilization, agriculture, and laws to the land. He married his sister, Isis, who was known for her wisdom, magic, and healing powers. Together, they represented harmony and balance in the world. Osiris's brother Set, the god of chaos, disorder, and violence, was jealous of Osiris's power and popularity. Set plotted to overthrow Osiris and take control of ancient Kemet. He tricked Osiris into a coffin (a beautifully decorated one), and after luring him inside, Set sealed the coffin and cast it into the Nile River, where it was carried away and eventually became lodged in a tree. When Isis learned of her husband's fate, she searched the land for his body. After much searching, she found Osiris's coffin in the city of Byblos (modern-day Lebanon) and brought it back to ancient Kemet. Unfortunately, Set discovered this and, in a fit of rage, dismembered Osiris's body into fourteen pieces, scattering them across ancient Kemet. In her grief, Isis and her sister Nephthys (Sutekh's wife) worked together, using magic to collect and reassemble Osiris's body. They embalmed him and performed rituals to revive him temporarily, long enough for Isis to conceive their son, Heru (also known as Horus). Osiris, however, could not fully return to the land of the living and became the ruler of the Underworld (Duat), where he judged the souls of the dead. After Osiris's death and resurrection, Heru (often depicted as a falcon or with a falcon head) was born to Isis, and he grew up to be a powerful and heroic figure. Heru eventually challenged Sutekh for the throne of Ancient Kemet, leading to a great battle between the forces of good (Heru) and chaos (Sutekh). Heru triumphed, reclaiming the throne of Ancient Kemet and symbolizing the restoration of order.

The Osirian Drama is rich in symbolic meaning, especially in relation to death, rebirth, and renewal. Osiris's death and resurrection symbolize the annual flooding of the Nile, which brings life to the land, while his descent into the underworld represents the inevitable return to death. The myth is also associated with the concept of ma'at, the divine order and balance of the cosmos, which Osiris and his son Heru seek to restore by defeating Set. The Osirian Drama is not just a tale of divine intrigue but serves as a foundation for ancient Kemetic religious practices, especially those related to death and the afterlife. Osiris became one of the most important deities in the ancient Kemetic pantheon, and his story influenced later religious thought, particularly the ideas of resurrection and eternal life in Christianity and other traditions. The Osiris Drama is a myth about the struggle between life and death, chaos and order, and the hope of resurrection and justice. It shaped much of ancient Kemetic spirituality and continues to be a central narrative in the study of religion and mythology.

The story of Osiris is a perfect example of how everything moves in cycles, each part connected to the other. It also represents the eternal struggle between light and darkness. This same concept is the foundation of these codes. Though each code stands on its own, they are all linked, forming a unified guide for Black men to step out of the shadows and into our rightful place in the light. The ancient myth of Osiris and Set reflects the battle Black men fight every day in America. Osiris, a king of honor, discipline, and leadership, stands for everything a Black man should embody. His brother Set, representing chaos, deception, and destruction, mirrors the forces that have worked to dismantle strong Black men. In this ongoing struggle, the feminine principle, represented by Isis, serves as a force of restoration and empowerment. From this myth, we extract the essential codes of conduct that every Black man must uphold to reclaim his throne. Integrity is the foundation. Black men have faced the same attacks, from the criminalization of their identity to the false narratives pushed by the media. To counter this, a Black man must be unshakable, standing firm in his principles without needing validation from outside sources. Just as Osiris remained the true king despite the betrayal, a Black man's integrity makes him undeniable.

Work ethic is another pillar of strength. Black men once stood as the backbone of industry, but systems were put in place to break their ambition. Set appears today in the form of welfare traps, corporate obstacles, and prison pipelines designed to kill drive. But a true Black man, like Osiris, refuses to accept stagnation; he builds, even when forced into exile. Through relentless effort, he proves that no force can keep him buried. Emotional discipline is critical. Black men face daily disrespect, yet reacting emotionally only plays into Set's trap. The system benefits from Black men being impulsive and easily controlled. By mastering emotions and moving with logic and purpose, a Black man reclaims his power, just as Osiris did when he ascended as the Lord of the Afterlife. Character is defined by follow-through. We, as Black men today, must stand firm on our word, making sure our actions line up with our values. When we move inconsistently, we weaken our foundation and open the door for Set's chaos to spread through the community. Just as Osiris remained steadfast in his purpose, Black men must uphold their commitments in fatherhood, business, and leadership. Gossip is a tool of destruction. Set used deception and slander to turn people against Osiris, a tactic still used against Black men today. Modern society encourages a gossip culture, weakening men by engaging them in meaningless chatter. Instead of discussing another man's downfall, a Black man must focus on building his own empire. Respect is commanded, not requested. Seeking validation from a system controlled by Set leads to disappointment. Respect comes from action, self-mastery, and an unbreakable will. When a Black man embodies these traits, the world must acknowledge his presence, just as Osiris' name remains eternal. A woman does not make a man; she reflects the man that he is. Isis loved Osiris not because he completed her, but because he embodied divinity. Weak men believe a woman's love will give them strength, but true strength comes first. Set represents the weak man who blames women for his failures instead of holding himself accountable. A Black man must move with purpose, and the right woman will reflect his greatness.

A Black man must be willing to die for his responsibilities. Osiris's death was not in vain; he sacrificed himself for the legacy of his people. Black men must embrace this principle, protecting our families, communities, and future generations at all costs. Cowardice allows Set to keep Black men weak and scattered. Responsibility is sacred; if a Black man is not willing to stand for something, he has already lost. A man's word is his contract with reality. A Black man's word shapes how he is perceived and respected. Set's influence is strongest when men lie, deceive, or fail to keep their promises. A Black man who values his word builds a reputation that cannot be destroyed, leaving behind a legacy that stands the test of time. Excuses are the language of the weak. Black men today have every reason to complain, but excuses accomplish nothing. The system is against us, but that is not a reason to fold. Excuses are Set's weapon, justifying inaction. A true Black man acknowledges obstacles but finds solutions, ensuring he rises from every setback.

A Black man must be proactive, not reactive. Osiris ruled with foresight, while Set acted out of envy and impulse. Black men in America must anticipate challenges before they arise, always thinking five steps ahead. Reacting emotionally or impulsively only benefits Set's system. Kings plan; pawns react. A man's worth is determined by what he produces. Black men who do not create, whether wealth, knowledge, or leadership, are useless to their communities. Set thrives when Black men consume more than they produce. The measure of a man is what he builds, and only builders are remembered. Brotherhood demands accountability. Horus avenged Osiris not just for personal reasons but to restore balance. Black men must hold each other accountable, correcting weaknesses and ensuring high standards. Brotherhood is sacred, and silence in the face of failure is betrayal. The only way to defeat Set's influence is by making accountability a law. Black men must be their brothers' keepers. Finally, discipline over desire is essential.

Osiris' manhood was stolen by Set, symbolizing the castration of Black men in America. Lust, reckless fatherhood, and pleasure-seeking are traps ensuring that many Black men never reclaim their throne. A wise Black man understands that his seed is power and protects it accordingly. The battle between Osiris and Set is eternal, but the path of Osiris leads to restoration and sovereignty. By living according to these codes, a Black man reclaims his rightful place as a king, unshaken by the forces that seek to bury him. Osiris's journey is the blueprint for Black men in America: the fall, the resurrection, and the legacy. The 14 Codes are the tools needed to reclaim power and restore divine masculinity. Set's rule only continues if Black men refuse to resurrect themselves. The choice is simple: remain scattered or become whole again.

The mythology of Osiris in ancient Kemet and the historical lynching of Black men in America share striking parallels. Both narratives reflect a recurring cycle of power, betrayal, destruction, and ultimate resurrection. By examining these similarities, we can better understand the deep historical and spiritual dimensions of racial violence and its lasting impact on Black American identity. One of the most chilling similarities is the ritualistic nature of Osiris's murder and the lynching of Black men. According to the myth, Osiris was betrayed by his jealous brother, Set, who murdered him and dismembered his body, scattering the pieces across the land. This gruesome act was meant not only to kill Osiris but to erase his presence and prevent his return. Similarly, the lynchings of Black men in America were not just acts of killing; they were public spectacles of terror. Many victims were not only hanged but also mutilated, burned, and dismembered, with their bodies often left as warnings to others. The message was clear: Black power, whether political, economic, or social, was to be suppressed by any means necessary.

The fear of Black power is another key theme that unites these two narratives. Osiris was a divine ruler associated with order, fertility, and renewal. His leadership represented prosperity and strength, and his murder by Set was an attempt to dismantle that order. Likewise, lynchings were often targeted at Black men who had gained a degree of independence, wealth, or social influence. Whether a man was accused of being *"too successful," "too defiant,"* or simply *"too confident,"* the underlying motive was always to keep Black people subjugated. White supremacists, like Set, sought to prevent the rise of Black leadership and prosperity by instilling fear through brutal acts of violence.

However, just as Osiris's spirit lived on, the memory of lynched Black men has fueled movements for justice. Osiris, though physically destroyed, became the god of the afterlife, representing eternal justice and resurrection. His story did not end with his death, and neither did the stories of those who suffered at the hands of racial terror. The names of men like Emmett Till, Sam

Hose, and George Stinney continue to be invoked in the fight for civil rights and justice. Their deaths, while intended to suppress Black progress, instead ignited movements that demanded change.

The role of women in reclaiming and preserving these legacies is another profound connection between the two histories. In the Osiris myth, his wife, Isis, meticulously gathered his body parts, restored his form, and conceived their son, Horus, who later avenged his father and challenged Set's rule. This mirrors the real-life role of Black women in the struggle against racial violence. Mothers like Mamie Till-Mobley, who insisted on an open-casket funeral for her son Emmett to expose the brutality of his lynching, ensured that these acts of terror did not go unnoticed. Black women have been the keepers of history, ensuring that the spirits of their lost loved ones were not erased but instead honored and avenged. White supremacy functions much like Set's rule, built on deception, destruction, and disorder. After Osiris's death, Set took over the throne, ruling through chaos rather than order. Similarly, the lynching era was not simply about individual acts of violence; it was about reinforcing an entire system of oppression that kept Black people in a constant state of fear and subjugation. This strategy was meant to break the spirit of a people, but, as history has shown, it failed.

The Osiris story is ultimately one of resurrection. Though he was murdered and dismembered, he lived on in the afterlife, and his legacy continued through Horus. This mirrors the resilience of Black people in America. Every lynching was meant to kill not just the body but the spirit of Black resistance. Yet, the spirit survived. From the ashes of terror rose the Civil Rights Movement, Black Power, and a continued fight for justice. The battle between Set and Horus is ongoing; the struggle between white supremacy and Black liberation persists. But just as Osiris's spirit endured, so too does the strength and resilience of Black people. The lynching of Black men in America is more than a historical crime; it is a chapter in a much older story. It is the battle between power and those who seek to destroy it. It is the cycle of destruction and rebirth. And it is a reminder that no matter how many times they try to kill the body, the spirit of Black resistance never dies.

The 14 Codes lay down the foundation for rebuilding from the ground up. They give us, as Black men, the values and discipline needed to regain our identity and power. The Codes show us how to take back what's ours not just a seat in society, but our role as leaders in our homes, our neighborhoods, and far beyond. Just as the Osiris narrative depicts the cyclical nature of death and rebirth, the journey of Black men is a never-ending battle to reclaim what was stolen from them: power, pride, and purpose. This is a journey of self-discovery and resilience, where each setback is an opportunity to rise stronger than before. The destruction of Black manhood did not come without resistance, and that same resistance remains. The 14 Codes offer a pathway out of the chaos, urging men to embody strength in all things, from work ethic to character. They teach that to rebuild, a Black man must first confront the ashes of his past and reject the false narratives that have been imposed upon him. Osiris's rebirth symbolizes the rebirth of Black masculinity, out of the fire and rubble, stronger and more purposeful than ever.

This fight for reclamation is not one fought alone. The 14 Codes push Black men to hold themselves accountable and to each other, creating a brotherhood of resilience. Accountability is a critical part of this rebuilding process, as the Codes demand that a man show integrity, character, and strength of purpose. Just like Osiris rose again after being torn apart, we, as Black men, have to rebuild ourselves from the ground up relying solely on our will and drive. Every Code is a direct stand against the forces trying to break us. When we live by these Codes, we make it clear: our past pain won't control our future. True strength comes from pushing forward, no matter what tries to stop us.

The Codes also stress that Black men must not just rise from the ashes; they must build upon the foundation of those who came before them. The strength of our ancestors, who endured unimaginable suffering and hardship, serves as a source of inspiration. Each step toward rebuilding is a step closer to honoring those sacrifices. The 14 Codes encourage men to take on the responsibility of legacy building, not only for their own futures but for the generations that will come after. This is why the fight for reclamation is so vital: Black men are not only rebuilding their own lives but constructing a foundation for their children and grand-children to inherit. The Codes teach that when Black men rise, they rise with the weight of their ancestors' hopes and dreams on their shoulders.

The process of rebuilding is never linear, nor is it without its challenges. The path to strength is often riddled with setbacks, failures, and self-doubt, but the resilience built through adherence to the 14 Codes helps men push through. The destruction of Black manhood was designed to make men weak, soft, and docile, but the Codes teach Black men to reject that narrative. The Black man is not meant to bend or break; he is meant to stand tall in the face of adversity. Each Code is a reminder that resilience is a practice, not an innate trait. It is through action and discipline that a man rebuilds, constantly sharpening himself against the grind of life's challenges.

Black men must understand that their journey of rebirth is not one for personal glory alone but for the collective good of their community. The Codes encourage unity, reminding men that they cannot rebuild in isolation. The strength of the individual is tied to the strength of the collective, and Black men must support one another in this rebuilding process. By adhering to the 14 Codes, Black men are laying the groundwork for an empowered community—one where men are strong, reliable, and accountable. The Osiris story shows that true power is not just found in individual strength but in the power of a community that stands together through hardship and destruction. Rebuilding Black masculinity is a communal effort, one that will only succeed if every man plays his part.

This rebirth is not about erasing the scars of the past but about using those scars as tools for growth. Just as Osiris's journey was filled with pain, betrayal, and loss, Black men must confront the history that shaped them. There is no skipping over the pain, but there is power in transforming that pain into something greater. *"The 14 Codes"* show that pain does not have to be a hindrance; it can be a catalyst for strength. Every wound becomes a reminder of what must never happen again. Rebuilding Black manhood means accepting the past but never allowing it to define the future. The past is a teacher, but the future is where Black men have the opportunity to create their own destiny. As Black men embrace their rebirth, they must also understand that the world will not make it easy. *"The 14 Codes"* teach that the path to strength is one that requires vigilance and sacrifice. The world may attempt to break them down, but the Codes provide the armor needed to survive the assault. Just as Osiris faced obstacles at every turn, Black men must be prepared for the trials that will come their way. The Codes are the tools that help them navigate these challenges, ensuring that they remain steadfast and unwavering. Resilience is not about avoiding hardship but about rising every time you are knocked down.

With everything stacked against us, we, as Black men, have to stand in our power without shame. The 14 Codes don't tell us to wait for approval they demand that we claim our strength and move with authority. This is what rebirth looks like: knowing that our power isn't something to hide or water down it's something we carry with pride, for ourselves, our families, and our people. Ain't no room for apology. It's time for us to step up, take our rightful place as leaders, and handle the weight that comes with it. The Codes aren't just guidelines—they're a call to rise up and take full control of our lives and our communities.

The story of Osiris is one of betrayal, dismemberment, and rebirth, a tale that echoes the experience of Black men in America. His wife, Isis, who represents the Black American woman, gathered his remains, but the one part she couldn't find was his phallus, the very symbol of his masculinity and ability to reproduce. This final act of castration wasn't just about physical destruction; it was an attack on his ability to create and sustain a future, mirroring what has been done to Black men in America. From slavery to modern times, Black men have been systematically broken apart—physically, emotionally, and spiritually. The auction block was the first stage of dismemberment, where families were torn apart, ensuring Black men could never fully pass down their legacy. Just like Set cut Osiris into pieces, enslavers shattered the Black family unit, making Black men disposable and their presence in the household unstable. Lynching and castration followed, serving as brutal reminders that Black men's power and influence were threats to the established order. Even after slavery, Jim Crow laws continued this mutilation, limiting Black men's ability to lead, provide, or even defend themselves without violent repercussions. The message was clear: a strong Black man was too dangerous to be left whole.

The economic and social structures of America have acted as the modern Set, constantly working to keep Black men fragmented. Mass incarceration became the new form of dismemberment, ripping fathers and sons from their homes and scattering them into prisons like Osiris's lost body parts. Welfare policies discouraged Black men from being in their own households, forcing Black women to raise families alone in exchange for government assistance. The war on drugs introduced yet another form of destruction, flooding Black communities with substances that ensured Black men either fell victim to addiction or were locked away for trying to escape poverty. Even those who *"made it"* faced corporate castration, where they had to surrender their identity, voice, and masculinity just to keep a job or avoid being labeled a threat. Every move was designed to ensure Black men remained fractured, unable to reclaim their full power.

Hollywood and the media played the role of Set's propaganda machine, reinforcing the image of the weak, absent, or hyper-aggressive Black male. The strong Black man was either ridiculed, erased, or villainized, just like Osiris was demonized by Set's reign of chaos. Black male sexuality was either turned into a stereotype or stripped entirely, reducing Black men to caricatures instead of multidimensional beings. Music, television, and movies all worked together to either emasculate Black men or turn them into perpetual sources of violence and dysfunction. This was psychological castration, ensuring that even when Black men weren't physically destroyed, they would never feel whole. Just like Isis searched for Osiris's missing piece, Black men today are searching for the parts of themselves that were stolen. Despite all this, Osiris's story didn't end with his destruction; he became the god of resurrection and the afterlife, a symbol of rebirth. This is why Black men must see themselves in Osiris, not just as victims but as those destined to rise again. Even though Set tried to erase him, Osiris still fathered Horus, the avenger, who carried on his legacy and reclaimed the throne. Black men must recognize that, despite centuries of attack, we still have the power to restore ourselves and our communities. The process starts with acknowledging the ways they've been broken and actively working to piece ourselves back together. The system was designed to keep Black men in a state of eternal death, but resurrection is always possible.

Just like Osiris's journey, the path to restoration is not easy, but it is necessary. Black men must reject the roles given to them by our oppressors and redefine masculinity on our own terms. This means embracing responsibility, leadership, and discipline, rather than letting outside forces dictate our identity. It means strengthening brotherhood, holding each other accountable, and rebuilding the family unit that was stolen from them. Education, economic empowerment, and self-sufficiency are the modern tools of resurrection, allowing Black men to reclaim our power piece by piece. The days of waiting for someone else to restore what was taken are over; Black men must be our own *"Isis,"* searching for and reclaiming what was lost.

The attack on Black masculinity has always been about control, ensuring that Black men never rise beyond the limits set for them. Just like Osiris's dismemberment was about keeping him from ruling, the systemic castration of Black men has been about keeping us from reclaiming our place as leaders. This is why society encourages weakness, emotional instability, and dependency, because a fragmented man is easy to manipulate. When Black men refuse to accept these conditions and instead work to rebuild themselves, we disrupt the very foundation of this system. We prove that no matter how many times we are cut down, we will always find a way to rise again. The resurrection of Osiris is not just a myth; it is a blueprint. It teaches that even when everything is taken from you, there is still a way forward. But that path requires action, discipline, and the refusal to accept *"victimhood."* Too many Black men are waiting for someone else to fix them when the truth is that no one is coming. The only way to reclaim what was lost is to build it back yourself, stronger than before. Osiris didn't stay dead, and neither should Black men. The only question is: Who is willing to do the work?

Black men have been conditioned by a system that undermines our strength and ability to lead. This is not by accident but by design; our leadership has been repeatedly suppressed through laws, media, and societal expectations. Yet, deep within every Black man is the instinct and potential to lead. The time for apology is over. For too long, we've been expected to shrink, to apologize for our existence and our power. It's time to reject the notion that we must apologize for claiming our rightful place as leaders. Leadership isn't just a position; it's an action. It's about showing up and making decisions, standing firm in the face of adversity, and inspiring those around you to rise. Black men must take the reins in our families, communities, and the wider society. It's time to be the examples of integrity, discipline, and accountability that we were always meant to be. No longer should we expect anyone to validate our leadership or wait for permission to step up. We lead because it is in our nature, and it is our duty to do so without hesitation or excuse.

We cannot lead effectively if we remain passive or disconnected from the people we serve. Leadership is about responsibility, and Black men must embrace that responsibility, understanding that every decision and every action impacts those around them. Whether within our homes, at work, or in our communities, we must be the ones setting the standard, not waiting for others to do it for us. The very act of leading creates a ripple effect that transforms the people and environments we influence. This is the foundation of strong Black manhood: unwavering responsibility. Part of the issue today is that Black men have been conditioned to doubt our worth and question our authority. For generations, society has told us that we aren't fit to lead, that our place is beneath the structure of power. This narrative has poisoned the minds of many, making them hesitant to step into leadership roles. However, the true measure of leadership isn't about the title; it's about your impact. If you can lead a household, guide a community, and challenge systems of power that have long sought to suppress you, then you are fulfilling your purpose as a Black man.

The history of Black men is filled with examples of unapologetic leadership, from our ancestors who fought to preserve our dignity to the civil rights leaders who faced death to secure our freedom. These men didn't ask for permission to lead; they did it because the necessity was clear. Today, that same spirit needs to be reignited. We stand on the shoulders of giants, and we owe it to them, as well as to future generations, to continue pushing for our rightful place at the table of power. Our leadership must be uncompromising, not shaped by the trends or limitations of society but by our own values and vision. Too often, Black men are told to temper their authority or to soften their words. This only serves to perpetuate the myth that we cannot be leaders without apology or compromise. Leadership isn't about being liked; it's about being respected. We must own our power, our voice, and our actions, and lead unapologetically in every space we occupy.

The leadership we need doesn't come from conforming to someone else's idea of what a Black man should be; it comes from embracing who we are, flaws and all. The 14 Codes provide the structure, but it is the decision to act on them that will make the difference. We, as Black men, have the power to shape our own destiny to lead the way for our families, our communities, and our nation. But that can only happen when we stop waiting for approval and start asserting our role unapologetically.

For too long, we've been told that in order to lead, we must fit into a certain mold: stoic, non-emotional, subdued. But leadership is dynamic. It's multifaceted. It's as much about the mind as it is about the heart. It's about knowing when to speak up, when to listen, and when to take charge. Our emotions, our experiences, and our unique perspectives are not weaknesses; they are sources of strength. Black men must lead with our full selves no fear, no masks. We have to stand in our truth, own our nature, and use that strength to guide and uplift the community. To lead unapologetically means to stand firm in the face of criticism and opposition, knowing that the path is not easy. But we cannot shrink away from it, because every time we step back, we further reinforce the narrative that Black men cannot be trusted with power. We've seen the consequences of Black men stepping away from leadership: broken communities, disjointed families, and systemic oppression. This is why we must refuse to be silent and allow others to lead us. The moment we stop looking to external sources for approval is the moment we begin to unlock our full potential.

The true challenge of Black manhood today is the willingness to fight for our place without compromise. The world may attempt to tell us we are not fit to lead, but we must reject that narrative. We are the sons of kings and warriors, the inheritors of traditions that predate this country. When we walk in unapologetic leadership, we honor those who came before us and ensure that we are setting a clear path for those who will come after. This is not just about us; it's about ensuring that our children, our daughters, and their children have role models and leaders to look up to. Leadership doesn't require the world to agree with you. It requires strength, clarity, and the courage to stand by your convictions. By taking unapologetic leadership, we stop asking for permission and start creating the world we want to live in. We do this not just for our own benefit, but for the generations who will inherit the lessons we leave behind. It is our responsibility to pass down this unyielding vision of leadership, to make sure that Black men from this point forward are not only ready to lead but also do so with full authority and conviction. We are not waiting for validation; we are taking the lead, boldly and unapologetically.

When I think about the future, it's not just about what I leave behind, but about what I instill in those who come after me. My daughter needs to see what it means to be a man who stands firm, who leads with integrity, and who knows his worth without apology. I wrote this book for her, for every Black daughter who needs to see what a strong Black man is. It's not just about physical strength, but about mental fortitude, resilience, and understanding the purpose of his existence. Black men have been conditioned to be weak, to be submissive, and to let the system dictate our value. But I refuse to allow my daughter to grow up in a world where Black men are shadows of what they're supposed to be.

The 14 Codes are not just a collection of principles; they are a blueprint for reclaiming strength and dignity. As a father, I have a responsibility to make sure my daughter grows up seeing examples of Black manhood that are unshaken by the forces that try to dismantle us.

She should never have to question what it means to be strong, to be a man of character, and to hold space in this world with conviction. The world will try to confuse her and mislead her about what a Black man truly represents, but I want her to always know that strength is in our blood, in our heritage, and in our ability to rise from destruction. We cannot afford to let this legacy die with me. Too many Black men have fallen victim to the erosion of their power, and the time for that to change is now. Each generation must know its role in the larger narrative of Black manhood. This is about more than a set of rules; it's about survival, empowerment, and the reclamation of a status that has been systematically stripped away. If I can set the foundation for my daughter to see the potential in Black men, then I've done my part. This legacy must be passed down; it's not just for us; it's for them, too.

The importance of passing these values down is bigger than me and my family. Black men have been reduced to a caricature of weakness, and this has had devastating effects on the community. If we don't restore our strength now, if we don't hold each other accountable and show the next generation what true leadership looks like, we will continue to see our community suffer. Every Black man who stands firm, who adheres to these codes, creates a ripple effect. That ripple is felt in the household, in the community, and in the world. When we get right, the world gets right. This blueprint is for the sons who will come after me. The

14 Codes are not just for today but for tomorrow, the generation after that, and beyond. I want my grandson to read this and see a reflection of what his great-grandfather stood for, what his father stands for, and what he should stand for. These values are eternal; they transcend time, circumstance, and the limits that the system tries to place on us. Future generations need to know that they have the power to shape their destiny, and that power lies in the choices they make and the men they decide to be.

I'm not interested in simply being a man who exists. I want my daughter to see a man who is unapologetic about his leadership. I want her to see the strength in the face of adversity, the determination that comes with knowing who you are and what you stand for. The system has worked tirelessly to dismantle Black masculinity, to strip us of our power and make us forget who we are. But I will not let her forget. This book is a tool, a weapon for her to use, to know that Black men are meant to be great and that she should demand greatness from them.

This is the responsibility that I take seriously. This isn't just for me or for the men who are here today; it's for the men who haven't been born yet. I've always had a vision for the future of Black men, and that vision is one where we're no longer soft, no longer malleable clay, but men of steel. The blueprint I've laid out in *"The 14 Codes"* is the foundation on which future generations will stand. It's a call to action to build Black men into the men they were always meant to be. The only way to do that is to ensure that this message never dies. Every Black man who embraces these codes becomes an example for the next. We owe it to our children, especially our daughters, to show them what strength really looks like. It's about more than just being physically present; it's about being mentally strong, emotionally controlled, and committed to the betterment of the community. This legacy doesn't end with one generation. It's a torch that must be passed, one man to the next. When Black men stand strong, unapologetically, they raise up those around them, especially the women and children who depend on them.

My daughter deserves a world where Black men are not just existing but thriving. She deserves to see Black men stand at the forefront of society, unapologetically claiming our space as leaders. This book is not just about codes; it's about the future. It's about setting the standard for what a man should be and ensuring that our children never forget what it means to lead, to rise, and to stand on the shoulders of those who came before them. Our women and children deserve nothing less than our best, and our best comes from adhering to the principles that make us who we are.

We are at a crossroads, and this book is the marker. It's the starting point for a new generation of Black men who know their worth and demand respect. It's time for Black men to rise out of the ashes of destruction and become the leaders they were always meant to be. I've written this not just for today but for the future, so that when I'm gone, my daughter will have this to look back on and know that her father, and all the men who came before her, fought for this legacy. This is the future we must build together, one man at a time, one generation at a time. In the end, this book is my contribution to a world where Black men rise to our true potential. It's the foundation for my daughter, for my grandchildren, and for the men who will follow in our footsteps. It's a legacy of strength, resilience, and leadership that will never be erased. This is just the beginning.

The 14 Codes are not just a guide; they are a call to action. Each Code is a weapon, a tool, a foundation to rebuild Black manhood. It's time to stop talking about change and start being the change. Black men must move beyond mere survival and become the leaders they were always meant to be. These Codes demand action, not words; they challenge men to rise above weakness and to build themselves into pillars of strength and accountability. To live by these Codes is to embrace a commitment to both personal excellence and the collective good of the Black community.

We've allowed the system to erode the essence of Black masculinity for far too long. From slavery to modern-day oppression, the fabric of Black manhood has been under attack, twisted, and reshaped to fit the needs of a society that never intended for Black men to lead. This blueprint calls for a reclamation of what was lost: our honor, our integrity, and our sense of purpose. Black men must stop looking for validation outside of themselves and start demanding respect. The world isn't waiting for us to catch up; it's waiting for us to take charge. We must do this for ourselves and for the generations that come after.

The 14 Codes are the antidote to the poison that has been injected into our minds for centuries. They strip away the false narratives that have made us soft, distracted, and broken. They're not just words on a page; they're instructions for a life of purpose, discipline, and fortitude. Each Code represents an element of the strength that has always lived within us, but that we've neglected or forgotten. To live by these codes is to stand as a fortress against the pressures of modern society, which seeks to undermine Black masculinity at every turn. It's time to be uncompromising in our adherence to these principles and unapologetic in our stance.

This journey isn't just about you; it's about every Black man who came before you and everyone who will come after. You carry the weight of a legacy that is greater than anything you could ever imagine. The 14 Codes serve as a bridge between the brokenness we've experienced and the power we are meant to hold. It's time to resurrect the greatness that was stolen from us and build something lasting. The power of these Codes lies not just in what they teach us individually, but in what they allow us to give back to the community.

When we stand as men, we raise the entire community with us. Reclaiming leadership means embracing responsibility. A leader is never passive; he takes action, sets an example, and holds others accountable. It's about waking up every day and demanding more of yourself, not just for the sake of self-improvement, but for the sake of your people. It's time for Black men to step into our rightful roles as the backbone of our families, our communities, and society. Too long have we been marginalized and disrespected. The time to lead is now; there is no more time for waiting, no more excuses.

To live the 14 Codes is to live a life of impact. Every action you take, every decision you make, must be aligned with the power of these principles. You aren't just living for the moment; you're living for your future, your children, your community. The time has come to stop apologizing for your existence, to stop seeking permission to be great. This world will try to convince you that you don't matter, that you aren't enough, but it's up to you to prove them wrong. Rise up, live with purpose, and show the world the strength that Black men possess. Every Black man who lives by these codes creates a ripple effect that spreads far beyond his own life. The legacy we build today shapes the future of Black men tomorrow. These codes are not just for this generation; they are for all generations of Black men, from the past to the future. By embracing these principles, we not only strengthen ourselves but also fortify the foundation of Black manhood for the generations that will follow. It's about creating a lineage of strong, accountable men who will carry the torch for years to come. Our strength today becomes the legacy of tomorrow.

There is no more time for hesitation or self-doubt. This is the moment to take ownership of your manhood, to step into your power with both feet planted firmly on the ground. Every Black man who takes these Codes seriously will leave a mark that is indelible, undeniable, and profound. It's not just about being good enough; it's about being great. And greatness doesn't come from waiting around or hoping for change; it comes from doing the hard work and committing to a life of purpose. The world needs strong Black men now more than ever. We've seen the consequences of Black men failing to embrace their leadership, disunity, weakness, and destruction. *"The 14 Codes"* are the cure to that ailment, the answer to the question of what it means to be a Black man in America. It's time for Black men to be the warriors we were always meant to be. This is our moment to rise, to lead, to be unapologetic in our strength. The *"Codes"* are the blueprint, and now it's up to us to build the future. We are the foundation for what's to come.

The final piece of this is the most important: passing this legacy down. This book isn't just for you; it's for your children, your grandchildren, and every generation after that. You are the keeper of this knowledge, the guardian of these principles. When you stand firm in the 14 Codes, you create a path that others can follow. It's time to start building that path, one step at a time. The world will look to Black men as leaders once again. It starts now, with you, with this book, with these Codes. Step into your power, and don't ever look back.

14 books every Black man needs have in their home:

- The *"Isis Papers"* by Dr. Frances Cress Welsing
- *"Post-Traumatic Slave Syndrome"* by Dr. Joy DeGruy
- **The United-Independent Compensatory Code/System/Concept: A Compensatory Counter-Racist Code** by Neely Fuller Jr.
- *"The Autobiography of Malcolm X"* as told to Alex Haley.
- *"Message to the Black Man"* by Elijah Muhammad
- *"Black Labor, White Wealth"* by Claud Anderson, Ed.D.
- *"PowerNomics"* by Claud Anderson, Ed.D.
- *"Think and Grow Rich: A Black Choice"* by Dennis Kimbro and Napoleon Hill.
- *"The Mis-Education of the Negro"* by Carter G. Woodson
- *"Outwitting the Devil"* by Napoleon Hill
- *"48 Laws of Power"* by Robert Greene
- *"The Art of War"* by Sun Tzu
- *"The Prepper's Survival Bible"* by Dale Mann
- **Any Holy Book i.e. Bible, Torah, Quran or Egyptian Book of the Dead, etc.**

REFERENCES

Welsing, Frances Cress. The Isis Papers: The Keys to the Colors. Third World Press, 1991.

Fuller Jr., Neely. The United Independent Compensatory Code/System/Concept: A Compensatory Counter-Racist Code. Neely Fuller Jr. Publications, 2016.

Fuller Jr., Neely. The United Independent Compensatory Code/System/Concept: Word Guide. Neely Fuller Jr. Publications, 2010.

Ginzburg, Ralph. 100 Years of Lynching. Black Classic Press, 1988.

Allen, James, et al. Without Sanctuary: Lynching Photography in America. Twin Palms Publishers, 2000.

Keyes, Ken. The Hundredth Monkey. Vision Books, 1982.

Faulkner, Raymond O. The Ancient Egyptian Pyramid Texts. Oxford University Press, 1969. CaBoom, Carmen. Christopher Jordan Dorner Last Resort. CreateSpace, 2013. Manifesto of a Madman: Is Dorner Crazy or Concerned? by C. Jeff Oakes (2013) Christopher Dorner's Manifesto (2013).

Revenge Killings – Chris Dorner: The Cop. The Serial Killer. The Manhunt. by Peter Vronsky and RJ Parker (2015).

Baldwin, James. Notes of a Native Son. Beacon Press, 2012.

Barnes, Nicky, and Tom Folsom. Mr. Untouchable: My Crimes and Punishments. Weinstein Books, 2007.

United States Congress. House Select Committee on Narcotics Abuse and Control. Organized Crime and Illicit Traffic in Narcotics: The Nicky Barnes Case. U.S. Government Printing Office, 1978.

Slade, Grady, Jr. Black Inventors: Hidden In Plain Sight. Independently published, 2018. Haber, Louis. Black Pioneers of Science and Invention. Harcourt Brace Jovanovich, 1970.

Fouché, Rayvon. Black Inventors in the Age of Segregation: Granville T. Woods, Lewis H. Latimer, and Shelby J. Davidson. Johns Hopkins University Press, 2003.

Dray, Philip. Capitol Men: The Epic Story of Reconstruction

Through the Lives of the First Black Congressmen. Houghton Mifflin, 2008.

Christopher, Maurine. Black Americans in Congress. T.Y. Crowell Junior Books, 1976.

Phillips, Patrick. Blood at the Root: A Racial Cleansing in America. W.W. Norton & Company, 2016.

Stockley, Grif, Brian K. Mitchell, and Guy Lancaster. Blood in Their Eyes: The Elaine Massacre of 1919. University of Arkansas Press, 2020.

D'Orso, Michael. Like Judgment Day: The Ruin and Redemption of a Town Called Rosewood. G.P. Putnam's Sons, 1996.

Rothstein, Richard. The Color of Law: A Forgotten History of How Our Government Segregated America. Liveright Publishing, 2017.

Loewen, James W. Sundown Towns: A Hidden Dimension of American Racism. New Press, 2005.

Charles River Editors. The Tulsa Massacre of 1921: The Controversial History and Legacy of America's Worst Race Riot. Independently published, 2019.

Nelson, Timothy E. Blackdom, New Mexico: The Significance of the Afro-Frontier. Purple Fern Books, 2022.

Washington, Booker T. Boley, a Negro Town in the West. Reprint edition, 1908. Shaw, James. Boley: Oklahoma's Famous Black Town. Black Wall Street USA Press, 2010.

Royal, Alice C. Allensworth, the Freedom Colony: A California African American Township. 2nd ed., Heyday, 2016.

Gauthier, LaFlorya. A Biography of Isaiah Thornton Montgomery. LifeRich Publishing, 2021. Crockett, Norman L. The Black Towns. University of Arkansas Press, 1992.

Fletcher, Marvin E. America's First Black General: Benjamin O. Davis, Sr., 1880-1970. University Press of Kansas, 1991.

Davis, Benjamin O., Jr. Benjamin O. Davis, Jr. American: An Autobiography. University of Washington Press, 1991.

Dvorak, Jack. Black Heroes of the American Revolution. Chicago Review Press, 2008. Worthy, Clifford. Black Knights: The Story of the Tuskegee Airmen. Routledge, 1996.

Shellum, Brian G. Black Officer in a Buffalo Soldier Regiment: The

Military Career of Charles Young. University of Nebraska Press, 2010.

Shellum, Brian G. Black Cadet in a White Bastion: Charles Young at West Point. University of Nebraska Press, 2006.

Malcolm X and Haley, Alex. The Autobiography of Malcolm X. Ballantine Books, 1965. Marable, Manning. Malcolm X: A Life of Reinvention. Viking, 2011.

Dyson, Michael Eric. Holler If You Hear Me: Searching for Tupac Shakur. Basic Civitas Books, 2001.

Shakur, Tupac. The Rose That Grew from Concrete. Pocket Books, 1999. Hoye, Jacob. Tupac: Resurrection 1971–1996. Atria Books, 2003.

McQuillar, Tayannah Lee, and Fred L. Johnson. Tupac Shakur: The Life and Times of an American Icon. Da Capo Press, 2010.

Robinson, Staci. Tupac Shakur: The Authorized Biography. Crown, 2023.

Davis, Jody. Yummy: The Last Days of a Southside Shorty. Lee & Low Books, 2010. (Graphic novel by G. Neri, illustrated by Randy DuBurke).

Time Magazine. "Murder in Miniature," by Nancy Gibbs. Time, September 19, 1994.

Payne, Les, and Tamara Payne. The Dead Are Arising: The Life of Malcolm X. Liveright Publishing Corporation, 2020.

Parker, John P. His Promised Land: The Autobiography of John P. Parker, Former Slave and Conductor on the Underground Railroad. Edited by Stuart Seely Sprague, W. W. Norton & Company, 1996.

Still, William. The Underground Railroad: A Record of Facts, Authentic Narratives, Letters, etc. Philadelphia, Porter & Coates, 1872.

Du Bois, W.E.B. Black Reconstruction in America, 1860–1880. Harcourt, Brace and Company, 1935.

Alexander, Michelle. The New Jim Crow: Mass Incarceration in the Age of Colorblindness. The New Press, 2010.

Egerton, Douglas R. Gabriel's Rebellion: The Virginia Slave Conspiracies of 1800 and 1802. University of North Carolina Press, 1993.

Robertson, David. *Denmark Vesey: The Buried Story of America's Largest Slave Rebellion and the Man Who Led It*. Vintage, 1999.

Bloom, Joshua, and Waldo E. Martin. *Black against Empire: The History and Politics of the Black Panther Party*. University of California Press, 2013.

Seale, Bobby. *Seize the Time: The Story of the Black Panther Party and Huey P. Newton*. Black Classic Press, 1991.

Brown, Scot. *Fighting for Us: Maulana Karenga, the US Organization, and Black Cultural Nationalism*. New York University Press, 2003.

Pharr, Wayne. *Nine Lives of a Black Panther: A Story of Survival*. Chicago Review Press, 2014.

Parks, Rosa, and Jim Haskins. *Rosa Parks: My Story*. Puffin Books, 1999. Barnett, Ferdinand L. "Race Unity." 1879.

Brimner, Larry Dane. *Accused!: The Trials of the Scottsboro Boys: Lies, Prejudice, and the Fourteenth Amendment*. Astra Publishing House, 2018.

Norris, Clarence, and Sybil D. Washington. *The Last of the Scottsboro Boys*. NewSouth Books, 2003.

King, Coretta Scott. *My Life, My Love, My Legacy*. As told to Rev. Dr. Barbara Reynolds, Henry Holt and Co., 2017.

King, Coretta Scott. *My Life with Martin Luther King, Jr.* Holt, Rinehart and Winston, 1969.

Rickford, Russell J. *Betty Shabazz: A Remarkable Story of Survival and Faith Before and After Malcolm X*. Sourcebooks, 2003.

Shabazz, Ilyasah, and Kim McLarin. *Growing Up X: A Memoir by the Daughter of Malcolm X*. One World, 2002.

Cox, Clinton. *Undying Glory: The Story of the Massachusetts 54th Regiment*. Scholastic Inc., 1991.

Abdul-Jabbar, Kareem, and Anthony Walton. *Brothers in Arms: The Epic Story of the 761st Tank Battalion, WWII's Forgotten Heroes*. Broadway Books, 2004.

Baker, Kyle. *Nat Turner*. Abrams ComicArts, 2008.

Styron, William. *The Confessions of Nat Turner*. Random House, 1967.

Kaye, Anthony, and Richard J. Downs. Nat Turner, Black Prophet: A Visionary History. Hill and Wang, 2023.

Oates, Stephen B. The Fires of Jubilee: Nat Turner's Fierce Rebellion. Harper Perennial, 1990.

Haas, Jeffrey. The Assassination of Fred Hampton: How the FBI and the Chicago Police Murdered a Black Panther. Chicago Review Press, 2009.

Chadwick, Bruce. The Creole Rebellion: The Most Successful Slave Revolt in American History. University of New Mexico Press, 2022.

Shabazz, Malik Zulu. The Book of Khalid: The Untold Story of Khalid Abdul Muhammad, Militant Prophet to Today's Radical Generation. Foreword by Farrah Gray, Malik Zulu Shabazz Esq., 2020.

Massing, Michael. The Fix. Simon & Schuster, 2000.

Muhammad, Elijah. Message to the Blackman in America. Muhammad's Temple of Islam No. 2, 1965.

Evanzz, Karl. The Messenger: The Rise and Fall of Elijah Muhammad. Pantheon Books, 1999.

Gregory, Dick. Nigger: An Autobiography. E.P. Dutton, 1964.

raft, Doreen Rappaport. Freedom Fighter: The Story of David Fagen, American Soldier. Scholastic, 1999.

Hoffman, Phillip W. David Fagen: Turncoat Hero. American History Press, 2017.

Morey, Michael. Fagen: An African American Renegade in the Philippine-American War. University of Wisconsin Press, 2019.

Alexander, Michelle. The New Jim Crow. The New Press, 2010.

Allen, James, et al. Without Sanctuary: Lynching Photography in America. Twin Palms Publishers, 2000.

Anderson, Claud. Dirty Little Secrets: About Black History, Its Heroes and Other Troublemakers. PowerNomics Corp. of America, 1997.

Baldwin, James. Notes of a Native Son. Beacon Press, 1955.

Beckert, Sven, and Seth Rockman, editors. Slavery's Capitalism: A New History of American Economic Development. University of Pennsylvania Press, 2016.

Fuller, Neely, Jr. The United-Independent Compensatory Code/System/Concept: A Compensatory Counter-Racist Codified Word Guide. 1984.

Ginzburg, Ralph. 100 Years of Lynching. Black Classic Press, 1962.

Gregory, Dick. Nigger: An Autobiography. E.P. Dutton, 1964.

Greene, Robert. The 33 Strategies of War. Viking, 2006.

Greenlee, Sam. The Spook Who Sat by the Door. Allison & Busby, 1969. Haber, Louis. Black Pioneers of Science and Invention. Harcourt, 1970. Hill, Napoleon. The Law of Success in Sixteen Lessons. The Ralston Society, 1928.

Nasheed, Tariq. Foundational Black American Race Baiter: Myths and Memoirs. Krispy Life, 2021.

Rogers, J. A. 100 Amazing Facts About the Negro. Helga M. Rogers, 1934.

Smither, Gregory D. Slave Breeding: Sex, Violence, and Memory in African American History. Xlibris, 2005.

www.ingramcontent.com/pod-product-compliance
Lightning Source LLC
Chambersburg PA
CBHW060512160726
47991CB00001B/10